SCOTTISH HISTORY SOCIETY

Travels in Scotland, 1788–1881
A Selection from Contemporary Tourist Journals

# Travels in Scotland
# 1788–1881

*A Selection from Contemporary Tourist Journals*

*Edited by*
*Alastair J. Durie*

SCOTTISH HISTORY SOCIETY
2012

THE BOYDELL PRESS

First published 2012

A Scottish History Society publication
in association with The Boydell Press
an imprint of Boydell & Brewer Ltd
PO Box 9, Woodbridge, Suffolk IP12 3DF, UK
and of Boydell & Brewer Inc.
668 Mt Hope Avenue, Rochester, NY 14620, USA
website: www.boydellandbrewer.com

ISBN 978-0-90624-530-9

A CIP catalogue record for this book is available
from the British Library

The publisher has no responsibility for the continued existence or accuracy of URLs for
external or third-party internet websites referred to in this book, and does not guarantee that
any content on such websites is, or will remain, accurate or appropriate.

Papers used by Boydell & Brewer Ltd are natural, recyclable products
made from wood grown in sustainable forests

Designed and typeset by Tina Ranft

Printed and bound by
CPI Group (UK) Ltd, Croydon, CR0 4YY

# Contents

# List of Illustrations

## Mary Allison, Trip to Butterbridge, 1881

# Acknowledgements

In the preparation of this volume, I have incurred many debts, notably to the staff at Glasgow City Archives, whom I also thank for permission to publish the transcriptions from Bald and the Tours. Great support came from the Special Collections Department of Glasgow University, particularly Julie Gardham, and I acknowledge the readiness with which permission was given to reproduce Elizabeth Diggle's journal and that of Henry Underhill. The technical assistance of the Photographic Unit at that university was essential to the provision of the illustrations.

There are the many archivists and local studies librarians who have helped: Murdo MacDonald of Argyll and Bute, Sybil Cavanagh of West Lothian, George Dixon of Stirling, and of course the staff of the reader services at the University of Stirling who have borne my many and esoteric queries with remarkable forbearance. They can all now relax. My wife, Kate, has laboured long and hard to decipher the handwriting of Mr Bald (from whom we will both be glad to take a break), and to track down obscure phrases: 'Æolus' for what seemed to read as 'Colus' was a particular triumph.

*Map of Scotland.*
*Inset: Argyll and Loch Lomond.*

# Introduction: Tourist Travels in Scotland

## Overview

Tourism in Scotland, in its growth from an elite to a mass experience, was as much a success story of the nineteenth century as the rise of shipbuilding, steel and textiles, all of which have long been discussed and analysed in depth. Yet tourism as an industry also created substantial employment, some of it urban, but much of it in rural and highland Scotland, and generated a stream of income, albeit on a heavily seasonal basis, for many groups in society. It is not surprising, therefore, that having been relatively neglected, in recent years the development of tourism to and in Scotland has become a flourishing area of study for both the professional academic historian and the wider community. Some broad surveys of the subject have recently been published which draw on the ever increasing number of accounts of the growth of tourism in particular resorts, coastal and inland, from Dunoon to Aberdour, Iona and North Berwick. Some types of tourism have received particular attention, such as sporting and health, and transport studies, of the railway companies or individual branch lines, or the recent study of MacBraynes, are extremely valuable. To add to the well known classics of travel in Scotland – Dr Johnson's Tour, Pennant, Wordsworth, Mendelssohn, Verne, Fontane – there is a steady stream of travellers' accounts, of varying calibre and interest.

These help to show the way that this new industry, although in different ways and to differing degrees, affected all classes and all areas. Some localities – for example, the Highlands – were places to which people went, some places from which they came: the towns of industrial Lanarkshire or west Fife. Others were both sending and receiving; as early as the 1850s the influx of summer visitors to Edinburgh may well have been matched by the outflow of the professional classes to their holiday retreats. Different places attracted a differing clientele, as did different types of tourism; the seaside drew the many, the grouse moors welcomed only the few. But the reality is that by the end of the nineteenth century tourism in one form or another had long since ceased to be the preserve of the wealthy few. The lower the income, the less the level of participation, but even the poorest child might get a Sunday School trip or an institutional outing. Clearly the lower down the social and economic scale, the less room there was for manoeuvre; options as to where and for how long were limited by time and money. But they could think of themselves as tourists, however humble. 'Tourism' is a generously inclusive term which takes in all forms of travel for pleasure and leisure, from the measured touring of the moneyed to distant parts through the organised excursions of the middle order to the days out of the masses to the seaside. There was for the select the expensive stay at a big spa or hydro hotel, for the middling orders, either by necessity or choice, cheaper boarding with a landlady, for some free accommodation with a friend or family. Whether focused or informal, scheduled or casual, expensive or cheap, tourism in one form or another – tour, vacation, excursion holiday or outing – touched most lives, from the summer vacation at a coastal or inland retreat of the professional and middle classes to the day away of the urban worker.

Much of it focused on the big cities and the popular coastal resorts, but even quite remote rural and Highland communities began to rely on the visitor as a key source of income, consistent or casual. Crofters, ghillies and farmers might not ever take much of a break away themselves, but there were worthwhile pickings to be had from this new trade. Some let their homes during the season, moving out to backyard bothies, as, for example, the crofters on Arran did, a source of income of which their landlord took note. The old traditions of hospitality without thought of return were eroded as the flow of visitors increased; food, fire, shelter or a bed could provide monetary return, small perhaps, but of some significance. This was bonus money, milking the tourist, who as a general rule could afford it. Age was no bar to playing a part in this new industry, from children selling stones on Iona, through young men acting as attendants to hill climbers, to old women selling lemonade. In the 1870s 'Ramshackles' MacGregor, an elderly, part-paralysed ex-soldier, used to make a nice summer living by coming forward with a ladder to allow tourists to dismount from the Callander coach at the foot of the Lanrick Brae, a steep pull. The tips that he harvested were, once the season finished, turned into an extended carousal.[1] Guides, self-appointed or selected, male or female, appeared everywhere on the tourist trail: city guides, and those at the big houses, or castles, or battlefields, could count on a steady flow of income, and the enterprising could increase their take by offering 'authentic' souvenirs, as the custodian of Doune castle did. In the 1820s the tours at Holyrood Palace were in the hands of four young women, dishing out explanations 'like parrots'. They were not slow, as one visitor observed, 'in making some money from visitors who must have a well-laden purse'.[2] There was a penumbra to the industry of begging in that the sight of poverty did prompt a response in the form of constructive philanthropy. For example, Thomas Cook's visitors raised funds for fishing boats to assist the locals on Iona.

---

1   James MacDonald, *Character Sketches of Old Callander*, 3rd edn (Stirling, 2006), 98–9.
2   *The French Macdonald* (Lewis, 2007), 124.

# The rise of tourism: a summary

The pleasure visitor or 'tourist' started to become a familiar figure in Scotland in the later eighteenth century. The term was first used at that time strictly to refer to someone doing a scenic and cultural tour, following a schedule of sights and experiences predefined by taste and experience. It widened thereafter to become almost synonymous with 'holidaymaker'. There is some evidence to suggest that numbers visiting Scotland were already on the increase by the 1770s. In 1759 Lord Breadalbane noticed 'it has been the fashion this year to travel into the highlands, many have been here from England, I suppose because they can't go abroad'.[3] The flow accelerated in the 1780s. 'All the world is travelling to Scotland!' exclaimed Elizabeth Diggle, who made her tour in 1788. The outbreak of revolution in France and the wars that followed, which led to a complete disruption of the Grand Tour, did much to divert attention to destinations within Britain. Travel to the North had been perhaps mostly only a reserve option initially for the traveller, but one which was explored more often during periods of war when touring on the Continent was discouraged. Nevertheless, the positive attractions of Scotland as a tourist destination did begin to play an increasing part. Most of the early visitors had travelled for landscape and scenery with waterfalls, caves and views high on their agenda. Many favoured literature and heritage with the lure of Ossian a particular pull, and yet others were drawn by scientific curiosity, or by the culture and intellectual life of Edinburgh. Travel was not easy, although the main roads did markedly improve, and accommodation was uncertain, unless of course the visitor came armed with a letter of introduction that could secure hospitality. This was a courtesy that would be reciprocated, but bore heavily on those whose residences were either in popular locations or en route to them, or who themselves were in demand: Sir Walter Scott's wife complained that life at Abbotsford was like a hotel 'without the money'. Indeed the promotion of Scotland and provision of amenities fell largely on the landowning classes. Some landowners had inns or hotels that were in effect annexes to their great houses. As part of their image, landowners improved their grounds, laying out walks, promenades, private and public drives, forming viewing points, providing hermitages and shelters, and so on, a tradition that was to continue as with the Queen's View at Killiecrankie. The scale of tourism is hard to determine, although there is indirect confirmation in the number of guides to Scotland which were being published, and some fragmentary statistical evidence from the few surviving visitors' books of the period, as for New Lanark.

3   James Hollway and Lindsay Errington, *The Discovery of Scotland* (Edinburgh, 1978), 63.

It would, however, be a mistake to see tourism in Scotland in this emerging phase merely as the cultural preserve of the foreign and English visitor, a conclusion which reflects the nature of the sources and their writers. Not all visitors were interested only in the landscape, literature and heritage. First, it is clear that there was a significant subset of young men by the turn of the eighteenth century for whom Scotland meant sport: hill climbing, fishing, deer stalking or shooting. The remarkable Sarah Murray found one bright day in August the scene at Dalnacardoch (near Dalwhinnie) full of life with the horses and attendants of 'sportsmen who were come to the Highlands to shoot'.[4] The North was beginning to become a playground for wealthy visitors. Second, upper- and even middle-class Scots themselves were beginning to appreciate their own country, whether the scenery of the Trossachs or the seaside. The upper-class medical enthusiasm for saltwater therapy had been imported and by the later eighteenth century the sea-bathing machine was to be found at quite a number of seaside resorts from South Queensferry to Lossiemouth. Some Scottish spas, as at Moffat, Bridge of Earn and Strathpeffer, enjoyed modest patronage, but only from the Scottish gentry. Few, if any, English health seekers would have been tempted north: the general view was that the quality of the Scottish waters was offset by the dullness of the company.

There is a third dimension, but one which is largely submerged, namely the extent to which ordinary Scots were taking time for trips or 'jaunts', whether to a fair or race meeting, or even a preaching or communion, a recovery of the holy day. This would not normally be regarded as tourism proper, but it shared at least some aspects, including the key notion of time for pleasure taken away from home and from work. Health, folk-medicine and culture still drew people to spas and holy wells, despite the hostility of the religious establishment to what they saw as popish superstition.[5] The annual outing by country folk of the North-East to the wells of Dalblair and to the sea-bathing nearby in the 1830s, as described by William Alexander, may well have been a survivor of a tradition once more widespread. There was a great deal of tourism that has slipped below the radar, of people returning to

---

4   Sarah Murray, *A Companion and Useful Guide to the Beauties of Scotland* (Hawick, 1982), 89; first published in 1799 and revised in 1803.

5   See Dr William Buchan, 'Mineral Waters of Scotland', in *Domestic Medicine* (Glasgow, 1819), 681:

> The sanative quality of good water, so abundant in Scotland, was in the dark ages ascribed to the wonder working power of some certain saints, whose names were imposed upon the salubrious springs, and thus did cunning and imposture usurp that honour, and that worship which is so justly due to the Author of life and the beneficent fountain of all our mercies. Nor has the light of Protestantism yet been able wholly to dispel this superstition. Almost every parish has still its sainted well, which is regarded by the vulgar with a degree of veneration, not very distant from that which in Papists and Hindoos we pity as degrading, and condemn as idolatrous.

the countryside during the harvest and combining some seasonal work with leisure. In the eighteenth century it may have been only the upper classes who discovered the seaside and its virtues for themselves; the ordinary people already knew of it. In short, forms of tourism which were not elite, albeit limited and informal, already existed in embryo, as adjuncts of recreation and of health rather than separately recognised. The roots of tourism were in place, which is not to deny what was to come in terms of the scale of expansion, the degree of formalisation and recognition as an activity in its own right, the participation across class, age, gender, place and income. Similarly, what had been haphazard became commercialised. A sign of this is the emergence of the profession of hotelier; whereas the early traveller used inns or coaching houses, the tourist wanted hotels. It is interesting to question which was the first 'hotel' in Scotland. According to Denby,[6] the use of the term, a French corruption of 'hostel', dates from 1765 and was originally used of superior inns which were places to stay, rather than just to pass a night. In Walker's view the first usage in Scotland is to be found at Glasgow in 1781, the Tontine hotel.[7] Almost as many hotels as churches – commercial, railway, sporting and hydropathic – were to be built in Scotland during the nineteenth century.

## Tourism transformed: the transport revolution

Thanks to rising disposable incomes, more free time and better transport, tourism in one form or another pushed its way up the agenda for many individuals and households in nineteenth-century society. Time away for touring, vacation or holiday became a 'need', an accepted part of the annual cycle of life for more and more people, a desire to travel from which many resorts, regions and countries in Europe benefitted. But Scotland did, it would seem, particularly well as a tourist destination, even and especially amongst those who had a choice of experience and of location. As a general rule, the Scottish working classes had neither the income nor the free time to range very far. There is a nice Edinburgh poem which catches the excitement of where a family might go: 'the wifie cried for Aberdour – week's rest by the sea wad health restore', but money is tight. A Highland jaunt is out of the question, a jink to Leith Links is indignantly rejected, and a trip to Roslin is the compromise.[8] The restrictions on holiday choice of the urban masses was to the benefit, for example, of the Clyde resorts. For the worker, the Continent was out of the question and only at the end of the nineteenth century during the

---

6  Elaine Denby, *Grand Hotels, An Architectural and Social History* (London, 1998), 26.
7  David Walker, 'Inns, Hotels and Related Building Types', in Geoffrey Stell et al. (eds), *Scotland's Buildings, A Compendium of Scottish Ethnology*, 3 (East Linton, 2003), 142.
8  James Lumsden, *Edinburgh Poems and Songs* (Edinburgh, 1899), 96–7.

Glasgow Fair did Blackpool and Scarborough start to experience a substantial influx of Scottish holiday-makers. But higher up the income scale, there was more choice and horizons did widen as transport improved; as travel times shortened and services became regularized – and publicized – destinations once out of reach became possible. People took advantage of this new freedom and opportunity. There was the engineer from Lasswade near Edinburgh in 1851 who took his family to see the Great Exhibition in London, a mere 24 hours by train (as against what would have taken his father several days by coach or steamer). It opened his eyes 'to a country of which I had seen nothing and known almost as little'.[9] The railways in Britain and on the Continent changed what was possible and for whom, a development not always to the liking of the socially superior, who preferred travel to be their preserve. 'What beasts the English are – the middle orders when they go touring. These railroads are the great curse of this country' was the snobbish remark of one.[10] Excursionists on the Continent aroused a similar response ('devil's dust tourists'[11] was one label) from those not accustomed to sharing the experience of travel with those not of their rank. For their part, the respectable middle classes were not too enthused about the arrival of the cheerful masses at their resorts.

Money gave choice, but it remains true that urban families tended to be remarkably loyal to the same holiday resort in Scotland year after year – Elie or North Berwick for the professional elite of Edinburgh – and indeed, from one generation to the next. But others discovered England, and once their appetite was whetted may have then looked further afield. The same railway and steamship facilities that allowed easier travel to Scotland and through that country for English and foreign visitors could also, and did take away Scottish travellers to England and the Continent. Travel agencies such as Thomas Cook's from the 1840s brought Tartan Tours to Scotland but also were later to offer the same kind of conducted tours to Switzerland, Palestine and the Middle East. The appeal of these carefully costed and timetabled tours cannot be overrated, especially to those who were both inexperienced travellers and who had limited free time and restricted budgets. Cook took the worry out of travel. But that could work both for and against Scotland. There was no protection or preference for the home market; although overall demand was rapidly expanding, destinations could rise – and fall. Tourism was a highly competitive industry.

Scotland's success, for it was success, did owe much to better transport, 'a perfect

9   Jeffrey A. Auerbach, *The Great Exhibition of 1851* (New Haven, CT, 1991), 138.
10  Letter of Thomas Babbington of St Albans, 15 October 1864, Glasgow City Archives, TD 1/913.
11  The phrase was used of Cook's tourists by James Lever, British consul at La Spezia in Italy in 'Continental Excursionists', *Blackwood's Magazine*, February 1865, 231. Cited in B. Cormack, *History of Holidays, 1812–1990* (London, 1998), 34.

revolution in favour of the traveller'[12] as one contemporary writer called it. Inaccessibility has its charms, and it is remarkable how, despite all the difficulties, early travellers, including those like Dr Johnson neither in the first flush of youth nor in good physical condition, did find their way around. But easier transport did encourage a much greater enthusiasm. The coming of the railway is usually held to have been a key factor in the growth of tourism in Britain. There is certainly no doubt as to its role in Scotland: in opening up areas to visitors and summer residenters, carrying them and their considerable luggage; in moving large numbers of excursionists, weekends and day trippers; in promoting resorts and events. Any mainland resort of any size and pretension pressed for a rail service, whether a spa town, seaside resort or inland retreat: Moffat and Strathpeffer, Gullane and Dornoch, Peebles and Grantown all successfully secured stations. Tourist marketing, which was in this period undertaken largely by the carriers rather than the destinations, could and did influence where tourists went and the railway companies played a key role in the promotion of Scotland through poster, handbooks and special fares. While none developed its own resort, towards the end of the nineteenth century they did invest in luxury sporting hotels, as at Cruden Bay, Turnberry and of course, the last and most opulent of all, Gleneagles. While summer tourist traffic could be very considerable, it is debatable quite how profitable over the year many of the small branch lines were. From the end of September until the following spring, without the tourists and their luggage, traffic could be light indeed. The shortness of the tourist season in Scotland was a problem for all involved in the industry, both for employment and for the finances. Highland hotels closing over the winter meant that they had to make their revenue during the season, which in turn led to complaints about the level of their charges. The growing late-Victorian taste for Christmas and New Year celebrations, which some of the bigger and better hotels began to harvest, was to be a welcome source of business ahead of the dead time of February.

Where Scotland's transport experience differs from that of England is in the much more significant role of the steamship. The coming of the steamship in the early nineteenth century lifted Scottish tourism to new levels and greatly extended its reach. Whereas in England, although steamer sailings to Margate, for example, were valued, the railway was the decisive force in the development of tourism, in Scotland that responsibility was shared with the steamships. Their service opened up in particular the West Coast firths and islands, making – as handbooks dubbed it – Oban the 'Charing Cross of the Highlands'. Bute and Arran were the focus of heavy summer traffic from Glasgow. There were also significant steamer services

---

12 *Murray's Handbook for Travellers in Scotland* (4th edn, London, 1875), 'General Introduction', ix.

on the east coast from Leith to Fife and on inland lochs – Tay, Katrine and Ness. Steamer services from London and Liverpool helped the visitor from the south, although that was a role largely superseded from the 1840s by the cross-border railways. The development of steamers capable of transatlantic sea voyages allowed and induced growing numbers of American tourists from the 1860s. The freedom from wind and tide which the steamers brought, their convenience and regularity, greatly enhanced tourist choice, allowing a confidence in their forward planning, saving on both waiting and travelling time. It was this that brought many destinations such as Iona, Staffa and Skye within range for the tourist whose time was limited.

In no part of the Western world was the steamer such an element in the cultural life of a whole region and for all classes as was true of the Clyde. Edinburgh's Portobello beach was within easy walking range of all classes in Edinburgh, but the Clyde resorts were a step too far; and for the Glaswegians a mix of coach (later train) and boat services developed.[13] The steamers pioneered the excursion or the pleasure day from Glasgow, and by the later nineteenth century there was offered by the competing companies a range of options[14] and destinations from Glasgow itself or Greenock or Dunoon or Oban to suit every taste, time-span and purse. They ranged from a week's sail amongst the Western Isles, or a circular tour coordinated with the railway companies, a day outing or evening cruise. This intensity of activity reached a crescendo during the Glasgow Fair, when a trip 'Doun the Watter' was on most Glaswegians' agenda. The better-off travelled cabin-class, the others (and the economical), steerage. 'The cheap steamers are the working man's highway to the sea air', said James Caldwell, MP in 1890.[15] The most popular sailings for the 'all the way' boats were to Rothesay, Dunoon, Brodick and Millport but there were dozens of piers elsewhere in the Firth of Clyde, as at Dumbarton, Kames, Strachur, at which the steamers could call. The Broomielaw at its peak was home to over two dozen steamers, some which functioned like floating trams.[16] Piers were built to allow regular landings at all states of the tide and some, as at Portobello, also acted as centres of entertainment, promenades, amusements and even theatres.

13 A.J. Durie, *Scotland for the Holidays: A History of Tourism in Scotland, 1780–1939* (Edinburgh, 2003), 48–63.
14 See, for example, David MacBrayne, *Summer Tours in Scotland* (various editions). The handbook for the 1897 season lists day sailings from Glasgow, special tours from Oban and circular tours in connection with the Caledonian and North British Railway companies.
15 Cited in A.J.S. Paterson, *The Golden Years of the Clyde Steamers* (Newton Abbot, 1969), 69. Also Ian McCrorie, *To the Coast. One Hundred Years of the Caledonian Steam Packet Co.* (Fairlie, 1989).
16 Joy Montieth and David McRorie, 'The Linnet', in *Clyde Piers. A Pictorial Record* (Greenock, 1982), 63.

Even the much maligned roads made their contribution. There was a substantial improvement in the road network of the later eighteenth century thanks to turnpikes. There was matching progress in the infrastructure of posting inns, where horses and guides could be obtained, and of decent hotels, though the quality of surfaces and rooms alike varied and tended to become poorer the further north and west of Perth that the traveller went. 'Take a linch pin', was Mrs Murray's advice. 'Provide yourself with a strong roomy carriage, and have the springs well corded.'[17] Difficulties and dangers were commonplace. It was not just the quality of roads in some areas – and of the horses – that posed a problem[18] but the hazards of ferry and sea crossings. When the Wordsworths toured in 1803, their horse was terrified by its treatment at the hands of the Connel ferrymen and unsafe near water thereafter.[19] The Argyllshire archives at Lochgilphead contain a series of complaints about this crossing, which appear largely to have stemmed from the temptations of the inn on the north side where the men waited for business. On 20 October 1890 a Mr Macphail complained about the frightening treatment given to his daughter and a friend by a tipsy boatman who fell off his seat and dropped his oar overboard so that his daughter had herself to take an oar.[20] Ferrymen in Scotland (not the girls who rowed) had always had an ill reputation for surliness and insobriety, and this was a continuing grievance, abated only by road and rail bridges which took away their livelihood: hard on them, but a relief to all travellers. Most longer distance traffic was captured by the railways, with by the 1870s grass growing over the main Inverness road north of Pitlochry. Coach services were important as feeders to the rail stations and the resorts, and of course in the more remote areas. Coaching services survived only for the sightseer and excursion party: as an Argyllshire land factor observed in November 1881, 'a tourist coach pays best in the most outlandish place.'[21]

Transport helped to make tourism, but there was also an interplay. Tourism *induced* a provision of transport facilities, whether 'summer only' coach trips from the resorts for the tourist or special rail outings, or day cruises on the water. The arrival of the bicycle in the later nineteenth century was to enliven many rural communities accustomed only to the occasional cart or drove of animals on their

17  Mrs Murray of Kensington, *Companion and Useful Guide to the Beauties of Scotland* (London, 1799), 11.
18  See Elizabeth Diggle on the way from Montrose to Blair, late at night, 10 June 1788, 'the horses failed near the top of the hill & down we went, chaise, horses & all, backwards and I was frightened to death but not otherwise killed for a tree stopped us after a while'.
19  Carol Kyros Walker (ed.), *Dorothy Wordsworth, Recollections of a Tour Made in Scotland, [1803]* (New Haven, CT, 1997), introduction, 140.
20  Argyll and Bute Archives, Lochgilphead: CA/11/227.
21  Argyll and Bute Archives, BO 43.4: Evidence to the Oban Road Trustees, 244: 'The wheel traffic on the roads is chiefly during the months of July, August, and September, in connection with the tourist traffic.'

roads. Crowds of middle-class and artisan cyclists from the towns, male and female, were to be found on summer evenings or at weekends, fanning out from the cities. It brought business for many little country inns 'that had gone almost to decay',[22] assisted by the Cyclists' Touring Club which provided in its handbooks lists of recognised places for food, drink and accommodation. By the 1890s, thanks to mass production and a growing second-hand market, there may have been as many as 150,000 cyclists in Scotland.[23] The motor car made a much noisier entrance in the 1890s, an asset to touring, but a mixed blessing in terms of smell, dust, mud and danger to bystanders, their walls and dykes, cats and dogs. Inexperienced drivers in the era before any driving test were a danger to themselves and their passengers; smashes and casualties were common. Two touring cyclists from Paisley will have spoken for many when they cursed the motor traffic on the road between Perth and Inverness: 'the motors were innumerable and intolerable. What with the stink of their petrol, the bray of their hooters, the pother of their dust, and the illimitable lordliness of their occupants, they added appreciably to the terrors of life.'[24]

That tourists could travel did not mean that they would come to Scotland. But Scotland had a good range of attractions which gave it a strong appeal. In addition to the landscape and scenery, there was the work of Scott, arguably the single greatest literary 'pull' for any country anywhere, which placed Scotland on the map for history and romance. The rebellions of 1715 and 1745 became glamorous, and the gallant cause was worth its wealth in tourist gold. Scottish spas, with the possible exception of Strathpeffer, attracted few non-nationals, and it was golf rather than sea-bathing (an acquired taste only for the hardy) that drew English visitors to the Scottish coast. Field sports, salmon fishing, grouse shooting and deer stalking did greatly interest the upper classes and new money alike, and, endorsed by Balmoralism, were the only high cards that Scotland could play to retain their allegiance. And played they were to advantage. Scottish moors and lodges were sought after, and railway traffic north was never heavier than on the eve of the Glorious Twelfth. Contemporaries called this sporting flow 'a golden stream'.

To the person new to travel, Scotland was an inviting destination. There was no problem with money, nor with culture (though the Scottish Sunday or Sabbath was to outsiders bleak), nor with language. As tourism advanced and increased, so Gaelic faded. A Methodist lady, travelling in June 1807, noted that the very intelligent woman who had rowed her on Loch Lomond said that Gaelic was very

22 Sir Archibald Geikie, *Scottish Reminiscences* (Glasgow, 1906), 310.
23 See Alastair Dodds, 'Cycling', in K. Veitch (ed.), *Transport and Communications; A Compendium of Scottish Ethnology* 8 (Edinburgh, 2009), 557–62.
24 Walter A. Mursell, *Two on a Tour* (Paisley, 1909), 37.

little in use with them now, 'especially among the young people'.[25] Above all, Scotland was safe. Travel in parts of Southern Europe could be hazardous even in peacetime. Theft and robbery, and even kidnapping and murder, were not unknown; and the botched rescue in 1871 by the Greek government of one party of wealthy tourists ('the Marathon murders') which resulted in the deaths of three Englishmen created a sensation.[26] Nothing like that, nor the endemic low level violence of parts in Ireland, threatened the tourist in Scotland. The Highlander may have once been a raider or rebel, but those days were long past. Indeed instead of wrongs against tourists, it may have been the other way round: the Police regulations of Argyll set out very clearly what could be done should a traveller set himself to depart without paying his bill. Tourists collected souvenirs, often without any thought or sense of doing wrong, whether rare flowers or chips off tombs. Their picnics left litter behind, their days-out were too often made riotous by drink, and a good time for them could too easily be a bad time for the place that they had visited. The tourist in Scotland more often sinned than was sinned against. Yet, it must be stressed that both the tourist and the host were mostly well behaved, with even the Glasgow Fair passing off with remarkably little incident.

## Tourist diaries and journals

Important though the industry became, and spectacular its rise, our knowledge of tourism, and indeed of Scotland itself, would be very much poorer without travellers' and tourist accounts. Were it not for the journals and diaries specifically kept by visitors during their travels, or as summer sections in a yearly journal, or the letters sent home or to friends, we would know little indeed about tourism in pre-modern Scotland. It was the subject of comment and of concern in the press, but neither national government nor parliament took any significant interest in this new industry, a general state of detachment which was only to change after the Second World War. No public money was put into it, no official body – unlike on the Continent – was set up to promote it, nor was it the subject of inquiries as to its prospects or working conditions. No national or regional statistics were gathered, in the way that figures for coal mined, or ship tonnage launched, or cotton cloth were assembled. Some local councils were more involved, primarily through the provision of civic amenities and marketing publicity; town clerks of seaside towns

25 Arthur R.B. Robinson (ed.), *Seeking the Scots. An English Woman's Journey in 1807* (York, 2006), 62.
26 See the important article by Martin Blinkhorn, 'Liability, Responsibility and Blame: British Ransom Victims in the Mediterranean Periphery, 1860–81', *Australian Journal of Politics and History* 46:3 (2000), 336–56.

and spa resorts issued local guides and lists of accommodation. But what they could do was limited by lack of resources. Blackpool Corporation secured in 1879 – how is not known – the authority to levy local taxation specifically for advertising, but this was a unique concession.[27] Other resorts in the United Kingdom could only envy Blackpool's ability to mount well-funded advertising campaigns each and every year. The legal system saw little of tourism, except when hotels came into bankruptcy, and if the law was little concerned, the churches were only marginally more interested, except – but significantly – over the vexed issue of Sunday travel and behaviour. Although at the local level, in tourist resorts like Moffat, occasional counts of visitors were taken, there was, for example, no systematic collection of regional or national statistics to show how many visitors went where and for how long. Books for visitors to sign, with their name and address, were kept at castles, great houses and other points of attraction and can be used to show numbers and the place of origin. Amongst those that have survived from the nineteenth century are visitors' books for New Lanark, Abbotsford, Doune Castle, Heriot's Hospital and the Glasgow Necropolis, but most, sadly, have disappeared, simply thrown out, or cut up for the signatures of the famous. Visitors' lists for the summer were published, usually on a weekly basis, in local newspapers at the more respectable resorts, which caught the middle class and professional summer residenter, those renting longer term accommodation or staying for a while at hotels. For the excursion and day-tripper trade, the best source of information was the local or national press. The arrival and behaviour of a large excursion party in a town like Peebles or North Berwick was nearly always reported in the local paper, with either approval or disgust.

The insights and detail provided by visitors' recollections is, therefore, of prime value. Every educated tourist, as well as sending letters, would have kept a record of some kind, at least a pocket book of recollections, to act as a reminder or souvenir of their travels to inform themselves and their friends or family. A few from the outset were designed for publication, and others (the great majority) were not. Some did reach the press, brought out perhaps on the strength of the author's name, or just because of the interesting nature of their material. Though many have vanished, every year seems to bring more to light. Recent examples include: the travels in 1807 of a Methodist lady from Hull, a banker's wife; the 1825 diary of the Napoleonic Marshal Macdonald returning to his father's birthplace in Uist; and the edited text of a Polish tutor's four years in Scotland between 1820 and 1824.[28] There are diaries

27 John K. Walton, *Blackpool* (Edinburgh ,1998), 82–3.

28 Robinson, *Seeking the Scots*; Jean-Didier Hache, *The French MacDonald. Journey of a Marischal of Napoleon in the Highlands and Islands of Scotland in 1825* (Isle of Lewis, 2007) and Mona Kedslie McLeod (ed.), *From Charlotte Square to Fingal's Cave. Reminiscences of a Journey through Scotland, 1820–1824. By Krystyn Lach-Szyrma* (East Linton, 2004).

and journals, or collections of letters and scrapbooks, which either have not yet surfaced or remain in archives[29] and private hands (as is Thomas Adam's 1857 excursion), only some of which have been located and listed. The very valuable survey undertaken by Robin Gard[30] of travel diaries and collections of correspondence, including much Scottish material, held in the county record offices of England and Wales, needs both revision and expansion to take in material held in Scotland. Indeed, a similar survey and trawl in North America, given the scale of tourism to Europe from the 1860s onwards, would certainly be rewarding. But, even as it is, there is no shortage.

Pleasurable – mostly – to read, they can shed light on how people travelled, what sort of accommodation they found, how far Scotland was geared to cater for tourists and holiday-makers like them, and the appeal of the localities which they visited. Taken together (and the historian needs to base assessment and interpretation on a range rather than just a few), diaries and related material do help to show the transition over time in tourism from an experience of the privileged few to something that everyone (other than perhaps the very poorest) hoped to enjoy. The value of the tourist eye has long been appreciated: what they saw, whom they met, visitors and locals, what they experienced by way of food and service, what points of interest or concern that they found, the small things that they notice, as well as the big issues. An assumption that is easily made is that the bigger the name – say Dr Johnson, Wordsworth or Keats – the more important the diary or journal, but this is not necessarily so. Some read better, and others are more colourful. But for the historian, it is what was seen that matters. The big name, and the reputation, may explain why an account has been preserved and published but they do not guarantee the value! At the lower end, there was no qualifying test as to how well a person could write when they wrote for themselves or their circle. There are those that are just trite and banal.

What follows, therefore, is merely a selection which is the tip of the iceberg, indicative and, it is to be hoped, helpful. No claim is made that these are fully representative, although they are not monochromatic in terms of class, or quality. There is no European or American visitor amongst them, nor any Cook's tourist. None is a sporting enthusiast, drawn by grouse or golf, none a botanist or geologist, none a family with small children or a honeymoon couple. Indeed, none has left any trace of their travels; their arrival or departure is not marked, as was common

---

29  See, for example, P.G. Vesey, 'Visitors and Voyages: a Personal Selection of Travel Diaries and Related Material in the Scottish Record Office', and A. Hilley, '"Scotland's Name is Poetry to Our Ears": German Travellers in Scotland c 1800–1860', both in *Scottish Archives* 2 (1996).
30  Robin Gard, *The Observant Traveller. Diaries of Travel in England, Wales and Scotland in the County Record Offices of England and Wales* (London, 1989).

with distinguished visitors, by a paragraph in the local paper. They are in that way representative of what was ceasing to be the preserve just of the elite. Being 'on tour', as Elizabeth Diggle's 1788 *Tour* shows, had been a measured and leisurely sortie, either relatively or entirely unconstrained by money or time. Bald is a very different kind of traveller, keen from his Glasgow home and business to take any opportunity on foot or with horse for a short jaunt or longer foray; to the hills or the coast, across to Stirling or to Edinburgh. That there was an established circuit for visitors interested in a 'peep at the Highlands' is reflected in the choice of route taken by the family party in the 1817 tour; both that and the follow up in the following year are assisted by developments in accommodation, information and in transport, within and to Scotland. Within just a few years of its introduction, the steamboat was playing an appreciable part in inland and coastal tourism. The coming of the railways was further to aid travel; although coaching and walking (quite remarkable distances) were still the greater part of Thomas Adam's process in 1857 to Loch Maree. The way in which Scotland had been brought within easy range is shown by the Underhills; not for them a stage by stage trip over a week or so by coach, or a two-day sea voyage, but an overnight rail service from Wolverhampton. Better transport shrank Scotland, and let visitors see more in a given period, even if a cost of that was more rush and less reflection, and a tendency to run across the same people with overlapping itineraries. It is clear, as the Underhills' experience shows, that tourist parties did criss-cross each other; this could be helpful when they swapped information as to what to see and where to avoid, which hotels had good service and which did not, thus allowing itineraries to be adjusted. But time mattered, and mattered most to those who had the least free time: it is no accident that Mary Allison, a storeman's wife, counts her holidays not in months or weeks but day by day.

As with every source, there are a number of considerations which should be taken into account. However well written, they should not be taken as 'gospel'. They have their value, and their limitations. A key issue is that they are from the perspective of the *visitor*, not the *visited*, looking from the outside, rather than looking back at the visitor. It would be good to have an innkeeper or hotelier's diary, those receiving tourist and visitors, to round out the picture. As to writing styles, there is no mandatory template, nor indeed any necessary relationship between quality of writing and the value of the account to the historian. Bald, for example, is to today's taste very wordy, aware and proud of his use of language. He has a fascination with long words: not for him the deception of simplicity. Was it just for himself that he shows off so? Most readers will be irritated by his cloud of words. Yet his journal is immensely valuable for what it reveals of how tourism and travelling was evolving in the last decade of the eighteenth century.

The essential questions which need to be asked of these diaries and journals, as with any source, are: who was the writer? For whom was it written? How and when was it written? Some understanding of who the writer was is important, as they are not necessarily objective in their reporting; they are offering responses. The written record, consciously and unconsciously, reflects things such as the education of writer, both in a narrow and a wider sense. The reader sees Scotland through their spectacles, which are tinted by culture and class, prismed by their prejudices and values, constricted or enlarged by their vision, tunnel or peripheral. The capacity to observe is particular to the individual, and some are much more aware than others, but their record is also shaped by their own sensitivities, gender, age and experience, level of education, regional background, their reading and peer group. Their response can also reflect their state of health, the weather, or their religious perspective! Some show a willingness to listen, as Thomas Adam did, and to look beyond the stock and conditioned reflex, beyond what for instance, the guidebook indicated that they should find interesting or 'picturesque'. But some do not; they respond as they are expected to respond. Given that these writings are likely to be coloured by the background, personality, finances or health of the author, the more that can be learned of their circumstances, the better. Key questions to consider include from what section of society were they, and from which area? What age were they, and in what physical condition? Their experience of travel generally or of Scotland in particular is relevant: were they a first-time traveller, or more seasoned? Was there perhaps someone in their party who had been that way before? Were they drawing on – and had they learnt from – what others had found about how and where to travel?

But in this legitimate desire for background lies a problem. For some of the writers there is a degree of biographical information. But for others there is very little or none at all, and indeed some accounts (such as the 1817 and 1818 Tours) may not even have an author's name, forcing the reader to rely on what can be gleaned from internal evidence. Allowance also has to be made for the process of composition. Some travellers wrote up a full journal as they travelled, complete with coloured or crayon sketches or later scraps, photographs, *cartes-de-visites*, souvenirs, pressed flowers. Others kept a rough notebook, which they later revised into a final and more polished record, which was a way of extending and revisiting the pleasure of the holiday. Some wrote letters which have the virtue of immediacy, later perhaps consolidated into copy books to record outgoing mail, as is the case with Elizabeth Diggle. A later generation was to collect and to send postcards; experiences caught in a sentence or two. Accounts written up subsequent to the visit may flow better, but they also run the risk of copyist's mistakes with words missed out or misread. Equally, the temptation to rewrite or to embellish experience is not always resisted. It may not be the conversion of what might have been into what did happen, but there can be a tendency to exaggerate or dramatise a minor mishap into a full blown crisis.

For whom is an obvious question. Those not written for general consumption, but for personal use as a record and reminiscence, or for very limited circulation within a small family circle had, or may have had, an authenticity beyond the travelogues that are to be found aplenty in literature of the period. But even if the record was designed only for their own private use, a degree of discretion or censorship may have been exercised; not all that happened finds its way to the record, for whatever reason. Where the record was for private or family use, there is also the problem of allusion; the writer uses abbreviations or references which make perfect sense to him or her and to the friends in the know, but which are obscure or meaningless to those outside the circle.

It can, of course, be tantalising and frustrating when some things, remarks on which would be expected, do not appear, and others about which it would be good to know much more only flit briefly into sight. Either way, these accounts provide a marvellous jumping off point for further enquiry, explanation and comment. Sometimes follow-up research in local sources can help to fill out the picture, but not always. Dorothy Wordsworth, on her second tour of Scotland in September 1822, mentions that the coach from Stirling to Castle Cary – where they were to get the canal boat to Glasgow – was driven by an elderly Negro, an 'honest blacky'[31] whom she declared to be 'welcomed wherever he goes'. But of the background or circumstances of this Thomas himself nothing further can be learned, either from Dorothy, informative as she often is, nor indeed from local literature or lore or newspapers. While these accounts provide glimpses when a full report was wished for, and are silent when comment was anticipated, nevertheless we should be grateful for the light that they do shed and what can be taken from them.

31 E. de Selincourt (ed.), 'Journal of My Second Tour in Scotland', *Journals of Dorothy Wordsworth* (London, 1943), 348.

# Editorial method

The selected tourist accounts which follow have been arranged in chronological order and each is prefaced by a short introduction, which deals with authorship, provenance, style and particular issues of transcription and of editing. As a general rule, however, the following have been adopted as standard practice throughout. Original spelling and some stylistic features such as dashes and underlinings have been retained. Square brackets have been used for editorial additions and explanations: a word or phrase missing or indecipherable in the original is rendered [****]; a word partially illegible or incomprehensible is shown [?thus]; sections omitted are clearly indicated thus [ ... ] and [sic] is used to highlight original spelling. Place names have been a particular challenge; some are spelled phonetically according to what the traveller heard and some have changed or faded away. Where it is clear what is meant, they have been left – for example, Inveraray or Inverary – and on occasion, modern equivalents have been suggested [thus].

# Note on the illustrations

The first group is a selection from the many photographic 6 x 9 cm 'scraps' which Henry Underhill pasted throughout his account, probably having purchased them en route. They illustrate the sights and scenes which he and his party saw, and are placed in the journal at the relevant sections of the tour. There is one mistake; curiously the view of Ben Nevis is pasted in twice, once correctly and other well out of sequence. Some of the prints have faded, a few are damaged, and others have stray glue on them, so what follows is a selection only. It is to be regretted that there are none here of Inverness, nor of Balmoral, for example. The originals mostly lack captions unless provided by the photographer, and whereas the town views are easily recognised, some of the country scenes are less certain and can only be identified by where in the text they are placed. Captions have accordingly been supplied along with a line of comment.

Some of the views would have been familiar to visitors at any time since the turn of the century, but equally some of what Henry Underhill saw, and the photographs catch, was either new on the scene in the later 1860s – the Highland Railway at Killiecrankie – or about to be swept away, such as the Old College in Glasgow. They have, therefore, a value beyond their place in Underhill's journal.

The second group are line drawings done by Mary Allison herself which are embedded throughout her letter to her niece. They have her captions in her own hand. Sadly, the condition of the manuscript means they are a little faded, and sellotape mars some of the drawings, but nevertheless they are a valuable part of the account.

# ELIZABETH DIGGLE:

## *Journal of a Tour from London to the Highlands of Scotland 19 April to 7 August 1788*

## *Introduction*

Elizabeth Diggle's journal is a consolidation, perhaps made by the family rather than her, of the thirty-two letters she sent to her sister and other relations back in Kent during her extended tour in the spring and summer of 1788. And what a remarkable tour it was. It was just after the middle of April that she had set off from the south of England in her own carriage transport, accompanied by her aunt and a servant, Joseph. Her first letter, which is dated 19 April, is from Hartfield: 'here we are, aunt and niece at the Salisbury Arms'. It was an early start to the tourism season. Not, however, until early August, nearly four months later and with many hundreds of miles under the wheels of her carriage, did she finally return. Scotland was her destination and the reason for her tour, but the first leg through England was no light undertaking: getting to the north, by way of Leicester, Nottingham, Durham and Newcastle, took her more than ten days before she was able to reach the border at Berwick. May, June and the early part of July were spent in Scotland, with an added-on sortie up to Aberdeen, showing that she was not pressed for time, before crossing back into England, this time by the west coast at Gretna on 7 July. The final leg of her return – by Carlisle, the Lakes, Buxton and Oxford – was not unduly hastened by a desire to get home, taking in as it did Chatsworth, Warwick Castle and Blenheim Palace.

It was a formidable expedition for a single lady, even if accompanied by her aunt and a servant, and for someone whose health was not entirely robust. Not quite well at Murthly in Perthshire where she was dosed, and over-tired at Aberdeen (letter of 10 June), she was advised by a physician to take two days' rest, which she did not enjoy, as the accommodation was so overcrowded. True, she had ample money (or drafts which were honoured and converted into cash) to soften the experience of touring and possessed letters of introduction to ease her way into society. The relative isolation of being in this distant and different country was lessened by letters from her family, which caught up with her from time to time, by the ability to buy reading materials and by the courtesy of the landowning class.

The challenges, however, of travel, accommodation and of the weather were very real and took their toll. It is small wonder that at Carlisle she noted that her hat was faded, her coat pinched, her carriage all faded, her servant's jacket turned into a brown one and 'we make as shabby a figure as need be'. The final letter in the journal sent from Oxford on 7 August promised that she would be galloping to Broadstairs – perhaps the family home – 'as shabby and dirty and shocking as possible', and then on to Margate, where her sister and her children (for whom she was bringing back some Highland dolls) had spent the summer: 'how we shall look amongst the spruce Margatians, I can only conceive'.

We know all too little about Elizabeth Diggle, of her circumstances and background, only what can be gleaned from the letters. She seems to have been single, rather than married or a widow, middle-aged and reasonably well-off. But her situation was no obstacle to travel or indeed enjoyment; as Jane Austen observed, 'a single woman of good fortune is always respectable, and may be as sensible and pleasant as anybody else'.[1] She had the means and the time to travel, the ambition to go far and, without children, the freedom to go much further than her sister, for whom sea-bathing at nearby Margate was all that was possible. Although the home counties were clearly familiar territory to her (Bagshot Heath, Ascot and Margate are mentioned), we do not know for sure whether she had been further afield. There are some allusions to dressing like the French, manners like those of French society, and the way that Edinburgh shop fronts were painted in a resemblance of Paris, from which one can infer that she had been in France. Certainly, the confidence and competence of her travelling suggests no lack of experience. There are also at the end of the journal, but in a different hand, notes for a journey from Basingstoke to Bristol and another for an excursion to the Isle of Wight, but nothing to confirm whether these were for her, or indeed ever undertaken.

What shines through the letters is her liveliness of spirit, her enthusiasm and acuteness of observation. Elizabeth would, one suspects, be very good company. She walks, climbs, dances reels, reads and generally mixes, to take full advantage of her travels, attending church, going to the theatre, visiting museums and picture galleries, looking at natural wonders, going round great houses and castles. What was also on her agenda, and what indeed for many tourists was part of the accepted schedule of activities, was the inspection of the burgeoning industrial and manufacturing enterprises. We can too easily assume that tourism at this period was essentially only scenic and cultural, focused on nature and art, history and architecture. While on occasion, there may have been an element of breaking up a long day's travel by looking at a works or factory, these new ventures, what was made and how, really

---

1   Jane Austen, *Emma* (Glasgow, 1965), first published in 1816, 80.

interested many people of Elizabeth's class. Her tour takes in, for example, Carron ironworks, a cotton mill at Wolverhampton, Wedgewood's pottery manufactory at Etruria (with which 'she was much pleased') and the button-making section of Boulton's Soho works, where she saw – but made nothing of – the steam engine.[2]

But while Edinburgh and its society enthused her, she was decidedly smitten by the Highlands. In her letter 17, dated from Killin, 17 June, she declared 'I am quite in love with them & never shall like to live near London any more.' It was a sentiment that she repeated time and time again. While she found the buildings at Buxton were magnificent ('the place at present is very full of company many invalids, such a walking up & down. Such riding! Driving and bathing!'),[3] Derbyshire she wrote down as a mere 'ugly aping of the Scottish Highlands'. She disliked Manchester as a most disagreeable, noisy, bustly place. 'I do assure you the air as we advance south seems absolutely thick to me & is quite oppressive; there is a fineness in the air of the north of Scotland that cannot be described.' Even the English Lakes, though attractive, were not so sublime. She took a justified pride in what she had done: 'at Lorwood where we dined I saw three gentlemen opening the doors of the post chaise, examining our looks and pronounced that they belonged to travellers tho' I doubt much if they guessed how far we had been'. And she would have been aware that as a woman traveller she stood out; whilst in the Lakes she noted that there seemed to be 'a great number of men tourists at present, but very few women'. With her resources and resourcefulness, she had had a wide choice of where she went. A grand or mini-tour on the Continent would still have been open to her in 1788 although revolution and war were soon to close that option for the British tourist: it was her choice to go to Scotland, and it was a destination that did not disappoint.

## Note

Elizabeth Diggle's journal is a 128-page notebook held in Glasgow University Library as Ms Gen 738. There are thirty-two letters in all and what follows here is that part of the journal containing those letters written from Scotland (numbered 8 to 23), that comprise about two-thirds of the whole. Included also is a 'plan for the lesser tour of the Highlands of Scotland, with list of the stages', and notes on the calibre of accommodation to be found. Excluded is a schedule for an excursion to the visit the Isle of Wight from Yarmouth, which is in a different hand, and another from Basingstoke to Bristol, and thence to Berkhampstead.

2   Letter 31 from Derby, Thursday evening.
3   Letter 29, Chatsworth, 26 July.

# *Journal*

## LETTER 6, NEWCASTLE, 28 APRIL [1788]

… We made an excursion to Tynemouth castle which is a complete ruin standing on a rock hanging out over the sea. It was a lovely day, & we sat by the sea on a piece of rock rising up in the sand for an hour. It is a charming retired bay for bathing, but it is too early in the season for the machines are not yet come down. We dined at our <u>coal</u> hole where was a club assembled to celebrate the anniversary of the battle of Culloden …

## LETTER 8, EDINBURGH, 1 MAY

Yes, here we are, safe & well & comfortably settled for we arrived by eight last night. Our history broke off at Alnwick. The Castle was built by the late Duke of Northumberland upon the site & plan of the old one. I do not know whether it is their scarcity that makes these gothic buildings with their lofty towers & appendages inspire more sublime ideas & seem more proper for the residence of a duke than the lighter structures of modern times, but I incline to think it is owing to their very appearance. On the battlements of Alnwick are rude stone figures of warriors, differently armed who seem to threaten all who shall dare approach. The form of the building makes the rooms of uncommon shape, not the less handsome or commodious than the more regular, the inside finishing of the whole is perfectly conformable to the antique appearance of the building without. We proceeded from Alnwick to Belford, (a vile place by the bye) & therefore resolved to post on to [Edinburgh] next day. We crossed the Tweed at Berwick over a fine stone bridge. The town looks black & ugly but the river is beautiful. The country beyond B: is wild open & uncultivated for some miles, but no where I think as bad as Bagshot heath, it is diversified at least with hills on the one hand, & a fine view of the sea on the other. We passed over the curious bridge (Pease Bridge) which is thrown across a deep valley, & makes a good road where it would otherwise be impassable. Dunbar being the first scotch town we came to, we had there an opportunity of observing wherein the appearance of the people differed from those of England & in consequence remarked only that the women were without shoes & stockings & hats or bonnets, giving one in the latter respect an idea of France. It is a fine ride from Dunbar to Edinburgh, fine romantic hilly prospects, & yet the road is so contrived as not to pass over the hills.

## LETTER 9, EDINBURGH, 3 [MAY]

We have begun to profit of our letters, & nothing can be more flattering to the writers than the early & polite marks of attention we receive in consequence of them; nothing more pleasing to us than to make acquaintance with so many agreeable, & estimable people of both sexes independent of the immediate local advantage we derive from their attentions just now. We have been this morning to the Holy rood house, a fine building but sadly neglected. We saw Rizzio's blood, he & Mary, & the Countess of Argyle were supping in the boudoir, we saw, when the dear Darnley, (seven feet four) did this job. We saw his bones & stout ones they were, & two pictures of him & some of Qn Mary but there is a charming picture by Vandyke of Charles 1st & his Queen, it belongs to Ld Dunmore who has refused seven thousand guineas for it, as the woman said who showed it. This palace stands at the bottom of the castle, in which street the outside of the shops are so painted as to give it a great resemblance of Paris. The Castle commands a charming view of the Forth, the new town & the old town & the country which is a charming combination of things. We are going to the play this evening. The weather is very warm: the town is at least as nice & neat as London, it is now very empty as the principal families go out of town at this season. On Sunday we went to hear Dr Blair preach: on Monday dined at Sir W. Forbes with a large party and went after to the play. We went yesterday to see Newbattle & Dalkeith, they are both charming palaces. The air here is wondrous fine & clear - and here is the advantage of sea bathing but a mile off. I am sure here is no want of trees near Edinburgh nor leaves either & tis too warm now (in May) to have a fire. - They put macaroni, & ham, & veal together & so I was taken in when I asked for my dear mac. I am as stupid as an owl, & I'll tell you why, I have seen so many new people & things within this week, that they are all in my head pell mell, a castle upon a lady of quality, & a scotch bonnet upon a church etc etc the young ladies here in general draw & paint & are much accomplished. They have all fine teeth & are taller than you & I. I cannot tell what we shall do next, but I can tell you what you ought to do, & that is write, you wicked pair -! That knew we were to stay here and if we could not <u>see</u> any old friends we might <u>read</u> some, & so adieu! I wish you a good breakfast & pen, ink & paper as soon as the tea things are gone.

## LETTER 10, [EDINBURGH], 7 MAY

Here are seven mortal days that we have been fixtures & hoping you would make good use of that time to let us hear from you, & all we have had from the post office has been seven <u>nos</u>. If it were not for those vile negatives, I should say this is one of the most agreeable places I was ever in. We are just returned from the Botanic gardens which is at some little distance from the Town, & contains a space of five acres very well planted with all manner of shrubs & laid out into agreeable walks. There are several large greenhouses full of those exotics that will not bear the open air. Lectures in botany are read here for the benefit of the students that are at the University. Our ears as well as our eyes & noses were regaled in this delightful garden; I never heard so charming a concert of singing birds. We went yesterday to Roslin chapel, which is the most curiously decorated with wrought stone of any thing I have ever seen & pretty entire, however it came to escape the ravages of time & the rage of reformation; the old woman who shows it has been in the office fifty years & is as great a curiosity as the chapel & she told us the history of every piece of sculpture but in a tone & language not easily understood by us. The weather did not permit us to visit Roslin castle but it appeared to be a ruin situated in a woody vale, its neighbourhood is noted for fine strawberries & large parties are made to go thither from Ed[inbu]r[gh] in the season. We went afterwards to Craigmillar castle, a very old place apparently deserted by the owner, it is situated on a high rock, & commands a fine view of Edin[bu]r[gh]: the firth of Forth & adjoining country. We have seen the museum in the college thro' the politeness of Dr Walker the professor of natural history. There is a remarkable good collection of Otaheite[4] cloaths & utensils. They have not yet room to display any of these things properly & indeed the whole of the college is very old & too confined for the great number of students. We are just returned from a review, the day is fine & the scene gay & splendid, Edinburgh poured forth its multitudes, & I believe we should have been crushed to death if we had not been well attended by military gentlemen who took care to keep us in the front of the line. The Parliament house is a very handsome building in the old town; it has a very curious roof. The Exchange is a very handsome square near it. The assembly rooms are new & magnificent they are in the new town the ball room has the greatest profusion of glass lustres that I ever saw in one room: these rooms are not yet painted which is the case with many in the new town, I fancy it must be from great care to have the walls dry first, & yet they inhabit their houses. Sunday: We are just come from church only think the pews are placed circularly facing the pulpit, & raised one above another like a theatre; in the Kings arms the Unicorn is placed at the right sight [*sic*], in his post of supporter & the arms of Scotland makes the first quarter. O' I am so tired we have been climbing up a steep mountain called Arthur's seat, we were two hours & a half going up and down & so good night, for we are going to breakfast with a fine garden tomorrow.

4   Tahitian.

## LETTER 11, EDINBURGH, [****] MAY

I walked seven miles yesterday in the heat of the day & saw an original of
Queen Mary that was not enchanting & glass making & cutting, that seems like
a miracle. We have absolutely seen everything in Edinburgh, down [to] the
performances of the portrait painters [*sic*]. Every body insists upon our returning
to the races, but I cannot tell. I wonder whether I talk Scotch yet & my aunt says
I do. Indeed we have been very happy in Ed[inbu]r[gh] perfectly well
accommodated, and an ease in the manners of those we were introduced to
(bordering upon the French) that was quite the thing for a short acquaintance. I
forgot in my last to mention an excursion to Pennicuik, the seat of Sir —- Clerk
a few miles from Edinburgh, chiefly remarkable for a hall with the sides and
ceiling painted, the subjects entirely from the poems of Ossian: but the house is a
very handsome modern building & the situation sweetly romantic. At this short
distance from Ed[inbu[r[gh] the young female peasants go entirely without any
covering upon the head except a ribbon that binds up the hair & gives them a
very pretty simple picturesque appearance.[5]

Kinross, 15th We left Ed[inbu]r[gh] this morning & proceeded by a very
pleasant road to Barnbugle (Lord Roseberry's) the walls of the house are washed
by the Forth, but the park is beautiful & well wooded. Then to Hopetoun House,
a very fine large stone building standing on an eminence a small distance from the
river & has a good many pictures in it. Then we crossed at the Queensferry &
were landed in the postchaise by a capstan, an operation I did not much admire.
We came here to dinner, it is a small town on the side of Loch Leven, a very
beautiful lake, with a small island three acres round, where Queen Mary was
confined in a castle which is now a perfect ruin. The lake is charming, bounded,
partly, on the north by Mr Graham's plantations, (the proprietor of the lake, &
owner of a fine house near it) & on the south by barren hills. I shall draw the castle
in the morning before we go to Largo. The trout of this lake are the best I ever ate.
The road from Inverkeithing [*sic*] (where we landed) to Kinross (12 miles) is
barren & treeless. The moment one has passed one ridge of hills another starts up.
We passed near Broomhall but not in sight of it. We always have good orange
marmalade with our tea and spread thick on toast and butter. Every where near a
house are young trees & gardens; but here they told us today it was too early for
vegetables. We find the servants who show houses here refuse the accustomed fees.

---

5    Elizabeth Diggle may also have visited the Theatre as she comments in her letter of 20 July from
Liverpool that the theatre there 'was much better than that of Edinburgh. We saw the Follies of Day and
Richard Coeur de Lion. London performers. The ladies in the boxes were all so fine, in gold spotted
bonnets & you would have thought it a race ball.'

Perth, Sunday evening. We have spent two very agreeable days at Largo, and have had a very long jumbling stage hither, with hills rising above hills all the way before us, but this place is in a delightful valley watered by the Tay, & wonderfully populous it appears; indeed I never saw any thing equal to the number of children in every town and village of Scotland.

## LETTER 12, MURTHLY, 19 MAY

Largo is a sweet place, an excellent house, well situated in view of the sea, charming walks romantic den & &. The roads thro Fife are the worst in Scotland, so we had a long days journey across the country to Perth, we passed by the magnificent remains of the castle of Falkland, & a few miles before we reached, broke all once upon one of the sweetest views that can be imagined to eyes fatigued with looking upon hills, it was a most beautiful, rich and extensive valley, with the charming river Tay wandering thro' it, & the whole bounded by these said tremendous hills. We only changed horses at Perth & got here to supper. The situation of this place is beautiful the house large but old, both within and without. From breakfast to dinner we have such delightful rambles by the rivers side, or sit listening to the waterfalls & singing birds, on the edge of some den, there are such delightful places to sit down & trees & shrubs & flower … In the evening we dance reels, & I get great credit for my performance here, & at Largo. We know Scotch dishes pretty well now & they are very good. The Grampian hills rise behind the house & Birnham wood is on one side: the prospect most romantic, on the one side bounded by the Dunsinan[e] hills, beyond which it seems, for we cannot see it, the rich vale of Strathmore extends itself, & in it is the castle of Glamis. On the other side, but at due distance for beauty, we have other lofty hills, the Tay washes their feet & glides sweetly through the vale below, its banks well shaded with shrubs, and some of the hills also are well planted. Dunsinane is about eight miles from Birnam. We went yesterday to the famous rumbling brig, which is a few miles from hence & the property of Sir John; it is a most magnificent fall of water, a whole river indeed, tumbling down over stupendous craggy rocks, with the most curious irregular breaks. We scrambled over some of the most craggy parts, & then sat down, & read your last letters to the sublime accompaniment of the dashing water. … From hence we visited a building belonging to the Duke of Atholl near Dunkeld, it is called a hermitage, but has more resemblance to a fairy palace called up in a moment by the stroke of her wand, & suspended among rocks, & close to a noble cascade, the entrance is by a rude gothic porch, a painting of the blind bard Ossian being the only figure that strikes the eye, he disappears at the touch of an invisible spring, & you are introduced to a most elegant room adorned in the most improved stile of modern art. I conceive that both these apartments are meant as emblematic of the ancient & modern times. But I had too little time upon the spot, & too much subject for thought, to endeavour to trace the justness of the idea by observing the ornaments more particularly.

## LETTER 13, PERTH, 27 MAY

What does my œconomical Sister mean, by not writing for want of franks? Surely I may lay a little sum by for my own amusement & what pleasure do I rate so high as hearing from you? I only think a letter too cheap when it brings me good news from you. I am sure I get more satisfaction by it than by a half guinea Marchesi.[6] Well Miss Si is married and we are all come together from Murthly this morning & they proceeded half an hour since towards London, but Mrs B. says there will be nothing worth seeing as you two will be gone - I shall be with you in about half a century. I am glad to hear there is room upon the stairs for us, pray don't eat all the Lobsters. You will get letters by Mrs B, they will be rusty or musty, no matter. The parting of parents & children is too bad, it has unhinged me. We were really happy at Murthly, but it must be dull now; for the graces M: G: & H: are flown, the last is the ugliest. They say I climb the hills better than I did & I used to hold all twelve by the ears like a young Ossian repeating verses. We were three hours upon the Tay yesterday & I let my large fan fall in. If you can live in the kitchen garden I think it can't be far from the orchard. I have changed my Observers for the Loungers & Miss Bewelers poems, & paid six shillings into the bargain & bought a pair of shoes for five shillings & so I have not time to write any more.

## LETTER 14, MURTHLY, 1 JUNE

It is at last decided to lengthen our highland tour in case Miss R: should determine on meeting us at Edinburgh, for the races do not begin until the 21st July. Mean while we pray you continue well, we place the fullest confidence in your word that 'twas only Mr H's wickedness reported you otherwise. You will be surprised to see me date again from this place, but you would not if you saw it a month hence, if you heard the pressing importunities of this family for us to stay, & saw what a relief the addition of a few guests is, to a circle made gloomy by the absence of Mrs B:. We returned here on Thursday & were welcomed as old friends, & soon found it would be impossible to pursue our journey on Friday as we purposed, tomorrow is now the day, tomorrow it will probably be. Our route

---

6   Marchesi was an Italian castrato singer, then enjoying a huge reception in London. The construction of the phrase is that she took more enjoyment from her letter than from a half guinea ticket to hear Marchesi.

is to Aberdeen, Banff, Inverness. On Tuesday last we went to the ancient palace of Scone, which belongs at present to L[or]d Stormont, & has not much appearance of ancient grandeur about it, but is fitting up in a very comfortable manner for a family house. The church or chapel where the Kings of Scotland used to be crowned is entirely gone, the person who shewed the house far from pointing out any vestige of it could not tell us where it had been. But they shewed us in the house more needle work wrought by Queen Mary's <u>own hands</u> during her confinement at Loch Leven than I think she could have done in her whole life, at least I have certainly seen so much in Scotland. This at Scone was a bed, chairs, & tapestry the latter in fine tent stitch some scripture history. The next day we went to Castle Duplin, it is a delightful ride from Perth & the park is beautiful, so that we did not entirely lose our time tho' we could not gain admittance to the house the family being there. Here is great deal of linen manufactured in the neighbourhood of Perth two large bleaching greens called the Inches one on each side of the town are generally covered in the whitening season, they are prettily planted with trees, & make an agreeable promenade for the inhabitants. We returned hither as I said on Thursday, since when we have had several additions to, & changes in the family party, for people come here to visit their neighbours, & stay a day or two at a time without any previous notice; a very agreeable circumstance in a remote place with a large house, & quite in the stile of ancient hospitality: before inns were invented. On Friday we went to Dunkeld a few miles from hence, where the Duke of Athol has a very pretty seat, finely sheltered by lofty mountains, the principal of which called craggy Barn is cut into walks, so as to make the ascent tolerably easy, & planted with shrubs and fruit trees, we mounted to a very considerable height, tho' we could not hold out to the top, we were high enough to enjoy, I think, the principal advantage of a balloon flight without running any of its risque, a great variety of most beautiful & picturesque views. People come into this neighbourhood to drink goats whey, & ride on horseback for their health, here are very good accommodations at a house, prettily situated on the other side the river, for such temporary inhabitants; & such summer lodgings are advertised in various parts of the highlands. The mountains at this time are all covered with such quantities of broom & furze in full bloom, that they look like hills of gold, or rather like golden showers pouring down their sides. The pieces of the rocks that I have taken up to examine, have appearances of ore mixt with their stone; gold dust is found in the sands of the Tay but in too small quantities to be worth the labour of gathering tho' I saw some little things that were made of it.

## LETTER 15, CUPAR OF ANGUS, KINGS BIRTHDAY [4 JUNE]

Sunday I went to church, or rather kirk & heard an extempore preaching of two hours. Monday we were to have left Murthly but I was not quite well, so the good lady had ~~an opportunity~~ [*sic*] the happiness of dosing me, & keeping us a day longer. Will you scold to find we have tacked on a new tour to our old one, & are going further north? It is an addition of ten days because we did not well know what to do with our time till I heard whether Miss R: will come or not, & there are some objects worth seeing; so now we propose making the long tour instead of the short, as we are told roads & inns are supportable, & I have hired horses at Perth for a month, as I found it would be more convenient, & cheaper; I shall send them home from Glasgow or Edinburgh. We expected to find Murthly thin of company as it had lost five besides us; but we found two gentlemen who came in our absence, Mr S: of Garth a sensible man, and his son who is in an highland regiment. I wish I knew how to spell a scotch bill of fare, I would send you one. Give my love to the dear children, & tell them the highland dolls are at last accomplished & making the tour with us: I began to despair of getting them but have at last with some trouble done it. I saw a sign at Perth of a man of the south country offering a pair of breeches to a highlander. Wednesday eve. Now for Glamis. We dined at Cupar upon fine salmon, roast chicken, spinage, & a great gooseberry tart of new gooseberries wine beer etc for 2s 11d. Glamis castle is now almost a ruin, it is where Duncan was murdered by Macbeth, I could not get them out of my head; & here we are going to bed at Forfar; with all the magistrates in the new town hall opposite drinking the King's health.

Thursday eve [5 June] Those loyal gentlemen kept us awake sadly. We went from Forfar to Brechin a small town with a seat of Lord Panmure's near it: we drank tea at Laurence Kirk, the waiter came in with two large books, which he said Ld Gardenstone ordered to be given to strangers: upon opening them we found written for title 'The Album to be given to strangers' and so every body amuses themselves with writing what they like; isn't it very droll? But his lordship has been still more bountiful to the traveller in building & furnishing a library adjoining to the inn; the whole village appears to have been lately rebuilt, & the marks of improvement every where visible, are so many honorable proofs of his attention to the good of the community. The old cottages in this part of Scotland in general are wretched hovels, in Angusshire they are of turf & stones alternate with thatch & mud plaistered together, & the thatch is fastened down with a sort of net work made of hay or straw thrown all over, & secured with wooden pegs at the sides. The soil hereabouts is rose colour & very barren. We are going to sup upon <u>parting's</u>[7] & <u>collared eggs</u> in a small town (Stonehive) [Stonehaven] close to the sea, & so *buona nocte carissima*.

---

7   Partans or crabs.

Friday 6th Aberdeen. Our road this morning has been thro' a most drear country, but we were consoled by a fine view of the sea at our right, & thought perhaps you were viewing the same object at that time but alas! how distant! This town makes a good figure as one approaches it, & seems very populous, & enjoys the double advantage of salt and fresh water, the seas & the two rivers Don & Dee, as soon as we spied the latter we looked for the [?contented] miller's house and soon found it.

## LETTER 16, CUPAR IN ANGUS, 10 JUNE

See the mutability of all human schemes! My last from Aberdeen told you we were going on north; when behold I grew over tired, had the physician, he advised two days rest & I was obliged to give him two guineas & to follow an advice I could not admire; as I was obliged to rest in a lodging with an hundred other people the inn being full. During this bait it was resolved to go no further north but to turn upon our elastic heels. So Sunday the Doctor thought an airing to the college to see some books, pictures & a lion's skin the Duke of G[ordon] once wore at a masquerade would refresh me. By the by, Aberdeen is two large towns, the sea, the Don & the Dee all run up to it. I saw a man selling cloth by auction in the market place. The country round Aberdeen is too ugly. We went to Montrose yesterday, & had two boiled chicks, a pigeon pie, asparagus, partons, puffs, an epergne of nice sweetmeats, for supper, for one shilling & fourpence. From Montrose, which is a pretty town in a very pretty country, we took the road we had been. When we reached Murthly again (on the 11th) we found Mr S: arrived & I got my letters & catalogue of the exhibition, thank ye, & I shall answer my letters as soon as I can. But now came my troubles in the first place they kept us at M: a day more than I intended; & then Lady S: would insist upon Mr S: of G[arth] attending us to Blair & Taymouth for fear of the bad roads & then I was obliged to offer him a seat in the carriage as riding soon after dinner was disagreeable; the stage to Blair was long and hilly, & we did not get here till twelve at night, about eleven & a half the pull was steep, the horses tired, the stick not down (to please the post boy) and so the horses failed near the top of the hill & down we went, chaise, horses & all, backwards, & I was frightened to death, but not otherwise killed for a tree stopt us after a time. We have been this morning seeing Blair castle (the Duke of Atholl's) such hills! - but I must tell you about the famous pass of Killiecranky tomorrow as I shall see it again going to Taymouth, in the light. There Mr S: is to meet us to go to Inverary, I tried to persuade him it was not his duty to go, but my eloquence failed. You know rhubarb grows here as well, & as valuable as the Turkey, is it not odd? The Duke of Atholl has an acre of it, & he sells it for an hundred pounds;

but then it stays in the ground seven or eight years before it is fit to torment children with. The road from Dunkeld to Blair is very fine. Hills to the skies, no signs of living creatures, clouds half down the hills, rivers at bottom, rocks & woody banks, & for variety a highlander leading a cow to feed; shake these well together & you produce a highland scene, according to the most approved receipts. Adieu until tomorrow. If you plant fir trees upon a bleak moor not worth sixpence an acre, the leaves will manure it till it produce nice grass for sheep. They are planting the <u>scarcity root here</u>.[8] It is very like the red beet root & in times of dearth is to feed all living creatures, if Noah had but known of it! Don't you grow very wise as to have it remarked?

## LETTER 17, KILLIN, 17 JUNE

Here we are in the heart of the highlands, I am quite in love with them & never shall like to live near London I know any more. The pass of Killiecranky is a pass between two immense mountains with a fine road on one side of it, & the river Garrie running at the bottom, but so distant is that bottom from the road that it is no object either of sight or hearing to the traveller. From Taymouth (by the bye that is such a delightful place that I shall never forgive you for not following your Paris mother's advice) hither the whole length of Loch Tay is most lovely, mountains innumerable, wooded or cultivated rise almost perpendicular from the lake, with many cascades falling down their sides. It was too hot to travel in the middle of the day, so we staid till eve, & never was there a lovelier ride, the sun gilded the mountains a thousand ways, the birds sung, the highlanders peeped out from their wretched huts with merry faces to stare at us, & looked so happy I could not pity them for living in such places. This dear little Killin is a charming village at the head of Loch Tay, with two rivers running into it. Here is a pretty house of a nephew of Gen[era]l: M: N's with a very curious burying ground, it is an island very prettily planted with trees of the mournful looking kind & cut out into walks. We stopt to see a hermitage of Ld. B's [Breadalbane] by the side of the Lake my aunt and I went up in a cart for the chaise could not be dragged up so steep a place. It is more like a hermitage than most things of the kind that one sees & has facing it, a most stupendous waterfall of two hundred & twenty feet. Ld. B: can go an hundred miles on his own estate here.

Dalmally Wednesday eve. Oh dear, we have been in the vale of affliction all day, & afflicting enough it is to see thirty two miles of hills piled on hills, without

---

8   This was the term used for mangel-wurzel, with which experiments were being made. The author of the parish account for Dowally refers to it 'promising to be a useful green crop' in *The Statistical Account of Scotland* 20 (Edinburgh, 1798), 86.

a tree, any mark of cultivation or face, <u>human or beastly</u>. I wonder how on earth a pair of horses does to drag us over such hills & stages of twenty miles: here they have no remedy as we are far from post horses, but we have never once heard it was thought of. This said vale must be dreadful in winter, torrents pour on all sides from the mountains, & it rained hard today so we have seen it in all its glory. - Friday we spent yesterday at Inverary (the Duke of Argyle's) & left that beautiful place to pass thro' a most dreadful desert (Glencrow) with mountains that kept us perfectly shaded from a scotching sun. Soldiers' tents here & there, enlivened the scene, the men are employed to mend the roads which were originally made, & are still kept in repair by the military. We are now at an excellent inn on the banks of Loch Long. Oh, I must tell you they never put up signs here in the highlands, so Mr S: who was walking up a hill near the end of a stage, went into a gentleman's house by mistake to order dinner; & again tonight we debated, thought the house too good, then told the servant to ride on, then called him back, because Mr S: was afraid of affronting a highland chief. By the bye our beau always chooses to breakfast when we dine, & dine when we sup; & so as we are always obliged to send on before, that the chicken may be killed, & the fish caught; so the orders are, breakfast & dinner, & dinner & supper! the people run staring out to see gormand diners that make two meals at a time. Goodnight.

Saturday. We have had a fine ride by the side of Loch Long, & Gair Loch to the firth of Clyde, & passed Roseneath, another fine seat of the Duke of Argyle & Ardincaple Ld. F. Campbell. Monday we spent yesterday in viewing Lochlomond & were on one of the islands, & eat of fish that can be eat nowhere else. The lake is beautiful 24 computed miles long 24 islands in it; two of which are deer parks, one of which belongs to the Duke of Montrose & the other to Sir J. Colquhoun, who gets £250 a year for the salmon fishery; we had a fine view of all the islands from the one we were on.

Glasgow, Monday eve. O, dear the post office is shut, & I must wait till tomorrow for letters. Now we are in the lowlands & I almost fancy myself in England now I am among cornfields and hedges. We came this morning from Dumbarton ferried over the Firth of Clyde to Paisley where we saw them make muslims, tiffaries, chamberry, gannere [sic] & bordered handkerchiefs & aprons & so good night. We are here in an Inn as big as a castle, & Glasgow is a bustle enough to frighten us poor highlanders. What a delightful number of letters! & no bad news in any that's charming! - I was in agonies while the man was gone to the post office & my aunt was endeavouring to soften a disappointment which she thought possible by persuading me not to expect any letters as there might be none & yet all things well; but you are very good three great ones from you.

## LETTER 18, GLASGOW, 26 JUNE

Dearest Sister. It rained so, all day yesterday we could not stir, but two months & a half in the country have made me too patriotic to regret confinement upon account of a circumstance which will be so generally beneficial. We have been out today to see the inkle manufactury which is a good deal like common weaving, only the looms are upright, & one pull moves a great number of shuttles, weaving so many pieces of tape at the same instant. It is curious to see how expeditiously, by means of proper machinery, women & girls fold the pieces of tape & bobbins into the neat form we see them at the shops. We have been too at the public walk, a very spacious meadow, with fine rows of trees. This place is much more bustling than Edinburgh, & has a great many fine large houses in it. The cathedral, the only thing left in that form in Scotland is in a miserable ruinous state; the college is much handsomer I think than either that of Edinburgh or Aberdeen, but being the vacation had a sad deserted look. Friday, we have driven thro' a fine cultivated [line missing][9] which looks like chimnies to the infernal dwelling, all flaming & smoking like mad. We have seen the flax in flower it looks very pretty being light green with delicate little blue flowers. All the cottages in this part have a sun dial placed over the doors contrived with a head at top so as to look like a hoop petticoat.

Stirling, Saturday. Heavens! We are escaped from the infernal regions. Imagine the Carron works, a whole town of smoke & fire, & a thousand people at work, furnaces blazing on all sides, half seen through a black smoke, beings whose appearance I leave it to you to imagine, pouring liquid fire into caldrons, hammering red hot iron etc & an engine working that absolutely overpowered me by a louder voice than ever I had heard before & that had waked me at the inn in the morning with an idea that it thundered. Imagine enough liquid fire pour'd into a mould to make a thirty six pounder, for they are now making a stock for the Empress of Russia. These pleasant abodes of destruction in embrio, are planted around with cannon, furnaces, bells, grates etc etc, innumerables, to cool & harden. I had never been in <u>Enfer</u> before, & know not how to relish the idea, of so many of my fellow creatures passing their lives there, to supply me & others with grates, tea kettles, etc etc, but I endeavoured to reconcile it to myself, by observing that they grinned with seeming pleasure at our fears & amazement, as if it came from hearts free from care & sorrow & by resolving never to let the kettle stay on the fire & burn its bottom out, to give them another needlessly to make. Our ride from this dominion of Vulcan was thro' ten miles of the richest

---

9   Sadly, the bottom line of page 58 in the manuscript has been trimmed off by the book binder and is all but missing; it might include 'country to land'.

country in Scotland (the Carse of Gowrie) to Stirling which stands on a narrow hill with a castle at top like Edinburgh, - you cannot think how odd it looked to see one of those black figures, that would pass for a good devil at the opera house sketching a cupid, & carefully marking the arrows in his quiver, with a large nail, on a mixture of soot & sand, for a mould to cast the sides of stoves.

## LETTER 19, STIRLING, 29 JUNE

I fear the weather is as rainy with you as with us, & it would be some consolation to me to suffer patiently for my country's sake, as I ought, after enjoying so much fine but I think you should enjoy it too, after so long a stay in London. From Stirling Castle is the finest prospect in Europe. The Forth meanders at such a rate thro' the Carse of Gowrie, that a village four miles from this town by land is twenty four by water; the river goes so 〜〜 & in spite of that snake like look, as you may think it upon paper, makes a most beautiful appearance, the rock upon which the town & castle are built rises singularly in the middle of this charming valley, & it is skirted by the highland mountains, forming a boundary to the view neither too near nor too distant. The castle is strong, the Scottish Kings once kept their court here, their palace is so droll, at the outside stuck thick with large rude stone figures, half out the wall like battering rams; among them are statues of James 1st & his Queen naked, Adam & Eve to keep her in countenance. We left Stirling yesterday, I told you we were going to stay ten days at Loch Long, we are got within sixteen miles but it grew late, so we were obliged to stop for tonight at a small inn, on the side of Gair Loch. I believe we shall find it very comfortable to be settled at home again, to be sure of good beds every night, tho' in fact we have been pretty well off here; upon the whole very well, so is every thing in its turn, but the best thing in its turn will be seeing my dear Sister well & happy.

## LETTER 20, GLASGOW, 2 JULY

Here's a fine piece of work! When we got to Loch Long the woman had written, a letter which I never received, to say her lodgings were full & so we had nothing to do but to come back again, & decide what we should do with ourselves. My resolution to stay a fortnight for the races would not stand this new attack. So I have written to Edinburgh that we shall not come & we are now proceeding to England straight forward, which new scheme will bring us to you a month sooner. If you have sent off no letters to Edinburgh, send them off to Manchester instead, & if you have, you must repeat all the important things about the house over again, as I shall be longer getting them back from Scotland. Good night I shall write more tomorrow.

Hamilton. I sent for Mr Boswell's tour to see whether we followed in Dr Johnson's steps, & now I find that for exactness & prolixity I am not at all comparable to Mr B: the clock has struck ten & a half, I meant to have written you a long letter tonight, but we found the <u>long minuet</u>, the <u>propagation of a lie</u>, & <u>the Prince's bow</u>,[10] all drawn up in battle array to engage us. Not to mention wax candles & bread & butter two novelties. When we were returning to Glasgow after our Loch Long disappointment, Joseph was stopped by a servant who told him, Mrs R: had sent ten days before to the Inn, by Loch Lomond to order the people to give her compliments to us, & to say she had beds at our command at Bel Retiro, & expected the pleasure of seeing us. See how very polite of Mrs M; she had written to this lady to invite us, knowing the Inn at Lochlomond was very bad, & the people at the Inn had never told us, so we heard not a word of it till we had passed the house some miles & seen all the Lake. Mr S: you know is gone prowling to Mull. We just now met a gentleman walking a journey with two footmen behind him. The landlord of the inn at Glasgow has given me ten guineas upon my draft without knowing who I was; see what it is to have an honest face! We have just been seeing Bothwell castle the seat of Mr Douglas there is a large new house almost completed; the ruins of the old castle are left standing behind in the pleasure ground & the inside cleared out for a bowling green, bordered with flowers, the situation is fine on the edge of a hill, we find the country in general much more flat since we left Glasgow, proceeding south. I hope you are glad we are coming to you: I was going to say home, till I recollected I was a houseless wanderer. —- I have got a tooth pick of broom, & some ore to show you. I find my bowls are very precious, as they are only made in one place & very difficult to get, but they say I should have filled them with water or they will fall to pieces, I wish it may rain in M: street, don't you? We have seen Hamilton palace & Chatelherault, the latter is only a hunting seat belonging to the Duke, but from its exalted situation makes a fine object to the former which is an old building situated in a fine plain. I think I have hardly seen in Scotland a piece of ground so even as that part of the park which is before the house: & it is used for a race ground. In the house is quite as much appearance of comfort as magnificence.

## LETTER 21, DOUGLAS MILL, 3 JULY

In our way to this place we have seen some very fine falls of the Clyde. Imagine a whole river washing & foaming over a high rock, trees & shrubs hanging over the sides, with an old ruin overhanging the whole. It is a most

---

10 Scottish dance tunes?

beautiful scene. Sir John Lockhart Ross is building a house just by. Sanquhar, from Douglas mill here is the most frightful country possible, but Ld. Hopetoun does not think so, for his lead mines are very valuable, & the habitations of the miners are almost the only ones to be seen for twenty eight miles. At Elvanfoot where we thought to change horses, tho' a short stage; they chose to say it was very hilly & we must have four, that there were precipices six times as high as the house & if we once got down the boy said he would never undertake to get us up again with a pair. I told him when once we were down I should not probably wish him to take any trouble about getting us up again. However I at last agreed to take four & after much difficulty prevailed on them to take off a pair half way according to the landlady's agreement. The best of it is that we found this stage less hilly than most we have been in Scotland. So we thought it our duty to write a note to that effect to the landlord (who happened to be from home) cautioning him not to suffer his servants to impose upon strangers for the future. If they had any thoughts of dragging people up again, who had once fallen from the road down those said precipices it would require I suppose all the horses of the county. But don't tremble for our necks, for we have near taken leave of those dangers & are going on smoothly to Gretna Green.

## LETTER 22, ANNAN, 6 JULY

Here, then we are on the very borders of England at least a month sooner than I expected a week ago. — How we came to return so soon, to relinquish the races at Edinburgh, you have already been informed. Our intended call upon Lady Dumfries was found to be impracticable, as the nearest stage we were to Dumfries house was twenty miles and we thought it ridiculous to go so far upon the uncertainty of their being at home & it was too far to send to know, as we must have staid in a very indifferent inn at the time. So on we passed from Sanquhar to the magnificent but miserably neglected palace like house of Drumlanrig, the Duke of Queensbury's, who has visited it but twice, and so it should seem for the furniture & everything about it appears at least a hundred years old. A heavy rain added to the dreariness of the place, for we are now receiving the arrears of ten weeks drought, tho' not all in one shower, as you have in Kent I find; but in a genteel gradual manner so as to hold out the rest of our journey, I suppose. It is a most Delightful ride from Sanquhar to Drumlanrig by the side of a winding river, with woody banks & the country continues fine from thence to Dumfries which was our last stage & is a good town. Near that place is the ancient seat of the Earls of Nithsdale. We enquired for the family, they are not there, nor when they are there do they ever reside at their own house but at one they hire of the Duke of Q:, but the people at Dumfries told me Mr C was going to build, the old seat not being very old. Here is a church of England chapel at Dumfries with an organ in it. People are coming north at a great rate, it seems, I suppose that we shall meet with all the inns full for the future especially if we fall in with any assize towns or races, for the newspapers I sometimes pick up say such things are in season.

## LETTER 23, GRETNA GREEN, 7 JULY

I have only time to say two words here as we do nothing but change horses. They are making up the inn in a grand stile for the reception of future matrimonial pairs. I think I saw the blacksmith. All the post boys have fine waistcoats bound with gold. Aunt says it is their East Indies.

Carlisle. Monday evening at a town five miles from Gretna. All the world seems to make a point of issuing from their houses to stare when a carriage arrives & our driver as if he felt the disgrace of having two sober females behind him whipt his horses into a gallop that they might not see into the chaise. We have now bid adieu to Scotland, oatcake & naked feet. All the world is travelling to Scotland or Ireland. We have been to the Cathedral, 'tis not beautiful but has a neat modern window with a painted border. To the bookseller's and bought Goldsmith's history of the earth, very vilely printed and a clumsy pair of stuff shoes; & discovered that I have got two guineas and a half of light money & that I have no more light or heavy upon which discovery I have sent off the letters you sent me, & mean to profit by them to remedy the above inconvenience.

My hat is faded to pieces, my coat pinched, ink'd &, the carriage all faded, Joseph's jacket turned into a brown one & so we make as shabby a figure as need be. But the carriage always attracts the notice of gentlemen in the inn yards & the good construction of the wheels is admired by connoisseurs. I know that it has cost me already more than five guineas for a new axeltree, & &.

## ITINERARY

Plan for the lesser tour of the Highlands of Scotland, after visiting Derbyshire & the Lakes of Cumberland. You enter Scotland by way of Carlisle & Long Town … proceed by way of Gretna Green & Annan to Dumfries, where you leave the great irish road & pass thro' north dale to Drumlanrig, the fine old seat of the Queensberry family, & Sanquhar, from whence a very romantic track will lead you over the Leadhills to Douglas Mill & Lanerk in the neighbourhood of which you may visit three fine falls of the Clyde. The palace of Hamilton is your next object & you will see Bothwell castle in your way to Glasgow at which city you may employ several days, & from thence you should visit the works of Paisley. You will then approach the highland by Dumbarton & after traversing two parts of the length of Loch Lomond descend to Loch Long a considerable arm of the sea & an excellent new inn on its banks. The dreary & astonishing desert of Glen crow & the desolate scene of Glen Kinloss will introduce you to another great arm of the sea called Loch Fine, from a curve of which you will burst at once on the glorious paradise of Inverary. You will then pursue a mountainous track to Loch Awe & passing thro' the pleasant vale of Glenorchy ascend thro' a dismal solitude to Tyndrum, from whence you will follow the Tay thro Glen Dochet or the vale of affliction to Killin, & pursue Ld Breadalbane's new road on the southern bank of Loch Tay to his hermitage, soon after which you will arrive at his seat at Taymouth, which together with the environs will occupy you for some time. Cross the Tay at Aberfeldie, near which are the falls of Moness, & near its junction with the Tummel ferry over the latter river soon after which you will join the road from Dunkeld to Blair in your way to which place you will have an enchanting ride by the sweet seat of Faskally & thro' the pass of Kiliecranky. At Blair you will find a fine old seat of the Duke of Atholl, & should visit the York cascades in his grounds: at Dunkeld he has a less but more beautiful place which you will visit in your return. You will here leave Birnam wood on your right as you quit the highlands & descend to Perth, near which is the Palace of Scone. Cross the vale of Strathern & the Ochill hills to Kinross on the banks of Lochleven, & visit the rumbling brig & castle Campbell in your way to Stirling where you will find a noble castle. The Carron works, Hopetoun House and Barnbugle will be in your way to Edinburgh where you will employ several days in the finest city in Europe. You should make excursions from hence to Dalkeith, Newbattle, Roslyn & Pennicuik. A charming ride on the coast thro' the fertile scene of the Lothians will bring you to Haddington & Dunbar near which is the Bass isle, & after crossing the curious edifice of Pease Bridge & ascending the moor of Coldstream you will reach Berwick where a long bridge over the Tweed will bring you into England. In case you mean to go further north, you should go from Taymouth directly to Dunkeld & then up thro' Blair to Lochness & Inverness from whence you may come round by Bamff & Aberdeen to Perth.

List of the stages with the number of miles on a tour from London to the Highlands of Scotland with an account of the Inns of Scotland as they were in the year 1788
From:

| [Stage] | [Mileage] |
|---|---|
| London | |
| Hounslow | 12 |
| Slough by Windsor | 14 |

| | |
|---|---|
| Henley | 15 |
| Benson | 11 |
| Oxford | 12 |
| Woodstock | 8 |
| Chipping Norton by Heathrop | 14 |
| Burford | 11 |
| Frogmill | 16 |
| Cheltenham | 6 |
| Gloucester | 10 |
| Tewkesbury | 11 |
| Worcester | 15 |
| Stourport | 12 |
| [****] | 5 |
| Birmingham by way of Hagley and Leasowes | 18 |
| Litchfield | 16 |
| Burton | 13 |
| Derby | 11 |
| Matlock, by Heddleston | 20 |
| Bakewell and return to [****] by Chatsworth | 26 |
| Ashburn | 16 |
| Ham, Dovedale & back to Ashburn | 10 |
| Buxton | 21 |
| Castleton | 12 |
| Sheffield | 16 |
| Peneston | 14 |
| Huddersfield | 11 |
| Halifax | 8 |
| Keighley | 12 |
| Skipton | 10 |
| Settle | 16 |
| Kirby Lonsdale | 17 |
| Kendal | 13 |
| Bowness | 9 |
| Lowwood | 5 |
| Keswick | 18 |
| Penrith | 18 |
| Carlisle | 18 |
| | 520 |

| Stage | Mileage | Accommodation |
| --- | --- | --- |
| Long Town | 9 | Graham's arms, good |
| Gretna Green | 5 | Gretna Hall, good |
| Annan | 9 | Queensberry Arms, good |
| Dumfries | 15 | Red Lion or King's Arms, good |
| Drumlanrig | 20 | No Inn |
| Sanguhar | 9 | Queensberry Arms, good |
| Douglas Mill | 29 | Dougal Arms tolerable |
| Lanerk | 7 | Black bull, indifferent |
| Hamilton | 14 | Hamilton arms, good |
| Glasgow | 11 | Tontine good |
| Dumbarton | 15 | Good |
| Luss | 13 | Very bad |
| Lochloing | 10 | New Inn very good |
| Cairndow | 12 | Very bad |
| Inverary | 10 | Very good |
| Dalmally | 16 | Very bad |
| Tyndrum | 12 | Tolerable |
| Killin | 20 | Good |
| Kenmore near Taymouth | 16 | Very good |
| Blair | 27 | Very good |
| Dunkeld | 27 | Inn, at Inver, very good |
| Perth | 16 | Campbell's very good |
| Kinross | 15 | Kinross green good |
| Stirling | 24 | New Inn excellent |
| Carron works | 9 | Small, decent inn |
| Falkirk | 2 | Red Lion, bad |
| Linlithgow | 7 | Three crowns, bad |
| New ferry by Hopetoun | 13 | South ferry house tolerable |
| Edinburgh | 9 | Walker's hotel excellent |
| Musselborough by Leith | 8 | A decent inn |
| Haddington | 11 | New inn good |
| Dunbar | 11 | George bad |
| Press Inn | 15 | Good |
| Berwick | 12 | Red lion indifferent |
| Belford | 15 | |
| Alnwick | 14 | Visit Warkworth between these places |
| Morpeth | 19 | |

| | | |
|---|---|---|
| Newcastle | 15 | Visit Tynemouth |
| Durham | 14 | |
| Sedgefield | 11 | |
| Stockton | 12 | |
| Ayton | 12 | |

[Note: the table continues with the following distances in England: Goatham & return to Ayton 24; Normanby and return to Ayton 14; Thirsk 22, Easingwold 10; York 14; Tadcaster 9; Ferrybridge 13, Doncaster 15; Bawtry 8; Gainsborough 13; Lincoln 18; Sleaford 18; Bourn 19; Stamford 10; Shilton by Burghley 15; Huntington 12; Cambridge 16; Chesterfield 11; Bishops Sorford 15; Epping 15; London 16. Total 1397 miles]

This tour is planned with a view to include both the universities Manchester & Liverpool might easily be added on the way to Kendal, where the tour of the English lakes begins.

# ADAM BALD:
# *Journal of Travels and Commonplace Book, 1790–99*

## Introduction

Born in Glasgow on 14 December 1770, Adam Bald became a drysalter, or dealer in chemicals. The family firm that provided his comfortable livelihood[1] had been founded by his father Peter, and was to pass entirely to Adam shortly before Peter's death in 1811. There was another son, Andrew, but he had enlisted in the Army under some kind of cloud in 1794. It seems that neither his father nor the business was too demanding of Adam, allowing him plenty of free time to use as he wished. An enthusiastic member of the Royal Glasgow Volunteers, his journal records action with them, notably in repressing civil unrest in 1797, when he was part of the militia sent to Kilpatrick church to quell a riot by arresting the ringleaders. A few weeks later found him at Calder where the Volunteers, according to his account, had met a 'combination of petticoat soldiers' trying to protect their menfolk from 'being snatched' for military service. However, his greatest enthusiasm over half a century was for travel and travelling, something that he indulged throughout his adult life.

Adam Bald's accounts of his various travels in Scotland and elsewhere in Britain over some fifty years between 1790 and 1840 are immensely valuable but they are also a major challenge. His commonplace book, some 456 pages of it, held in Glasgow City Archives, promises much and looks as if it ought to be full of fascination. He has a life of endless dancing, drinking and entertaining – and travels away. There are descriptions of trips to the Lakes, climbing expeditions (up Ben Lomond) walking tours (to Inverary), seaside outings to the Clyde coast and rambles in and around Glasgow as well as sorties to London and Ireland. There are even a few drawings.

Sadly, the early appeal to the reader soon palls. There is his handwriting: dense, full of strokes. There is his prose-style: self-indulgent, very wordy and over-complicated, knee-deep in contrived pseudo-education. He has a stock of phrases which amuse him – but not the exasperated reader – such as 'raised our risible organs' for 'made us laugh'. There is his love for the world of Don Quixote;

---

1 On his death in July 1843 he left an estate worth some £6962.

everything is adventure . . . tediously so. There is his love of himself; Bald is fascinated by Bald. In his defence it is only fair to note that this journal was never intended for publication; it is his own private record and meant, in all probability, only for his own amusement. One can imagine him of an evening chuckling 'what a lad I was!' as he read his way through the text. The flow of the original for the reader is disrupted by his tendency to omit the personal pronoun: some I have supplied for ease of reading. There are added complications due to illegible words or those manufactured by Bald from a Latin base.

The commonplace book is not an easy read, therefore, for the decade for which the transcriptions are provided. Nor does the task get easier in the later sections of his journal, as he ages or after his marriage. His style barely evolves and does not improve; nor is his increasing fondness for the poetic form an asset. A trip to Dunoon in the summer of 1826 is celebrated over six pages of dire verse. The opening stanza gives the flavour of this form:

> Along the Coast in gaudy steamer paddling
> Some to the Isles, some nearer home doth bend
> Amidst vulgar crowds or gay parades to seek
> Some for retirement in the cozy glen.

Yet for all the difficulties and deterrents, there are gleanings of real importance which fully justify the transcription of some sections from the opening portion of the journal: the first 160 pages or so which contain his travels during the 1790s. Here is an account by someone neither of name nor reputation, but coming from the emerging mercantile or middle class, which was beginning to travel and to tour quite widely within Scotland and elsewhere in Britain. Tourism, other than the elite experience of the Grand Tourists to Europe, is often held to have been a product of the steamship and of the railway. But Bald is on the move well before these developments, travelling outside Scotland, for example, to Liverpool in July 1792 and to the English Lakes in September 1797. The last he especially enjoyed: 'if ever I may be enabled to retire from the cares of the busy world, the Valley of Patterdale in Ullswater is where I would like to retire'. He travels on foot or on horse, by gig or coach, boat and ferry, the last attended with a fair degree of risk, depending on the weather, water and the competence of the rower.

This section of his journal shows that as a young man, and unmarried,[2] his sorties start mostly as short-term impulses, getting away as much as getting to, rather than as the result of longer term planning. He knows that he wants a break

---

2   Bald married Jess Telfer in St Enochs on 7 June 1813. There were two daughters, a son Peter who followed him in the business and a 'natural son', Adam, for whom he made provision in his will.

from home and from work, but his destination is almost a last-minute decision. It can be a day away, or a weekend, or a longer trip. Over the years it is true that the tours become more scheduled (and longer) and by the summer of 1828, as a much older and richer man, he was allowing himself a two months' sojourn in the Highlands. In this progression, he is clearly not alone. He is a part of a group with an increasing taste for time away from work and home, and not just for days but for weeks; others besides him of his class and kind are on the move for pleasure and leisure, whether to the seaside or the hills: Scots exploring their own country. Bald himself does come across the longer distance tourist.[3] In August 1799 he and his cronies find themselves on Loch Lomondside at Rowardennan, which he describes as 'a romantic spot'. But in summer, as he remarks, it is often the seat of 'bustle, confusion and disappointment from the crowds of visitors from different parts of the world of different ranks and degrees huddled together in a small and but indifferent plenished inn'. There he encounters three Cornish girls, soaked after climbing the Ben, three beautiful young ladies 'of a genteel cast, posted to enjoy the sublime scenery of Scotland' with their father. He and his companions chat them up, without success. Theirs was clearly a lengthy and long-distance tour, a substantial undertaking in terms of time and of cost. But much of Adam Bald's early travelling in the 1790s, on which we focus here, is much lower down the evolutionary scale in terms of tourism. It is outings with friends, among family and their connections, of a kind that has left little or no trace.

His journal, therefore, offers a valuable window into the progression of tourism during the late eighteenth and early nineteenth centuries from an elite experience for just the moneyed few to a pleasure shared by more and more. In July 1791, for example, he makes his way to Gourock to stay with relatives who were spending their summer there, seized (in his words) by the 'saltwater mania' and a taste 'for naval amusements'. This is not the medicinal sea bathing of the gentry, but a more popular enthusiasm, cheap and cheerful. The foray to the Stirling area, with which the extract begins, is a young man's sortie – Bald was then aged twenty – at the suggestion of a friend, with whom he travels. They visit his friend's uncle at Logie, mutual acquaintances in and around Stirling, and add on a day for a visit to Carron ironworks. It is in the spring, a long weekend taken during the celebration of the half-yearly communion in Glasgow, holy days made holidays by him. Friday, the first day, sees them from Glasgow via Kilsyth to Bannockburn where they spend a night. They walk the next day to Logie. Sunday in Stirling is passed at church, in

---

3   This also holds true for England; Bald comments of the English Lakes that he had discovered there 'groups of town bred folks, both male and female who had been there for *weeks*' (letter to Thomas Lister, 8 September 1798).

the King's park and down to Cambuskenneth. On Monday they start with bowling and then go via Bannockburn to Carron, where they engage beds in the inn, and on the Tuesday take the canal boat back to Glasgow. He travels on foot, by coach and canal boat: he stays with friends and in an inn. He talks, goes to church, plays bowls (but not on the Sabbath), inspects Carron works and writes up his journal. And this is the record which is set out below. None of this travelling would have left any trace, except perhaps in the visitors' books at Carron, which have long since vanished. Yet it was a growing part of the new taste for travel spreading through society.

Not all historical sources are either immediately accessible or rich in findings, and some require distinct perseverance to yield any information. There are always challenges with journals and letters: even where the handwriting is clear, there are the gaps and obscurities that dog any such transcription. Some difficulties may lie in the words or phrases which were familiar to the writer, but the exact meaning of which eludes us today. But Bald presents a different challenge, requiring the reader to persevere through the thickets of his prose.

## Note

Adam Bald's Journal of Travels and Commonplace Book (TD 19/6) is one of a cluster of documents grouped together in Glasgow City Archives, which relate to the Bald family. These include some business papers (TD 19/4), a description of a journey to Liverpool in July 1792 (TD 19/1), a second journal of two further excursions to England in 1838–40 (TD 19/7) and a small octavo journal, May 1785–1822 (TD 19/3). The last shows Bald's magpie-like mind; it is a mixter-maxter of events (hangings and the like), weather (thunder and heavy rain), shipping and trade data, tables of distances and family happenings (births, marriages and deaths). An entry for 5 September 1798 records:

> A melancholy accident happened a few days ago to a number of young folks whilst on a pleasure sail from this to P[or]t Glasgow. About a mile from said town at nine o'clock PM, a sudden squall of wind upset the boat, when horrible! - seven out of eight were lost, Vizt Mr William Trueman, ropemaker Anderston, his beautiful sister Miss Catherine about twenty years of age, Mr Brown with Bogle and Jack, Mr Dick agent to the Paisley Bank, Mr Gilmour writer, Mr Carmichael clerk and a boatman. Mr Colquhoun calico printer was saved by clinging to the mast for about an hour.

The commonplace book is 456 pages long. The transcriptions offered here relate to the first section, and focus on Bald's travels within Scotland during the 1790s.

Some of the shorter trips are omitted, such as the accounts, in verse, of 'a pedestrian trip to Gartness from Friday 1 October 1790 to the Monday following – address'd to William Jamieson dyer there, and a Description of the Laird of Corshous's Kirn, above mentioned, Friday 15th October 1790'. Also set aside are 'A ramble to Campsie, Gartness Etc in March 1792' [p. 45]; 'A walk to Ayr with a Mr Lawson Sunday Oct 7th, 1792' [p. 84]; 'A five days ramble to Stirling etc with John Sanderson writing master Thursday Nov 1st 1792' [p. 86] and 'A trip to Gartness for four days from Saturday February 16th 1793' [p. 92]. Also his note for 1st August 1799, 'On Saturday last I join'd a Strawberry ploy at the Ibrox where there was an abundance of that delicious fruit'.

There has been some cutting within the longer accounts when Bald's descriptive enthusiasm was considered likely to try even the most patient reader too far. There has also been some tidying of his prose and spelling, but some tasters of his poetry remain from which the reader can judge whether they would have wished for more.

# *Journal*

## A TRIP TO THE NORTH COUNTRY FROM FRIDAY 9 APRIL 1790 TO THE TUESDAY FOLLOWING, WITH PETER WRIGHT, SON OF DOCTOR WRIGHT GLASGOW

It is too much the irreverent custom of the inconsiderate youth, and at times indeed of the more advanced in years of this part of Caledonia, to fly (as from a plague) the vernal celebration of the sacrament of our Lord's supper, considering myself to have joined the sceptical throng for no other means than merrily gratifying a youthful propensity to see a little of the world, which surely, before becoming a devotionist was not altogether criminal. Embracing therefore the periodical return of a relaxation from mercantile pursuits, in gratifying the propensity, by obeying the invitation of my acquaintance Mr Wright to a pedestrian visit to his clerical uncle of Logie near Stirling and other friends in and around that neighbourhood. For this purpose we set off one stormy morning in the month of April, propell'd on our way by the increasing blast, and almost invisible to one another by the dense clouds of dust which this vernal hurricane raised around us, and looked like the gypsy tribe by our hats fasten'd with our handkerchiefs, rais'd our risible organs when a waning blast indulg'd us with a glimpse of each other. In this situation the Edinburgh stage Coach came up, and luckily got a lift till near Kilsyth, where we breakfasted with an acquaintance of Mr Wright, which fortified and prepared us for scaling the soaring Tak-me-Down, the lonely, rugged, and forbidding surface of which was with difficulty got over, by the howling blast bluffing our eyes with showers of hail, which caus'd many an awkward stumble e'er we reached the summit of the Alpine road. About two or three miles from Stirling in the vicinity of Loch Coulter (partly an artificial dam for supplying the neighbourhood Mills) we dined with a Mr Rennie a relation of mine and five o'clock arriv'd at a Mr McLaughland's a highland Gentleman in whose house we lodged while in that neighbourhood.

Next morning (after breakfast) walk'd over to Logie (about three miles from Stirling) to visit my companion's reverent Uncle,[4] who cordially received us, and pass'd till two o'clock in the study of this eccentric divine amused with humorous and varied worldly stories, original and selected. Being summon'd to dinner we accompanied our clerical host who introduced us to two aged and rather antiquated looking dames, but in what relationship they stood to the divine never had the curiosity to enquire of my comrade, but he seem'd not to treat them with too much kindness, for no sooner than he swallow'd the substantials than we left our female friends to enjoy themselves as they might think proper and accompanied again the eccentric to his study (after a walk in the garden) where from a bole he brought a large bottle of whisky and continued sipping and laughing at his irreverent Jokes and stories till tea was announced when again joining the deserted Duennas at their sober beverage, left the romantic manse of Logie and arriving at our polite Stirling friends hospitable mansion about eight o'clock, pass'd the remainder of the evening in an agreeable manner with their kind family.

Next day being Sabbath went to Church with the Misses McLaughlands and after dinner had a sober walk in the King's park, thence adjourn'd to the Abbey of Cambuskenneth situated on one of the peninsulae form'd by the Forth founded by King David the first in 1147; and was one of the richest abbeys in the kingdom, but now in ruins and surrounded by fishermen and cottar houses who seem'd very devout or rather superstitious, as they would not (being Sunday) sell milk for the comfort of any intruding stranger to their venerable ruin on that sacred day, but had no scruple to give us a boat to carry us from their prayerful mansions, and indeed to lengthen our sail around some of the links of the winding Forth, the pleasure of which was heightened by the serenity of the evening and landing at what they call the Shore, the harbour of Stirling, march'd home in the twilight where our kind friends received and treated us with true highland hospitality.

---

4    When his nephew and Adam Bald called on him, the Reverend James Wright of Logie (1721–1800) was nearing seventy and his second wife was no younger, as the description implies. He was the author of some devotional verse, and provided Sir John Sinclair with the short three-page entry for the parish of Logie that was published in volume three of the *Statistical Account of Scotland* in 1792.

We pass'd next forenoon in the bowling green, and after dinner bade adieu to our highland friends, with grateful acknowledgement for their kindness and bent our course for Carron Works. In passing Bannockburn partook of a refreshment with my friend Mr Walker, and arriv'd at Carron about seven o'clock without one single incident worth noticing; bespeaking beds in the Inn, and after a cup of tea, saunter'd over to Bainsford a neighbouring village to enquire about a conveyance for Glasgow next morning. In returning to our lodgings were much delighted nay indeed transported with amazement at the wonderful and terrific effects of Carron works, blazing mountainous heaps of Coal and other minerals, with the glaring furnaces illuming the heavens and country around, blowing of their bellows and other infernal devices, made it appear as the dominion of Pluto, or a City in flames. To drive away the direful effects of our nocturnal ramble banqueted at the board of Bacchus till a late hour.

Leaving my friend Wright snoringly embraced in the arms of Morpheus, I went alone to encounter the noble crew of Carron's sooty labyrinth, and for maybe two hours travers'd within its extensive walls, in viewing the surprising machinery for forging implements of destruction to enable the ambition of Princes to hurt with horrific effects their sanguinary mandates on some restless and grasping neighbour tainted with the same warlike spirit as themselves. Leaving this scene of infernal bustle, found my companion at the Inn, who seem'd indignantly impatient at my long absence. After breakfast left these regions of fire and smoke and musingly saunter'd along toward lock No. 16 on the great canal, where the track and luggage boat from Grangemouth stops to take in passengers, reaching it in good time, seated ourselves near a good fire as the weather was so cold and snowy prevented us from traversing the deck of our sluggish boat to peep at the passing scenery. We kept playing backgammon till we came to Auchinsterry where stopping an hour for dinner and onlay of horse, slumber'd along again in our tedious voyage and arriv'd in Glasgow about six o'clock. Thus ended a five days perambulation and although in search neither of Historical information nor Quixotic adventures, yet mingled with a little of both allow'd us all the pleasure and amusement anticipated.

## EQUESTRIAN TRIP TO EDINBURGH ALONGST WITH MR CHALMERS MY BROTHER-IN-LAW FROM SUNDAY 23 MAY 1790 TO THE FOLLOWING MONDAY

The propensity of young men (emerging from scholastic thraldom) to visit distant places, seems to be so ingrafted to our nature that for parents to attempt to suppress altogether this youthful desire, feeds, rather than diminishes the travelling mania. For this reason I suppose my father consented to my accompanying my brother-in-law to a visit to our metropolis. Mounting my brother-in-law's horse (Mr Craig's) we left Glasgow about seven in the morning and after a pleasant ride, stopt about two miles from Bathgate and pass'd two or three hours with a brother's family of Mr Chalmers, thence jogged forward to Mr Jarvie's Inn at Bathgate, a most eccentric and agreeable man, his garden decked and ornamented in all the luxuriance of fancy. Trees cut out in the resemblance of different animals and seats in some of them sufficient to accommodate a pretty large party - passing an hour or two in the company of the fascinating Boniface departed from his whimsical repository and arriv'd at Heron's Inn Edin[bur]gh about nine o'clock pretty much fatigued, being unaccustomed to such a long equestrian journey but after a little supper (a wretched meagre one being serv'd up) with some wine dissipated the effects of the ride so far, as to be able to mount stairs to my bedroom where after a comfortable nap found my strength and spirits renovated to their usual vigour in the morning.

After breakfast call'd on Mrs Barr, a half-sister of mine, and passing an hour or two with her and family went out to view the beauties of this romantic and picturesque City. Traversing with gazing wonder and delight the capacious and ornamented streets of the New Town, as also the ups and downs of the ancient and venerable looking part of Auld Reekie with its towering and formidable castle. Well pleas'd with our forenoon ramble return'd by three o'clock to my Sister's to dinner and seven went with her and husband to the Circus, where after laughing at all the whimsical absurdity's of this place of entertainment adjourned again to my friends where passing a hour or two in convivial harmony, then steer'd for our respective pillows.

Pass'd the next forenoon in perambulating the bustling sea port of Leith where nothing is attractive to strangers save the walk to and fro, which is picturesquely grand, the towering and romantic Edina, with its dragon like Castle ready as it were to protect with devouring pounce its venerable train, and eyeing around with scanning watchfulness as the guardian of its outstretched and ornamented wings. Three o'clock being the usual hour for dinner in the quarter went and partook of family chat in Mr Dick's house, an acquaintance of Mr Chalmers where spending a pleasant afternoon, accompanied Mr M Barr to the Circus but soon being tiring of its amusements made an early retreat from the buffoonick place of entertainment, and pass'd to an early hour in the morning in social harmony with Mr Allan Barr.

About seven in the morning we took our departure from Auld Reeky, homeward bound and deeply impress'd with grateful acknowledgements for the kind and hospitable manner we were treated while sojourners there, had an agreeable ride till about two miles from Bathgate, breakfasted in a Mr Calder's thence adjourned to eccentric Mr Jarvies, and whilst Mr Chalmers was making some private business in the village, amus'd myself with this original and enlivening character in harmless diverting chit chat and sauntering amongst the fantastic enclosures till about two o'clock when accompanied Mr Chalmers to his brother's to dinner, after which having a stirrup gill with Mr Jarvie bent our way again to the west, and after only one other stoppage to tea about eight miles from Bathgate arriv'd in Glasgow at eleven o'clock, not so much fatigued as on my arrival in Edinburgh.

## [EXTRACT FROM] A PEDESTRIAN EXCURSION TO EDINBURGH WITH JOHN SANDERSON, DANIEL MCKINLEAY AND JOHN WRIGHT, FROM THURSDAY APRIL 7TH TO THE MONDAY FOLLOWING

> I being much tired, a Chaise wished them to hire
> But none except Wright would consent
> Therefore that proposal having met with a refusal
> To the door for a coach speedily went
> Where the Fly just come up, then I thought to have got
> With Wright in the inside or on top
> But alas none but one, on the top could get on
> The Wright he commenced to trot
> Squeezed aloft on the deck, on our way joyfully set
> Well pleased with a glimpse of Auld Reek
> Where as Seven struck the Clock, all safely we got
> But lodgings I had yet to seek
> Near an hour through the streets did I stray
>
> Next morn, all our ills from us fled
> Our best pulling on, to Breakfast sat down,
> When done, to St Bernard's Well[5] ran
> Where our stomachs did drench, but Oh! What a stench
> Like spoiled lye or stagnated dam
> Quite tired with the water, through the town made a splutter.
> To forget this sad case, to the Circus did haste

---

5    Fond though Bald was of sea-bathing, this is the only instance of him taking spa water, which may have been a novelty prompted by the publication of, and attendant publicity for, in the previous year, John Taylor's *Medical Treatise on St Bernard's Well illustrated with Select Cases* (Edinburgh, 1790).

There laughing we had in full store
For the Clown and the Taylor, with Harlequin Sailor
Did put all the house in uproar ...

## A TEN DAYS RAMBLE TO THE SEA COAST, 16 JULY 1791

It was the custom for valetudinarians in the inland parts of the country to
repair for the summer to the Sea coast, with the expectation of confirming a
state of convalescence and purifying their constitutions from the Morbifick
influence of a winter blast. For this purpose every spot on the seashore was
crowded with the diseased and emaciated part of mankind, but now the scene is
dramatically changed. Instead of the cadaverous looking sojourner, you meet
now the plump and jolly, sauntering the rocky shore, or climbing the heathery
hill, full of health and spirits, while the sickly race are confined to their gloomy
chambers, driven from their summer retreats by the intrusion of the gay votaries
of pleasure, illured to these marine haunts by the fascinating tales told them by
their friends on their return to Winter quarters. Thus what was intended for
our good, has now become one of the plagues of life, for nought now will satisfy
either married or unmarried or the aged and young but a trip for the summer to
the Sea coast.

For the purpose of witnessing these enchantments I set off in the Greenock
stage Coach, and had an agreeable ride to Crosshill the half way house, when
laying a good foundation of the Eggs toast and tea renew'd my excursion with the
addition of two young men, sons of a Glasgow Physical snob, Doctor Stevenson,
a celebrated Physician.

One of our fellow travellers, a Mr Merchant of Campbeltown, by his frank
and humorous behaviour made the few remaining miles of our journey glide
pleasantly along, and at one o'clock arrived in Greenock where our two medical
friends left us. Regaling myself with the rest of the passengers; and sacrificing an
hour or two to the jolly god, sallied out to view the wonders of their *petit* though
bustling sea port, traversing its uninteresting streets and lanes, directed our
course to the back walk, where falling in with the habitation of a Solitary mortal
who never visits the town, save when the cravings of nature prompts him to leave
his lonely hut, and then lay out with the greatest Oeconomy, the small tributes of
Pity presented to him by his daily visitors, and few must be his wants, as his only
occupation seems to be in perusing a few good books composing his library, and
in describing to the enquiring stranger the history of a few of the feathered tribe
the constant and only companions of this wonderful Voltaire. Being satisfied of
the voluntary seclusion of one of our fellow mortals, and bestowing on him our
mite, left him to follow the bent of his inclination. Near to his hermitage we

regaled ourselves with Strawberries, then conducted my fellow traveller Merchant to the harbour where he embarked for Campbeltown.

Being now left alone to the freedom of my own will sauntered towards the village of Gourock where meeting with some of my relations who had been seiz'd with the Saltwater mania, a visit to whom was chiefly the intention of my excursion. Before I had pass'd a few days amongst them was fully initiated in favour of these Marine retreats, for whom the cheering influence of bright phoebus, invited to the attractive enjoyments of fishing Sailing etc etc. I join'd the careless sojourners in these fascinating amusements, and when the silent evening suspended our aquatic pastimes joined the sprightly fare in tripping the light fantastic toe to fiddle or flute round Kempack's fairy stone, or when the lowering atmosphere drove us from our evening saunter, took refuge in the confin'd apartments of the happy inmates and with song and tale sacrificed to Momus[6] the remaining hours of the evening till the intervention of the slumbering god invited by exhausted nature to disperse the sprightly throng to their respective places of repose in order to reexcite their waning spirits for a renewal in the morning of the naval amusements of the village.

Thus a few days pass'd agreeably away, but having only a short time allow'd from the bustle of business, made me anxious to make the lost of my time by visiting some more of these marine retreats, such as Auld Kirk, Largs and Fairlie, but as I in a manner only pass'd through them can say very little of their attractions, but being highly delighted as I pass'd along the foaming coast with the Alpine scenery on the opposite side of the firth, where the beautiful Island of Bute o'ertopped by the towering and romantic mountains of Arran, and the shore skirted with the picturesque hills of Cowal, intersected with beautiful saltwater Lochs rous'd a desire within me to visit some of the dark and retir'd masses of those mountains. For that purpose I hasten'd back to Gourock with the expectation of finding some congenial soul to accompany me on my Alpine perambulation. On entering the Village met a Mr John Hamilton writer and his brother-in-law, Mr Andrew Duncan who at once agreed to join me in my visit to the Cowal glens.

Early next morning we embark'd in a small boat for Ardentinny on Loch Long where we arrived about nine o'clock after a pleasant passage and priming ourselves with a highland gill of excellent Usquiby commenc'd our Glen Cowal excursions, thorough a romantic wooded retreat of the Earl of Dunmore and after traversing two miles of a good road began to ascend a rugged winding path across the face of a steep mountain, and wandering with indefatigable

6   The Greek god of wit, irony and satire.

perseverance a cheerless track of about five miles, adorn'd with neither tree or shrub, and the solemn stillness enliven'd with the bleating of the fleecy tribe on the surrounding heights, and the murmur of the wimpling rills winding through the dark glen almost perpendicular neath our tottering step. Absorb'd in profound meditations on the sublimity of the mountain scenery, kept silently advancing till the joyful appearance of Loch Eck meandering through the sequester'd and picturesque valley of Strachur, let loose our bridled tongues to rejoice at the gladening prospect of Water - Woods and Cottages to the latter of which we bent our steps for information which way to proceed. On entering a wretched hovel on the banks of the Loch (where we expected nothing but rustic simplicity) were agreeably disappointed at the polite and hearty salutation of "welcome, welcome gentlemen to the highlands, come sit down and partake of our homely fare" looking around the clay built hut for the person who unexpectedly and kindly address'd us, were delighted at the smiling and gentlemanly appearance of two Jolly highlanders, contently regaling themselves with whisky and oaten cakes after an unsuccessful forenoon's fishing in the Loch. The Landlord and Landlady of the hut a hoary headed couple, seem'd transported at the appearance of unknown faces, expecting no doubt an increased sale of his Whisky. Sans ceremony we cheerfully accepted of the polite invitations of the two highland chieftains and soon the circling glass with the cheering conversation of those sons of the mountains, dispersed the gloomy effects of our previous march and with Song and Story enliven'd with rapturous warmth the old heart of our contented landlord, to such a pitch, as to pour forth in grateful strain a gaelic poetical rhapsody of his own composition, in favor of one of his highland guests, for some generous and unsought-for actions done to the anointed bard, and which he sung (by the frequent libations of the whisky potion) with the most unfeign'd animation, and which also inspired us enraptured visitors, to join with the liveliest joy the Chorus of their highland Cronochs sung for our amusement by these sons of Strachur. To repay in the same strain the musical effusions of our highland friends, Hamilton in his usual animated manner gave them the old Scottish Song of 'Tak your auld cloak about ye,'[7] a song peculiarly descriptive of our two aged cottagers and language cannot describe the joyful sensations [showing] in the faces of the tottering pair, as whom at particular parts of the song, brought to recollection some similar association of their pilgrimage, which often glisten'd

---

7   According to Robert Chambers, *The Scottish Songs* (Edinburgh, 1829), 11, this was an old song of which there were many versions. This anonymous ballad, from which the stanza quoted by Bald differs, was first published in Allan Ramsay's Collection of Scots Songs, *Tea Room Miscellany* (Edinburgh, 1723). A completely different version is to be found in John MacQueen and Tom Scott (eds), *The Oxford Book of Scottish Verse* (Oxford, 1966), 313–14.

their furrow'd cheeks with tears of mutual Joy and affection, and at the concluding stanza of the song, no longer could the seeming smother'd wailings of their heart be kept down, for with unfeigned ecstasy.

> Bell his wife, dear as his life,
> Crept to her sire right fondly
> Rise oh gudeman, with thy auld wife
> To thank them for their roundelay.

Our animal spirits being rous'd to such a pitch with mirth and happiness that we had almost forgot where we were and whence we were going, until reminded of our situation by the setting sun glancing in our cottage window, having an unknown rode [*sic*] to traverse, we bade the hospitable group adieu, and received from our two polite angling sons of Strachur recommendatory letters to certain publicans on the root. To show every requisite attention for our comfort and amusement, leaving their clay built cottage with wicker bedsteads doors and partitions, renew'd with frantick spirits our excursion amongst the wooded banks of the Loch. The road being rather rough which with our indiscrete usage at the board of Bacchus occasioned many awkward stumbles, and just as the setting sun was gilding the surrounding mountains with his departing rays, enter'd a small village or rather town as they are stated in that part of the world and observing a number of men and women having potatoes we invited them to a small public house where we expected to find another port to recruit our fading spirits but after priming them with bumpers of their mountainous spirit, found them incapable of amusement by their clownish and idiotical-like bashfulness, leaving them in astonishment at the cause of our invitation, pursued our rout and arriv'd about ten o'clock at our destined haven for that night, Mr Nelson's Inn Strathur, a two storrie slated house, which we did not expect to find amongst these regions of hovels. Tea being the most ready beverage for supper in an highland inn, we supped upon its refreshing extract and pass'd a few convivial moments over a bowl of good rum punch more congenial to our lowland tastes than the heating nature of their mountain dew. Sleep the balmy restorer of exhausted spirits showing by its slumbering influence over our blinking eyelids, that it was time to retire to bed, Hamilton being the eldest we gave him a choice of berth and Duncan and I slept in a double bedded room, but early in the morning were rous'd from our slumbers by a loud knocking at our door, on opening of which were astonish'd as well as affrighted to see Hamilton in a paroxysm of rage, at the sight of whom we recoil'd a few paces in a posture of defence not knowing the cause of his convulsed aspect, but seeming to employ no other weapon than his tongue, we sat down with amazement to listen to his invective levelled against his two innocent comrades for enjoying a sound sleep in a comfortable bedroom whilst he lay shivering and tossing all night, unable to shut his eyes by the whistling of the wind through innumerable apertures of his crazy apartment, and now pained all over by the excessive cold, tho we gave him the choice of his bed, no other comfort would be received from his comrades but taking a peep of his ley chamber, and to our astonishment, found they were building an addition to their house, which was neither plaster'd nor windowed, and to keep out the external air was hung all around with carpet, which the clouded imagination of Hamilton by his unguarded sacrifice at the shrine of Bacchus the preceding day had represented a fine tapestry. Consoling with him for suffering, and throwing out a few invectives against landlord at Strachur Inn, finished our patronage about seven in the morning and in half an hour thereafter arriv'd at a ferry on the banks of Loch Long where we intended to cross, but the morning being rather stormy, old Charon advised us to walk about a mile further to St Catherine's where we would be certain of a more safe and expeditious passage. Thanking him for his attention to our safety, proceeded up the Loch and after walking more than a mile saw no appearance of a ferry but a good deal surprised when a peasant told us, that we were still more than four miles from it, discovering when too late that the attention of the old boatman to our comfort was only a selfish propensity to save his own lazy corpus, as he would have had a pretty severe pull across the ruffled Loch. Impress'd with another unfavourable trait on the highland character, we saunter'd on and arriving at St Catherine's did not altogether regret the advice of the deceitful ferryman, for after a refreshment of some of the lowland comforts, Whisky and Seed cake, which we did not expect stretched so far northwards especially the latter luxury made us cross with spirit the celebrated Loch fine and arrived at Inverary about eleven o'clock yet not without a wet Jacket being often immers'd by the briny spray and pouring rain which made us doubt whether our opinion of the first ferryman was correct, for even in the more confined part of the Loch we found it rough enough. Landing in safety with the exception of the ducking; went to McIntyre's Inn, the second best in the town, recommended to us by the two friends of the Strachur band, getting breakfast and dressed in our best, sent our names to the Duke of Argyle (a usual custom) expressing a wish to visit his Castle.[8] Having received his permission, off we went to view the wonder of his palace where we saw nothing

---

8    Bald and his companions were part of a growing number of visitors to Inverary, its castle and pleasure grounds. The author of the parish account of Inverary for *The Statistical Account of Scotland, Volume 5* (Edinburgh, 1793), 290, noted that such was 'the resort of travellers to that place, that in 1790 a hundred had viewed the grounds in one week, and that two years later that figure had doubled'.

in its outward appearance, that excited our surprise, it is a building in the Gothick stile, of a bluish stone abounding in that part of the country. Being situate in the midst of a plain with some large trees scattered about it in the background cloud capped mountains skirt with extensive woods renders the situation of Argyle Castle delightfully grand. The inside of this venerable pile is furnish'd in the greatest polite elegance, the walls of some of the rooms are painted and gilt in a very rich manner, and others cover'd with elegant tapestry and paintings brought from Italy by the present Duke when on his travels. The family are very attentive to strangers for in order that they may see all the apartments worth notice, they shift from room to room. Being highly satisfied and pleased with the inside of the Castle of Clan Campbell's chief, mounted by ladder to the top of the battlements where an extensive and picturesque scene burst on our view. The Loch stretching below us. The beautiful village of Inverary the metropolis of Argyle, extensive woods, heath cover'd mountains, and the naked rugged precipices of Glen Croe form'd an interesting landscape. In our descent pass'd one of the young ladies of the family playing a favourite highland air on an organ fix'd in the staircase. This musical departing scene heightened the pleasure we enjoyed in the princely mansion. After leaving the Castle saunter'd to the summet of the conical Dunicuich. And although 700 feet high, a carriage can be driven to the top by a road winding along the wooded front, leading to a Gothic building on the knoll, for the accommodation of visitors, as a shelter from the precipitation of this humid climate. Here the grandeur of the scenery far surpasses that from the turrets of the Castle and fully repays the traveller's climb. After our descent from Dunicuich traversed other parts of the beautiful and picturesque policy's and return'd to our Inn by 5 o'clock to dinner.

Having now accomplished the main intention of our excursion and visit to Inverary, after a moderate dose of highland comfort, crossed to St Catherine's on our return home, after a more pleasant sail across than we had in the morning, found our way towards Strachur and e'er we reached it a furious storm arose, which rendered our situation utterly unpleasant. The howling of the wind through the wooded glen, the splashing of the troubled loch, the beating rain with the mournful bleating of the fleecy tribe, threw us into despondent reverie until the appearance of Strachur Inn broke the silent enchantment of Hamilton which brought to mind his former sufferings, fervently pouring forth his supplication for a more comfortable berth than in the preceding night we arrived at the Inn and after some refreshment, Duncan and I anticipating Hamilton's intentions of dispossessing us of our former beds made a premature retreat to our Rooms, and left him to muse on the unrelenting conduct of his comrades, but remembering the adage that 'self preservation is often a hindrance to beneficent actions' was the reason of our not offering to our enraged fellow traveller an exchange of berths. Having enjoyed a comfortable repose, we waited on Hamilton early in the morning to enquire for his welfare, when he assured us in a more pacifical tone that he had got a most refreshing sleep, by his taking the precautions before going to bed of closing up all the whistling crevices of his tapestered apartment. Leaving Strachur in good humour had a pleasant walk to the Poet's house formerly mention'd, where drinking whisky with the seemingly contented bard - continued our excursion and e'er we reached Ardentinny were overtaken by a tremendous storm of wind and rain, which we certainly could have attributed to the influence that Hamilton had with aerial powers who by his fervent ijaculation for our punishment had poured out their deluging effects on us by way of retribution for our selfish conduct at Strachur Inn, but he not accepting the fury of the elements thought it was only a casual operation of nature. Arriving at Ardentinny with well soak'd jackets, dissipated the gloomy effects of the blast by a bowl or two of good Whisky punch after which we thought of embarking here for Gourock but the swell of the sea being so great although the wind had abated, was persuaded by the ferryman to walk to Portemstock[9] about four miles from here where we would be certain of a safer and quieter passage than working down the coast against wind and tide, more convinced of the propriety of his advice than we were of the Loch long ferryman we forwarded towards Portemstock which we with difficulty reach'd about nine o'clock at night, for the late rain had swollen the bridgeless rivulets so that not without a good deal of trouble got across some of them. One of these mountain torrents in particular had almost bid defiance to our endeavours, when a peasant from one of the heights, observing our unsuccessful attempts to cross the growing flood, ran down to our assistance and conducting us to a fordable part of the stream, carried each of us safely on his back to the other side. Thanking and rewarding his unsolicited attention with a small pecuniary gift, arriv'd without any other impediment at our much wished for ferry and had a fairly rough passage to Gourock where we arrived about ten o' clock and were received with tears of joy by our friends who had dreaded some catastrophe had befallen us, during since our absence the inclemency of the weather. Fatigue being our only ailment a comfortable night's rest dissipated all our ills and got up early in the morning full of health and spirits. After passing other two days most agreeably in the marine retreat, embarked on a Monday afternoon in one of the passage boats for Glasgow and after a pleasant sail till about Dalmure where they

---

9    According to Slater's *Commercial Directory of Scotland* (London, 1867), 364, Portinstuck was another name for Blairmore.

were deepening the river, our pilot by some unskilful manoeuvre ran our small wherry between one of the punts and a galliot which threatened to crash us to pieces but escaping with only our gunwart drove in and a terrible fright to the ladies having got a good many on board, parmercy. Our boat arrived at the Broomielaw without any other obstruction about Eight o'clock pm where regaling at the board of Bacchus with some of the passengers till eleven, retired to our respective places of abode.

## [EXTRACT FROM] VISIT TO BEN LOMOND WITH ANDREW ORR AND JOHN URQUHART, 1 OCTOBER 1791

After Breakfast though Ben's top with dense fog was clad
Resolved we to reach it, a project sure mad
But as this was the cause of our journeying so far
Neither storm fog or rain would deter our friend Orr,
And also John Orhart for all I could say
Was determined with Orr to scramble up the great brae
That both could relate the vast wonder they saw
How great was their prospect- the length of a straw
But now to relate this Quixotic ascend
Persuaded to join the cavalcade of Old Ben
At ten we set off with a boy as a guide
And to carry our store of good whiskey and bread
O lead us to springs of pure water when thirsty
Washing down the Oat bannocks and qeenoching the Whiskey
When reaching half way Caledonia's famed hill
John Orhart and I resolved to sit still
For the fog was so dense and the day threatening rain
We resolved without Orr to return back again
But consulting awhile as Orr still did ascend
We resolved that to him outstrip thither would bend …

## A TRIP TO DRYMEN AND STIRLING ETC., 3 NOVEMBER 1791

About half past ten o'clock in the morning left Glasgow on foot and passing without any remarkable incident through the villages of Milngavie and Strathblane till about a mile from Killearn left the public road and following a foot path leading to Gartness, arrived there about three o'clock pm where taking some refreshment bent my course for Drymen to witness the froliky gatherings of a highland fair, and to meet my friend Gartness with whom perambulating among the loiterers of these periodical assemblies, who were lounging and gaping at some amusement the principal intentions of their visit, and in the absence of the more aged and business part of the throng who were by this time withdrawing to their respective and distant places of abode. Highly amused with the manners and these mountaineers, and the various rowdy howling amusements of a highland fair, adjourn'd to a public house with a number of Gartness's acquaintance where carousing for a little - went to another house at the foot of the town where a lively group were tripping on the light fantastic toe and joining them in all the hilarity requisite to please and to be pleased. My appearance created a good deal of diversion, for having on my head a hairy cap belonging to one of Gartness's men, on my entering all was speculation and conjecture who this outlandish-like person might be - some thought it might be one of the Mountebank or other itinerant attendants on a fair, whilst others imagin'd me a foreigner disguis'd in order to enjoy incognito the diversions of a country wake, but their speculative conjecture were closed up by my friends, Gartness introducing me to the almighty throng and entering into all their mirth and absurdities for two or three hours adjourn'd to a third house and clos'd the fair in a jovial manner chas'd with songs from a Mr Bruce head gardener to the Duke of Montrose and departing highly delighted with the days excursion arriv'd at the Pot of Gartness about two o'clock of the morning.

Next day was pass'd in an unsuccessful shooting perambulation through the adjoining woods and fields, where having kill'd with my Gun only a few small birds not game spent the evening most agreeably with the inmates of Gartness.

After breakfast on Saturday morning left the romantic dell of Kenroy And after an unmounted walk through the Villages of Buchlyvie, Kippen and Gargonik [Gargunnock] arriv'd at my friend Mr Walker of Bannockburn at Six o'clock pm and took up my abode with him for the night.

Next morning being clear and frosty perambulated in and about the village till breakfast time after which accompanied Mr Walker to Mr Cross's meeting house[10] St Ninians where having an excellent sermon from that Revd Gentlemen and in the interval of the fore, and afternoon's meeting partook of <u>bun and gill,</u> a Presbyterian custom, and at two went to church again, after which had another refreshment, and on our way homeward call'd on Mr & Mrs McGown our relations, who were sitting down to dinner, after partaking of their kind invitation to join them, steer'd our course for Mr Walker whose arriving about Six o'clock pm pass'd the evening in reading and religious meditation, and after family worship from Mr Walker retired to bed at ten.

10  The Revd Archibald Cross was, and had been since his arrival from Biggar in 1784, Minister of the Succession Bannockburn United Presbyterian congregation at St Ninians.

Monday being the time agreed upon for my return homewards from this short ramble about Eight in the morning having breakfasted, bade adieu to my friend Walker, and in passing Denny call'd on my friends Mr & Mrs Renny after resting with them sometime, continued my excursion and followed a new line of road cutting by Cumbernauld about a mile to the South of that Village, fell in with a man journeying on foot to Glasgow and with him trudged along in a very agreeable manner till we came to a part of the road not cut, and had to wade and scramble through meadow fields and heather for about three miles e'er we came to a public or Ale house (where after our scramble refreshing ourselves with <u>Pap</u> or Cake & whisky) and good black puddings, the latter of which my comrade in the absence of the good folk of the House stowed some of them in his pocket and in case of detection, that I may be thought equally guilty with him he stuff'd one into mine much against my inclination, but afraid of his resentment (being a goliath to me) in case of a positive refusal pocketed the affront, and continuing our rout[e] arriv'd in Glasgow at five o'clock pm where taking a parting gill with my comrade in one Dobbies in the High Street, separated at Six o'clock for our respective places of abode.

## A VISIT TO MY COUSIN ALEXR WALKER ON HIS MARRIAGE WITH MY SISTER MARGARET WHICH TOOK PLACE 24 NOVEMBER 1791

On Sunday 27th November at eleven o'clock in the morning I mounted my brother in law's (Mr Chalmers) horse on a matrimonial visit to my eldest sister who was married three days previous to this to her cousin Alexr Walker. After having clear'd the town spur'd up my beast to endeavour to outride a gathering storm to windward at same time it blowing a severe gale. By my exertion got into Kilsyth e'er the fury of the storm reach'd me, and by the time I had got breakfast the weather had so far cleared up as to enable me to enjoy my ride in a more quiet and satisfactory manner. About a mile to the north of Denny met a Chaise containing my Father, Brother and brother in law Mr Chalmers, returning homewards from the marriage, after speaking with them a little, rode on to St Ninians where I arriv'd about twelve o'clock, where stabling my horse and in half an hour after met Mr & Mrs Walker coming from church and joining them in the usual custom of bun & gill with an extra chappon[11] for their hymeneal Welcome, accompanied them to the afternoon sermon, after which mounted my

---

11 Quite what is implied here by 'chappon' is not clear. It could mean simply a container full, or the full measure of a chopin, a half pint Scots or a pint and a half imperial – which would be a very generous welcome indeed.

horse for Bannockburn for Mr Walker's where after dinner pass'd the remainder of the evening in reading and religious conference and after family worship from Mr Walker retired to bed.

Next forenoon being stormy and wet did not venture out till about one o'clock when our friend Mr Rennie from Denny came in, who having forgot some bills wanted one of Mr Walker's men to go to his house for them, but to oblige him at same time glad of an opportunity for a ploy offer'd my services to bring them which readily accepted of, performed the task without any other inconvenience than encountering a severe storm of wind and rain, but on my return having soon got the better of the drench'd effects called on my acquaintance Mr Milton. But being rather engaged return'd to Mr Walkers and after tea played at Draughts with him till bed time.

Early next morning Mr Walker set out for Doune fair, where I promis'd to meet him after breakfast, provided the weather was favourable at nine o'clock the morning being clear sunshine, set off for the fair, and after a pleasant ride arriv'd at eleven, and met Mr Walker on the crofts among the Cattle (being an extensive cowmarket) where riding with him a whole day up and down the fair, the stables being so crowded could get no accommodation for our horse, and as little for ourselves, left the market about five pm in rather a famish'd state and unfavourably impress'd with a Drovers life, but my friend Walker being rather of a saving turn prevented me by his parsimony and consequent shyness of mixing with the social group from forming an accurate opinion of the true character of these Cattle Merchants, reached Bannockburn about seven in the evening and after satisfying with dinner the cravings of our empty stomachs, and after some oatmeal silencing the still grumbling wrumbles of my not yet satisfied paunch with a supper retired to bed a little after ten.

The weather next morning being favourable for a ride left Mr Walkers after breakfast and bending my course towards Falkirk had an agreeable ride thither, after passing said Town was hesitating whether to retrace my steps or proceed further when observing the shivering topsails in Grangemouth made me resolve to visit that petite harbour and following the direction of a man that was passing rode a considerable way down an avenue but after perambulating about half an hour up and down this seeming labyrinth at last landed in midst of some stubble parks and reluctantly had to wheel about, till meeting the high way again on which I jogged till coming to a cross road following the one which I consider'd would take me to Grangemouth that after riding along it for about two miles found to my disappointment that it was the Borrowstoneness road in place of the Grangemouth and that I was only about three miles from the former town. Thinking it rather ominous I was not able to reach Grangemouth by the several checks I met with, proceeded on to Bo-ness where arriving about one o'clock only rode through its narrow dirty streets - obscured in the dense columns of smoke rolling from the salt pans. Afraid if I took dinner there of gulping down mouthfuls of the sooty atmosphere directed my way to Linlithgow where getting at two o'clock had a tolerable good dinner in Mrs Finlayson's Inn with a pint of Wine after it, then steer'd my steps towards Bannockburn, determining to trust no more to Cross ways or bye roads but jogged straight forwards through Falkirk, passing which a heavy shower of snow came on, but buffeting the storm proceed'd on my journey, till at last clearing up the scene became delightful. The moon peeping from behind a cloud contrasted with the terrifick effects of Carron Works render'd the picture truly sublime and shew'd my progress towards Bannockburn where I arriv'd at Six o'clock better pleas'd with my ride than I was on the former day perambulating the Cattle market of Doune from which Mr Walker arriv'd just as we had fortified ourselves accompanied by a brother Drover with whom sacrificing to Bacchus till ten o'Clock went to bed.

Having now satisfied my curiosity with the scenery in and about Bannockburn thought it was time now to steer homewards therefore on Thursday morning December first left Mr Walker at ten o'clock am, and called en passant on my friend Renny at Denny resting for an hour pursued my course with the apprehension of broken bones it being hard frost with a little snow and my horse not being prepared for the change made me frequently dismount to lead it down the frozen declivities of the road till after passing Kilsyth when a change of climate took place, for instead of sliding and skating among alongst the frozen highway now all was splashing and at Cadder a deluge of rain accompanied the remaining five miles of my journey, arriv'd in Glasgow at 3 o'clock pm.

## TRIP TO BANNOCKBURN, FRIDAY 24 FEBRUARY 1792

Mounted one of John Nielson's hacks new wynd at eleven o'clock am & after a pleasant ride till near Dennyloanhead I left the highway for a nearer cut to Denny but had soon cause to repent of my wish for an abridgment of my journey for when in the middle of the moor there came on a heavy fall of snow, and the road being wretchedly bad, render'd my situation truly disagreeable and more tedious than if I had continued the public way. However arriv'd at my friend Rennies at 2 o'clock and after dinner embraced the opportunity of a fair blink of pursuing my journey, but scarcely had I cross'd the Carron till an increas'd fall of snow blinking my peepers made the road rather narrow for my Romantic zigzagging alongst the whiten'd path, but my youthful blood treating scornfully the fury of the storm, urged on the faltering steps of my jaded beast and arriv'd at my friends Walkers of Bannockburn at five o'clock and pass'd the evening with them and Mr Renny on a agreeable chit chat.

The weather next morning being favourable for my intended trip to Auld Reeky left Mr Walker at eleven o' clock and after a pleasant ride to Linlithgow and comfortable dinner with a moderate primer after it renew'd my excursions and arriv'd in Edinburgh at five o'clock pm. Stabling my horse went to my brother in law Mr Barrs and after tea accompanied him to the Circus[12] where we were entertained with a new pantomime from Ossian's poems call'd Oscar and Malvenia, after which we spent the remainder of the night most agreeably with him and his brother Allan.

Next morning perambulated with Mr Barr, the different streets, lanes or avenues of this distant and picturesque city, and at twelve bent my way for Bannockburn, baiting myself and Aleck at Linlithgow arriv'd at Mr walkers at Six where after tea and family worship retired to bed. At eight next morning left Bannockburn on my return homewards - breakfasting at Denny with friend Renny and at twelve set out with him towards Glasgow by the Cumbernauld road where about three miles of the new cut not being finished render'd our journey very unpleasant for raining on at all the way then few miles was little more than a quagmire Mr Rennie parting from me a few miles from town as he was going to his farm at quarrly [sic]. Arriv'd at Glasgow 6 o'clock.

## [EXTRACT FROM] TWO DAYS RAMBLE TO RENFREW WITH WILLIAM FRAZER, WILLIAM STARK, ARCHIBALD HUNTER, JAMES MARTIN AND ROBERT HADDOW, THURSDAY 5 AND SATURDAY 7 APRIL 1792

> Twas at the season of revolving time
> When Presbyterians have the world to prove
> Their warm affection, for him who died for men
> And join'd with faith their stated feast of love
> Not so devout, the group above we hail'd
> Tough Sceptic like yet true believers were
> To please their fancy, snuff the vernal gale

---

12 According to *The Edinburgh Evening Courant*, 1 March 1792 at the Circus (doors opened at 6 and begins at 7) there was a programme of tight-rope dancing, etc. which was to conclude with 'The Grand Heroic Ballet Pantomime *Oscar and Malvina. Or the Hall of Fingal*. Carroll by Mr. Dubois, being his first appearance in that character'. The work, derived from Ossian, is described in the catalogue of the National Library of Scotland as performed at the Theatre Royal, Convent Garden in 1791 as 'airs, duets, choruses and argument of the new ballet pantomime'.

And leave behind them for a time dull care
Such were the reasons urged our youthful range
Not quite so bad as if apostates all
To Bryants' Inn we hither bent our way
Where with good porter drench'd our parched lips
And ordering dinner - further on did stray
At two return'd but off the bell we pull'd
Or e'er our dinner on the board was placed;
Instead of Salmon, with Salt beef were gull'd
Veal, Steak, and Broth our table also graced
With knife and fork each play'd so well his part
That soon the board with viands clear appear'd
Amaz'd, the waiter smil'd, to think how smart
So wondrous hungry as such loads to clear
But bowls of punch appeas'd the wondr'ing wait
And rous'd our spirits on to frantic mood
No longer trembled he the guzzling site
Afraid no gainer such gulps of food
In merry key we left the Borough town
And had rare sport in Barr's bleaching house
Each with the damsels had our tousling turn
Some thought us tipsy, others thought us wous.

## A FOURTEEN DAYS RAMBLE TO THE SEA COAST FROM FRIDAY 9 AUGUST 1793 - AND TOP OF BEN LOMOND

My annual propensity to visit the Sea coast, again urg'd me to the firth of Clyde along with a Jas Mitchell writer. At Eleven o'clock am set out on foot and had a pleasant walk to Crosshill about 12 miles from town, after a very indifferent dinner at One shilling a head we again renew'd our journey and reach'd Port Glasgow about eight pm where in Eaglesom's Inn we devoted to mirth and sociality the remaining hours of the evening.

10th About eight next morning after paying rather a high charg'd bill, we continued our rout[e], but had not proceeded a mile when it came on very wet, and had to take shelter in a house till it was over. Arriv'd in Greenock at eleven and breakfasted in the Black Bull Inn at 10d a head, traversed the town and harbour viewing its uninteresting features till near one o'clock when Mitchell, return'd with him towards Greenock whilst I paid a how do ye do to some of my friends. At five o'clock proceeded towards the West and at the entrance to Greenock meeting comrade Mitchell, return'd with him towards Greenock and drank tea in a Mr Scots of Fenert, after which bent our steps for Gourock and in Lyetts Tavern devoted the hours of the evening to mirth and good humour with a group of social sojourners.

11th At eight next morning saunter'd along the shore and had a salt water dip, return'd to Breakfast at ten - perambulated the coast till One - when lunch'd in a Mr Turnbull's, a writer [lawyer], sallied forth again till three when din'd in Mr Turnbull's, rose from our bottle at five, saunter'd till six, and join'd a Club of jolly mortals in a House at the east end of the village where sacrificing to Bacchus and Momus, retir'd to my lodgings at ten, when getting supper, soon thereafter lay down for repose.

12th Sallied out at nine o'clock next morning and bath'd, Breakfasted at ten, walked about till three when din'd - drank tea at six o'clock in my acquaintance Mr Boyd, after which accompanied him to Greenock which we left at 10, on our return to Gourock, and on our way thither fell in with Mr Farrie and his family, and adjourned with them to their house, where drinking some Grog, retired to my lodgings and getting supper went to bed.

13th After Breakfast next morning, saunter'd alongst the shore and took a bath at twelve. - At three din'd with Mr Mitchell and a Mr Brand, after which walk'd with them to Greenock accompanied with Mr Farrie, where we went on board of the Tender, to get an apprentice of Mr Brand's who had run away from him, and enter'd into his Majestie's service. On our getting on board of the Ship, went down to the Cabin and demanded the boy, but was refused without an order from the Captain who was then on shore. Left this miserable abode of nearly two hundred ragamuffins, who were stow'd together like herrings in a barrel, On getting ashore call'd on the Captain an old superannuated fool, and he likewise refus'd him without a silver oar[13], that is an order from the High Admiral. Mitchell told him that was quite unnecessary for the Water Baillie's warrant was the only silver oar known on the Clyde, and to his peril refuse the surrender of the boy which he still with the insolence of Office declin'd giving him up. Leaving the impassionated dotard for a while to enjoy his tyrannical insolence, return'd with a Messenger and lodg'd a protest against the conduct of the commodore, at the same time telling him that we would be at Mr Kechnie's Inn for half an hour and if in that time an order of liberation did not arrive from him he must abide by the consequences. We had not been long at the tavern till a polite apology came from the trembling hero, with an order to take away the boy being afraid he would have been serv'd like his predecessor on the station, who had been near losing his berth for a similar sneer at the Water

13  The silver oar was the symbol of Admiralty authority for a Commodore.

Baillie's authority. The boy having been got on shore, glad of his escape from such an infernal berth, we left Greenock about Ten o'clock and arriv'd at our respective lodgings at eleven.

14th After Breakfasting next morning at ten, play'd at Backgammon till One with Mr Brand, being so wet could not venture out: at said hour walked to Greenock with Brand & Mitchell on purpose taking a sail in the packet for Rothesay. On arriving at Greenock call'd on the Packetmaster to learn when he was to sail, and were told at four. Din' in McKechnies at three. Call'd myself on the Master of the packet at four to see if all was ready, but to my disappointment would not set off (he said) till next day. Return'd with a sorrowful heart to my two companions in the Inn who were also a good deal chagrin'd at the intelligence. Leaving them to wash away the disappointment with an extra glass, bent my steps for Gourock where I met two acquaintances (Dykes & Taylor) who were going to take a ride to Largs. Agreeing to make one of the party, return'd with them to Greenock to procure horses, which having done, we set off at seven o'clock and after a pleasant ride for the most part close to the shore, arriv'd at that pleasant marine retreat about nine, and taking up our quarters in Gibson's tavern, were but indifferently entertain'd with supper, and after sacrificing in moderation to Bacchus retir'd to Bed.

15th At six next morning we saunter'd down to the beach to look out for a boat to Rothesay, determin'd to see that town and no longer to trust to deceitful packetmasters, but to be our own commodores whilst our purses could afford to charter a boat, and here our designs were again nearly frustrated by the boats being left by the ebbing of the tide high on the beach. At last seeing no alternative but either to return to Greenock or venturing ourselves in a very small vessel like a canoe which was laying ashore, we resolv'd on the latter, and with care launch'd her into the water, and getting ready with four good hands, set off at Eight o'clock and arriv'd in Rothesay about two hours thereafter. Breakfasted in the principal tavern at One shilling a head, which charge was higher than customary, but considering the hearty breakfast we made was moderate enough. This borough is but small, yet clean and regular, most of the houses slated and the Ivy cover'd Castle, towering over the high part of the town gives a picturesque effect to this petite seaport. The safe and commodious harbour was almost destitute of vessels, being all out on the herring fishery. The interior of the island for the short way we penetrated seem'd to be pretty fruitful, but observed more potatoes growing than Corn. Return'd to our boat at 2 o'clock but were doubtful whether or not we would venture ourselves on it, as the wind was rather high and the least squalls we were afraid would overturn her. After a little consultation with the crew, set off with little sail, and arriv'd in safety at Largs after a pleasant two hours cruise. Paying eight shillings for the boat and after drinking health and prosperity to both sides of the Firth, mounted our steeds at five o'clock and after a pleasant ride to Auld Kirk partook there of some refreshment after which renew'd our ride, and reached Greenock about seven, paid our hire which was four shillings and six pence, then bent our steps for Gourock where we arriv'd about Nine.

16th Got up next morning at eight and bath'd, breakfasted at ten, after which walk'd about till one, when observing the Portenstock ferry boat, laying at the back of the quay and about to return to the Cowal shore, made me resolve on a saunter through the highland glens to Inverary. The boatman promised to wait on me for some little time, but e'er I had got myself equipp'd for the journey they had gone off without me. Determin'd however not to be baulked on my wishes to visit the capital of Argyle I hastened to Greenock and fortunately found the Ardentinny ferry or Packet boat about to set off. - we left Greenock at five o'clock pm with a fine breeze but right ahead of us, after beating to and fro for two or three hours it came on a dead calm, which render'd my situation not altogether pleasant, for as night was advancing, and only a couple of Oars, with a very leaky, clammy heavy boat, making about 20 or 30 pints of water every hour or two, and the tide running so strong against us on entering Loch Long caus'd our movement to be rather retrograde, which was rather discouraging. The grandeur however, of the surrounding scenery supported my dropping heart. It was now the silent hour of midnight when the busy world seek for repose on their downy or straw fill'd pillows but here slumbering on the peaceful ocean nought but the hull and rugged ballast of our boat seem'd to be the place of repose - should sleep entice and to stretch my wearied frame, therefore, endeavour'd by the sublimity of the scene to keep myself awake. This delightful romantic and mourill [*sic*] Highland scenery beguil'd the drowsy propensity of the midnight hour, cheered with the robust & sprightly highland nymphs with men and children composing my fellow passengers, returning to their native glens who commodating the situation of the Stranger as they styled me, plied their hardy strength to the lazy Oar and to rouse me from my meditations chanted some of the mountain pibrochs suitable to the occasion, echoing amongst the hills and join'd in the Chorus by the whole of our romantic crew. Alas! This joyous scene was soon o'ercast with melancholy gloom, for the moon sole cheerer of the silent night, spiriting on these mountaineers to the exultation of their joyous wakes at last sat behind the rugged precipices of the pellucid Loch and left us as it were in the regions of perpetual darkness. The lofty mountains which surrounded us now appeared a profound abyss into which we were sliding, and the twinkling lights from the solitary cots alongst the shore like as many guides to entice us into them. The damsels who had delighted me hitherto with their native Chronachs were now silenced by the awfulness of the surrounding scene, not a hush was heard save the splashing Oar and the murmurs of the mountain rills. Gliding softly towards one of the twinkling lights, soon found to our joyous satisfaction that it proceeded from Ardentinny ferry house, the place of our destination near which we all in safety landed, and reach'd the house at Three o'clock in the morning after a tedious passage of ten hours, the distance from Greenock being only nine miles. Rewarding my highland minstrels with some of their mountain dew for their unsolicited efforts to amuse me on the passage, left them in the kitchen to enjoy themselves as they thought proper. Feeling myself much fatigued wish'd to proceed to bed after eating a little supper, and using the precaution of getting clean bed Cloaths laid myself down for repose.

17th After a refreshing nap of four hours, saunter'd forth for a puff of fresh air, and met at the door Mr Ferguson, a highland gentleman, whom I had fallen in with at Greenock, and for some reason or other, supposed to be am'rous, had crept into the Portenstock ferry boat in place of the Ardentinny. As we were going the same road he join'd me at breakfast and fortifying ourselves for our Alpine tour with a glass of the doctor in our last Cap set off on our mountainous saunter through the pleasant retreat of the Earl of Dunmore and then across a steep rugged path, at times calling at the scattered lonely cots and partaking of their Highland hospitality, enabled us to pursue our stumbling steps with more spirit. We passed some farms under very singular leases. Three or four trees in a tuft growing on some conspicuous part of the farm, and as long as these trees vigitate the tack continues. Mr Ferguson being a native of this district, either believed or pretended to believe in the supernatural prowess of the inhabitants by shewing me some surprising feats of strength done by them, such as large trees cloven asunder by the single stroke of a broad sword, but which notwithstanding his protesting in the belief of such auld wives' stories, I imagined to have been occasioned by some electric explosion. We next came to a heap of stones piled on high as a monument of abhorrence for a murderous deed committed by a band of Robbers on that spot, and all who pass that way throws a stone of the Cairn to keep them from scaith during their pilgrimage amongst these mountains. Following my companions Superstitious notion I threw my precautionary stone on the heap when he constantly assured me I would be now perfectly safe in my progress through these Glens. At two o'clock arrived at a small village where Ferguson left being not far from his family mansion. At three reached the banks of Loch Fine and walking to a ferry about a mile further up, and had a pleasant sail across, the breadth being about a mile and a half for which paying three pence, delightfully sauntered alongst the banks of the loch for about five miles to Inverary where I arrived at 5 o'clock pm. Going to the principal Inn, had a comfortable dinner served up in five minutes warning at One shilling. This House is very large and elegant, yet notwithstanding it is insufficient to accommodate the strangers who present thereto in summer, on their visits to the Highland Glens, therefore they are building a large addition to the House, which when completed will in the main time compensate for the defects of the present one. The Landlord, (one of the Duke's old servants) has the whole of the premises for only paying the interest of the money expended in their erection. But when considered that only in the summer they can meet with any tolerable degree of custom this moderate rent may be deemed extravagant enough. The town is a neat clean looking place, most of the houses uniformly built and slated. It is in agitation to build an elegant Church with spire in the centre of the town, which when completed will add much to the beauty of this picturesque borough. Having in my former mentioned excursion to Liverpool fallen in with Mr Fisher on the homeward bound passage, a resident or manager of a Woollen factory in the neighbourhood of Inverary, at six o'clock walked about six miles down the Loch to the said factory, and meeting my friend Fisher, passed with an agreeable night.

18th. Left Fisher's next morning at ten, arrived in Inverary about an hour after and passed till 12 with an acquaintance I chanced to fall in with - pursuing my wandering career had a pleasant walk alongst the banks of Loch fine for several miles to a ferry where I crossed to save a walk of about 4 miles round the head of the loch. Stopt at Cairndow the first stage from Inverary and partook of a lunch after which continued my walk through the wild and sublime scenery of Glencroe where the frightful and inaccessible mountains seem to threaten destruction to the gazing traveller, whose steps are urged on with unconscious progress lost in wonder and amazement at the aweful grandeur and varied scenery of this romantic glen, lulled to delightful meditation by the murmur of the mountain rills and the bleating of the fleecy tribe wandering alongst the wrinkled fronts of the towering heights. Neither tree or shrub above this lonely retreat and a few wretched like huts, scattered at the bottom of the glen are the only symptoms of human beings inhabiting this frightful pass. My spirits began to droop a good deal at the solemn stillness and sombre shades which the advancing twilight generally brings into these Alpine regions. But soon with estatic joy beheld Loch Long glancing past the extremity of the Loch and spying through the evening shades the elegant town of Arrochar gracing the opposite banks of the Loch thither with hasty steps I steered my musing course and reached it in ere the curtains of night had obscured from my wondering eyes the grandeur of the surrounding scenery. On my arrival at the Inn was shewn into a very large and handsome parlour and immediately began to take notice of my day's perambulations which being observing by the gazing waiter - was probably the cause of an extra attention being paid me, afraid no doubt of an unfavourable report being jotted down in my note book - after a comfortable supper, retired to bed about nine.

19th Being refreshed by a comfortable sleep of twelve hours, adjourned to my former parlour and the time breakfast was preparing contemplated the romantic and delightful situation of Arrochar, much frequented in summer by travellers perambulating amongst our heath covered mountains and deep shaded glens. Being much pleased with the beauties at the head of Loch Long, and the hospitable receptions and treatment I met with in the elegant and commodious Inn, I left it about ten after paying a very moderate charged bill, nothing for bed. The day being very hot, had rather a sweating tho' yet pleasant walk to Invercruglie (about 6 miles from Arrochar) which I reached by twelve. The prospect here was truly inviting, the placid surface of the Isle studded Lomond, the bald and unclouded summit of the towering Ben, the clear unfoggy aspect of the distant horizon, were all so inviting that although I had been formerly on the top of the Ben, yet the present moment was so propitious for a View, my inclination for again ascending to the Aerial region, could not be restrained; therefore crossed over to the Rowardennan where I stopt for about an hour for a little refreshment. Not wishing to say to the folks of the house that I was going to ascend Ben Lomond without a guide, I put four biscuits in my pocket and paying my fare gained the track on the mountain by a circuitous path and kept ascending the stupendous height under an unclouded sun and not withstanding the fatiguing march, reached nearly its summit without almost stopping. Coming to a spring of fresh water at the bottom of the last storey of the venerable Ben, a valuable and refreshing treasure to my parched lips, but being much heated with my continued climb, dare not taste of the cool limpid spring, therefore soaked one of my biscuits in it which proved a safe and cooling refreshment. After this simple lunch, ascended the most difficult part of the mountain, the steep and rugged top of old Ben, the summit of which I gained at four o'clock. The extensive prospect which I now enjoyed was a full recompense for the fatiguing climb. Towards the north the scene was truly awful and sublime, naked rugged mountains piled as it were upon one another, beautiful and picturesque Lochs winding through the peaceful valleys and water glittering on the tops of the heights beneath me delighted my astonished eye. To the West a more refreshing, delightful and extensive landscape opens to view. Loch Lomond with its numerous islands stretching from the bottom of the mountain, Dumbarton Castle with the firth of Clyde refreshing the gazing eye, whilst Ailsa, Cantyre [Kintyre] and seemingly Ireland with the Atlantic Ocean glistening beyond the Western Isle, boundering the distant horizon and the more rich and cultivated scenery of the east and south, form one of the most grand and exhilarating prospects imaginable, and fully repays the fatigue in scrambling up the majestic mountain. Unwilling to leave the enchanting scene but as I had yet a long distance to trudge e'er I accomplished the plan of the day's march, and as the Sun was receding from that part of our whirling Orb, with reluctance I began to descend and on passing Bens crystal fountain soaked my remaining biscuit, and at six o'clock reached the bottom of the venerable height. On which I will never regret these four hours of my existence. Two hours I took to ascend, half an hour remained on the top, and one and a quarter to descend. When I reached the bottom by a path a little distant from the Inn, sat down for a few moments ere I pursued my course and contemplated the hazard of such a solitary undertaking which I would not advise any person to attempt for many casualties may happen which only company or an experienced guide can extricate you from, and these casualties such as fogs, sickness etc. etc. should they over come a solitary mortal, the consequences may be fatal. Thankful I had regained the bottom in safety, pursued my wandering steps alongst the shaded banks of the Loch. The evening was serene and calm, not a hush disturbed the solemn stillness, save at times the bellowing and bleating flocks as they homewards strayed, and e'er I reached the southern verge of the dark and sheltered wood of Salashi, the dusky shades of twilight had given way to the cheering influence of the rising moon. With delightful astonishment at the grandeur of the romantic scene kept passing onwards without dread or fear, and when at Drymen, left the highway and wandering about three miles alongst a solitary rugged road, lost in silent mediation, till the gladdening murmur of the Pot of Gartness roused me from my reverie and seating myself near the pellucid waterfall contemplated for some time with delightful sensations the grandeur of the evening scene. The moon with unclouded brightness darting her silvery rays on the foaming pot, through which the waulk mill echoing her industrious pound, with the Dyers cloth streaming from the surrounding trees made Romvoy appear as the den of enchantment. The twinkling lights from the Litsters cottage shewed that her social hearth yet teamed with animation, to reach which with difficulty crossed the roaring pot and met with a kind and warm reception from my worthy friend. Being worn out with my fatiguing walk after a little refreshment retired to bed.

20th It was late in the morning (9 o'clock) e'er I left my drowsy pillow. After breakfast I traversed the delightful banks of Endrick in fishing and returned by Two o'clock to dinner. At this part of the water they have a very simple and murderous method of catching salmon. Under the Fall or pot of Gartness they attach a large basket with ropes, the fish attempting to get up the fall, are at times driven by the force of the stream into the basket, and are there kept from rising by the great body of water tumbling upon them. By this method they catch at times a great many. I was witness this day of eleven being brought up at one haul. When the charming influence of bright Phoebus had receded from this delightful spot, putting a stop to the amusements of the field and river, adjourned in the evening to the blazing ingle and was entertained with songs of humour and amazing stories, sung and being told by a rival throng of lads and lasses, assembled as is customary in the evenings, at the end of their day's labour, to join in innocent diversion. Sleep the refresher of the human frame and restorer of exhausted strength stealing on the eyelids of the most heavy-headed of the meeting, denoted that it was time to bring forward the stimulant service of the evening. Large Cogs [wooden tubs] of potatoes and milk were instantly placed before us, which soon drove the sleeping tendency from the drowsy part of the gathering, and what they wanted of cheerfulness and activity before, did not now fail to shew their inclination for and abilities in the gormandising system, but the tendency for this pleasure was likewise soon satiated, and all now being seized with the nodding mania, retired to respective places of abode.

21st Arose next morning at nine, breakfasted at ten at twelve accompanied Mr Jamieson to Balfron, where he was going to a roup. After attending said roup for two hours, adjourned to a friend of Jamiesons where we dined, after which called on the buxome widow Strachan, and drinking tea with her, repaired after leaving her to the Inn and primed ourselves for our return to Gartness. Soon after leaving Balfron it came on a most dreadful storm of wind and rain, and having nothing to secure from the blast but an Umbrella rendered it owing to the violence of the gust but of little service. We left the high road and wading through miry and clayey fields almost to the knees, rendered the unaccustomed situation to be very disagreeable but Jamieson was not much better for the plaid he had round him was soon soaked through and through. At nine o'clock reached Gartness in a truly pitiful plight, wet to the skin, and bespattered over with clay from head to foot. On my arrival I waded with my Cloaths on into the river, and washing the clay off, retired to the house where getting shifted and supper retired to bed.

At eight next morning accompanied Mr Jamieson to Dalnar to breakfast. Returned to Gartness by Twelve. Left at two on my way homewards, where I arrived at eight o'clock after an agreeable walk. Thus ended a pleasant and most romantic excursion of eleven days.

## TRIP TO THE SEA COAST, FROM 12 - 22 JULY 1794 (GOUROCK, ROTHESAY, CAMPBELTOWN ETC.)

July 12th On Saturday July 12th left the Broomielaw at half past eleven am, in one of the fly boats, and after a pleasant sail, arriv'd in Greenock at five pm meeting my acquaintance Mr John Sanderson with whom I din'd after perambulated the town with him until Six, then drinking tea bent my course for Gourock where arriving at eight pass'd an agreeable evening with some of my friends.

13th At six next morning walk'd alongst the shore and bath'd returned at ten to breakfast. The forenoon being very wet [I] was confin'd for the most part of it to the house - clearing up in the afternoon, went to Greenock with my acquaintances Stewart & Craig, and on the way thither were overtaken by a severe squall of wind and rain arriving in Greenock retired to Steven's Inn, and washed down the drench'd effects of the blast with cann of Grog - after which call'd on Sanderson and drinking tea with him return'd to Gourock at eight o'clock.

14th Salli'd forth at seven o'clock morning and bath'd - breakfasted at ten - at eleven parted to the Ship Union, lying in Gourock bay bound for Grenada, a neat well built vessel - returned on shore at twelve - where falling in with six young men acquaintance of mine, scrambled with them and two young ladies to the top of the rising ground above the Village, taking a fiddler with us, danced and caper'd in a joyful manner for about an hour on top of the hill, when returning at three, din'd with my brother in law Mr Craig after which adjourn'd to Lyters tavern and pass'd till nine in a most agreeable manner, having the fiddler with playing some of enlivening tunes, at the sound of which the Ladies gather'd from all quarters of the Village and in a short time our music room was crowded with the sprightly youngsters of both sexes, but the fair ones were the most numinous of the jocund throng. All now seemingly wore out with dancing, another entertainment unexpectedly cast up. A boy passing the door with a basket of Pyes, was brought into our still panting throng, each of us male or female taking a Pye in our hands, and for want of forks thrust our fingers into the Stove to pluck out the substantials, while others taking a bite of the still smoking encrustations afforded a good deal of merriment at the comical gestures occasion'd by the scalding effects of the welcome yet burning morsel. Mr Hart an old superannuated fool making love to all the fair ones around and seemingly smote with the bewitching passion so as to be insensible to any thing but an endeavour to please the dear ladies in obeying their thoughtless requests, such as standing in the middle of the floor to shew (as they said) his handsome form, dancing and telling of foolish stories, which buffoonery was followed with similar stories and songs by others of our party, but by 12 o'clock queen Mab seem'd to have gain'd possession of our senses and by blinking and nodding evinced it was time to retire to our respective places of abode, then by shaking of hands and other usual tokens of regard the ball room was soon clear'd of the merry sojourners.

15th Had a bath at seven in the morning, and breakfast at ten - My Acquaintance Mr Lister and I agreed to make a short tour in the highlands, after breakfast we went to Greenock to arrange some little matters before setting out, on our arrival fell in there with a Mr Johnston of Glasgow; our mutual acquaintance who had engag'd a boat for Rothesay with Messrs Betch and Waddle of Govan, and prevail'd on us to accompany them. Glad of the opportunity, I hasten'd back with Lister to Gourock to see our friends and clear our way before our departure and where our Rothesay adventurers promised to call on us with their boat en passant. About an hour after our arrival in Gourock the Wherry appeared with our friends, but owing to a strong head wind agreed to postpone our voyage to next morning. At three o'clock had a feast of gooseberries in Darroch's garden. At six Tea and from eight to ten held a tavern Club, with a few jolly mortals and at eleven retired to bed.

16th Lister and I were rous'd from our slumbers at One o'clock in the morning by one of the boatmen tapping at our window as the Wherry was about setting off, we huddled on our cloaths the best way we could and embarking in our boat, set sail about two o'clock but having little or no wind our progress was not great, and the Oars yielded but little assistance in propelling our clumsy Wherry which render'd our situation during the chilly cold of the morning very unpleasant, for the den or cabin the front of the boat sent forth such a disgusting effluvia as to prevent our taking shelter in it, and laid ourselves contentedly in the bottom of the wherry like so many convicts till bright Phoebus gilding the Eastern horizon with his radiant beams soon rous'd us from our waking holes, and cheerfully enjoy'd the beauties of the rosy morn. About six o'clock a moderate breeze sprung up which wafted us by nine o'clock to the harbour of Rothesay, and breakfasted in the head Inn kept by a Mr Muir at ten pence a head. After breakfast I accompanied Lister and a Mr Neil Douglas of Glasgow (who came in the boat with us) to take a bath alongst the shore, after which fell in with a Mr Orr who took us through a Cotton Mill in the neighbourhood which was highly gratifying. Return'd to the Inn where meeting the rest of our fellow travellers drank a farewell glass with Johnston and Douglas who were going no further. Belch with a Mr Scot baker from Glasgow whom we fell in with at Rothesay agreeing with our boatmen for a passage to Campbeltown, whilst I, with Lister and Waddle wishing to see more of the interior of the highlands set off on foot with the promise and expectation of meeting Belch at Campbeltown. Bidding our aquatic friends adieu, directed our pedestrian course across the Island of Bute towards the ferry of Kilmichel [Kilmichael] (about ten miles from Rothesay). After walking about two miles we found to our disappointment when calling at a house to enquire our road, that we were on the wrong path, putting therefore about and regaining the proper course travers'd about eight miles of a pleasant tract and reach'd Kilmichel about five o'clock pm where we expected to meet the boat with Belch and Scot to carry us across the ferry, but as there was no appearance of them, went into the ferry house to get some refreshment. On our entrance they kindl'd a fire on the middle of the floor and in a few minutes had some excellent Beer scones ready for us, with which fresh butter eggs and milk we made a delicious repast, but made our stay as short as possible, for being nearly suffocated with the clouds of smoke rolling around us (for having no outlet but the door, or any crevice it found in the turf built walls) render'd our situation not altogether comfortable, paying our fare, went out to reconnoitre and observ'd the boat with our two aquatic friends about two miles from us making little way. As night was advancing and wishing to reach Tarbert (about ten miles further on) that night could not possibly wait on them. Therefore we crossed on the ferry about seven o'clock pm, and in a quarter of an hour reached the opposite side, when we began to ascend a pretty high mountain, and when on the summit a most captivating view burst on our sight, the sea underneath smooth as a mirror, the heath cover'd mountains surrounding us on every hand. When we had rested ourselves enjoying the sublimity of this landscape as long as our time would permit, were rather dishearten'd when looking forward to observe no path or object to guide us to our destin'd haven, but determined to proceed straight forward, we proceeded hastily onwards for more than a mile but still no appearance of the habitation of human beings depress'd our spirits a good deal. As there was no alternative but to advance, kept wandering on, and at last to our inexpressible joy a beautiful valley appear'd in view with a number of Huts scatter'd here and there, and a serene Sheet of water or small loch, with an old Castle gracing its banks. This unexpected sight rais'd our sullen reverie to frantic joy, as to make us wish to be one of the peaceful inhabitants of this sequestered spot, through which not a hush was heard, save some trickling rill, or shepherd's dog guarding the silent vale, and warning the rustic mountaineers of the approach of our intruding steps. Seating ourselves down on the declivity of the heights surrounding this picturesque hamlet, enjoy'd with estatic delight the suns departing rays glancing through an opening of the western barrier of the silent vales and gilding its heath cover'd hovels with its refulgent beams. After gazing for some time with enthusiastic delight at this sequestered spot we ventured amongst the scatter'd huts, and soon found "that it's no a gowd that glisters" and that the further off we viewed this seeming earthly paradise the more inward satisfaction we had, for on entering some of the crazy hovels, composed of clay and small stones huddled together found the rustic inmates living seemingly contented in the midst of filth and nastiness. Obtaining information which way to proceed, renew'd our perambulations over a barren waste for about two miles and to our joyful surprise observ'd at a little distance a respectable looking mansion to which we bent our course, and found it to be the residence of the Laird of Lamont. Enquiring how far from the ferry of Portcorqhy [sic, Portavadie perhaps?] were politely told by a servant maid, but at the same time express'd her fears of our not being able to get across that night owing to the state of the tide, and if we found as she stated, to return again and she would procure beds for us, and by that time her master who was at a neighbour lairds would be at home an give us a hearty welcome. Returning our sincere acknowledgments, for the kind invitation of the frank and buxome wench, wander'd towards the ferry, and found her apprehension was too well founded for the boat was far on shore and would not be launch'd till the return of tide, and to return to the hospitable mansion of Lamont was out of the question, for we were but noviciates to the enjoyment of true highland hospitality - therefore could not permit of intruding (as we thought) on the generous and general conduct (as we were told) of the much respected and ancient family. We therefore had to content ourselves with the accommodation of a wretched hovel of a ferry house, and on examining the beds which they had to give us, were rather shock'd at the their appearance for in a crazy apartment were two holes call'd beds but more like hog stys than anything else at the back of which a clay partition in such a ruinous state that as would have allowed a pretty large mastiff to have pass'd through several parts of it. The bed consisted of a little dirty straw, with a very coarse sheet, and an old brown woollen cloth for a blanket. At the sight of such miserable berths drove almost sleep from our drowsy eyelids, but having got no rest the preceding night, and altho' tremblingly afraid of catching the Scotch fiddle [sic] we nevertheless, but not without taking the precautionary step of stripping ourselves to the skin, laid ourselves down for repose, and in a short time fell fast asleep.

17th At six o'clock in the morning raising my blinking peepers, spy'd through one of the large holes in the back of my bed, our fellow traveller Waddle lying on the kitchen floor on a little straw, imagining something wrong had driven him from his little sty like bed, I raised myself on my elbow and to my inexpressible horror the sheet or rather sack underneath was covered with myriads of fleas, but fortunately had not touched my skin; yet had plagued considerably my fellow Lister, but not to such a degree as they done Waddle who appeared from head to foot as if he had been cover'd with measles, and which was the cause of him leaving his bed, and taking up his berth as mentioned from which he rose at 7 o'clock more fatigued than when he laid down. At half past seven we left this miserable hovel of Portflea (as we called it) ferry house, and had a pleasant sail to east Tarbert which we reach'd about nine. This is rather an irregular mean looking village, situate at the head of a small bay call'd Loch Tarbert. There is a small neat looking church, situate upon a rising piece of ground, which sets off to advantage the appearance of the place. This village is a great thoroughfare for passengers & cattle from the Island of Islay to the low country, saving the dangerous and tedious navigation round the Mull of Cantyre. For the accommodation of passengers, Shawfield the laird of Islay has establish'd neat packets which sail regularly once a week with the Mail etc from Islay to the head of West Loch Tarbet, which is only about a mile from East Tarbet where there is another vessel that sails for Greenock soon as the Islay one arrives. At ten we left this village and had an agreeable walk for two or three miles through a fine natural wood. At twelve reached an inn, a small thatched house in the parish of Kilcalmonell, where we had a lunch of Bread milk and whisky, all the house would afford, almost every house you meet with in this district sells a gill and is call'd an Inn. Pursuing our rout[e] arriv'd about five o'clock in the parish of Killin [Killean] where by the sea shore stretches a fruitful level tract of land where appear'd excellent crops. In passing a farm house were astonished by the appearance of a number of stout bouncing wenches, to know the cause of such an assemblage of females, went close to the house, and at the door met the landlord who informed us that it is the custom in that part of the country for a female out of every house to assist on certain days their neighbours in spinning and to crown the evening with a dance to which in the gloaming the rustic servants scamper with joyful hearts from the surrounding farms. We went to the barn to see this curious spinning servants factory, and to our great delight, witness'd twelve rosy smiling dames nimbly spinning and joining the chorus of an highland song sung by one of their number. Being much entertained for about a quarter of an hour with this industrious and contented meeting, inviting us to stay until eight o'clock and join them in the merry dance, when many more were expected. Being afraid of creating Jealousy amongst their favourite swains and anxious to get on our way, we thought it best to proceed on our journey, then bade them adieu after thanking them for their kind invitation, and had an agreeable walk for about six miles further to a small pleasant looking village called Barr [Glenbarr], where we stayed the night.

18th After a comfortable sleep of nine hours, we got up to renew our journey, and paying our moderately charged bill, set out at seven o'clock morning and after a pleasant walk to the village of Ballachandee [Beallochantuy] we took a bath amidst the foaming billows of the Western ocean, which rolls in here with amazing fury having to stop its course from America to the west of Cantyre and in the time of a storm from the north west driven in upon the Coast with such a prodigious noise that two persons walking on the beach cannot hear as we were told one another speaking. Altho it was nicely calm when we past still a great surge was breaking on the shore. Seeing no appearance of an Inn or bathing place at above village according as we were told, we wander'd on in search of it, with keen appetite for breakfast and sharpened the further we advanced. Going to a farm house to enquire for the Inn, were rather disappointed when told we had past it in Ballachandee and there was now none until we reached Campbeltown, but that if we would stop, we would be hastily welcome to their humble cheer. We at once accepted of their kind invitation and instantly was placed before us an abundance of Milk, Cheese, bread and butter with which without ceremony we made a hearty breakfast, and were rather surprised and not a little abashed when there was nothing to pay which this hospitable family resisted in spite of our efforts to rewards them for their kindness. Bidding them adieu with heartfelt sentiments of gratitude for their unsolicited hospitality, renewed our pedestrianism, and arrived at Campbeltown at One o'clock pm, and at our entrance fell in with Belch and Scot our two aquatic travellers and accompanied them to the head Inn and taking a lunch saunter'd with them through the town, but observed nothing worthy of notice except its safe and commodious harbour sheltered from the easterly winds by a small island at the mouth of the bay. There is a bar of sand runs from this protecting island to the mainland which is dry at low water and proven dangerous to a vessel unacquainted with the circumstance for at high tide there is not above two feet water on it. The town itself is a small dirty looking place. There is one established Church and a dissenting meeting house, with other two Churches in ruins. From the parish one runs the principal street, which is pretty broad and regular, in the middle of it stands a curious carv'd stone cross and in the centre of North end of said street, a neat looking gaol. On the quays there were a great stir, and in the harbour a good many vessels fitting out for the herring fishery which is the principal support of this place. At four returned to dinner and had a tolerable good one at ninepence a head. — Saunter'd out at five, and returned to supper at nine, when pass'd till eleven in social hilarity and retired to our respective places of repose.

19th We left Campbeltown at eleven o'clock forenoon in a small half decked boat which we freighted to carry us to Greenock for twenty five shillings which was the price of a passage packet, five shillings a head being moderate enough considering the distance. There being little or no wind made but little way during the day and when night was approaching were anxious to get ashore at the small fishing village of Carradale to stay all night rather as cram ourselves into the dirty and confin'd hole in the front of the boat, but our boatmen prevailed on us to stay on board as in all probability a breeze might spring up in the night time, which may carry us to the end of our voyage by the time we would be rousing from our slumbers in Carradale. Seeing the propriety of their entreaty we kindled a good fire and crept all down to the uncomfortable cabin, and pass'd two or three hours in a jovial manner singing songs, telling stories, and quaffing a little whisky we providentially brought on board - but without any other kind of store as we expected to have reached our destin'd haven that night. Observing some herring stored in a corner of the den, rous'd us to a sense of hunger and made us long to partake of them but no person for some time would own these, till Scot yielding to our enquiries at last said they were as a greeting piece to his wife at Rothesay and was sorry he could not possibly gratify our watering mouths. We told him that as charity begins at home and necessity knows no law, we meant to save the dreadful fate of casting lots who was to be sacrificed to appease our increasing hunger, seize upon his fish to prevent the direful consequences, which he still refused to give us. Being now well acquainted with his weak side, and all bent on fun, we began to write out the seeming too serious and dreadful tickets of Cannibalism, preparing as he was the fattest subject that in all probability the lot might fall on him. Seeing us such a determined set of fellows he crestfallen and with faltering voice bade us take what we liked of them. Getting a pan with some salt water, soon cook'd on our little fire a very savoury supper of herrings with a part of a loaf which the trembling Scot was also carrying to his dear rib as a sample of Campbeltown bread. Leaving as much of the herrings as would do for his greeting present to his wife, we after a good deal of laughter at this whimsical scene, stretched ourselves for sleep in the best manner this black hole could afford.

20th Next morning about One o'clock we began to rake our still drowsy eyelids, and popping our head out of our picnicking stew, the horrors of which we had forgotten during a two hours nap on a piece of old sail, found we had made a few miles in our slumber by a gentle breeze but no sooner had we awoke than it subsided again into a calm, and allowed us to indulge ourselves in contemplating on the rugged and romantic scenery of Arran. Rowing alongst its gloomy shore and whilst thus loitering on the peaceful Ocean, the hardy islanders had not yet risen from their slumbers, all was silent not a hush was heard save the dipping of our oars and bright Chanticleer [cockerel] more, welcoming from the mountain tops the solemn Sabbath and rejoicing at the rising sun, peering with a watery appearance from behind the Kerry [sic] mountains. The sublimity of the surrounding landscape amused us till about six o'clock when a moderate breeze sprung up, but right ahead, kept beating about two or three hours when again left us, but at two O'clock pm a favourable wind arose which carried us with some speed through the narrow channel of the Kyles of Bute and at Six o'clock landed Lister and Scot about a mile from Rothesay, being heartily sick of the voyage. Beach, Belch and I remained in the wherry and with a fine breeze made the Cloch ferry when again the wind failed us. Plying all hands to the lazy oars, reach'd Gourock about 1 o'clock in the morning where not a soul was stirring, and the Inns or lodging houses either through stubbornness or dread of strangers at that solemn hour of the morning refused us admittance by saying through the door they were all full, and could not admit us. We therefore had to trudge onwards to Greenock where we met with more consideration than from the Gourockers, by a welcome reception at Stevens Anchor Inn, and all three bundled into one bed.

21st At ten o'clock am we arose and after breakfast walk'd down to Gourock to bid farewell to some of my friends as I intended going that day to Glasgow - However on my reaching Gourock it came on very wet and was easily prevailed up to stay till next day. The evening was pass'd in a most innocent convivial and joyous manner in the society of a number of young ladies.

22nd And at One o'clock next forenoon left Gourock on my return homewards. Arriving in Greenock din'd in the Anchor Inn and at three set sail in the fly boat with a favourable breeze to Renfrew when it calm'd. Coming out I walked to Govan and gave a call en passant to Belch and Waddle who had come up the preceding day. Left them at nine and reach'd Glasgow at ten where I pass'd an agreeable two hours with the Harmonic Society and reach'd home about twelve after a most delightful romantic and variegated excursion.[14]

## RAMBLE AMONGST THE MOUNTAINS WITH MR DENNISTOWN, FROM 18 JULY 1795

18 On Saturday July 18th 1795 left Glasgow with Dennistown a light hearted mortal on a perambulation to the Western coast, arriving in Greenock took up our quarters in an Inn.

19 Early next morning we saunter'd in and about this petite seaport and breakfasted at ten. Paying our bill which was moderately charged, sauntered towards Gourock which we reached about twelve. Dined with our mutual acquaintance Mr Craig - after which perambulated the shore, and returned to Mr

14  Bald itemises (12 July) amongst the expenses of his excursion: 12 July pen knife £0 0s 6d and stick £0 0s 6d.

Craig's again to tea - walked till nine, returned and supped also with our friends. At 12 o' clock took a bath, and then retired to bed, where I enjoyed a comfortable sleep after the cooling dip.

20 At five morning went a fishing but catched nothing returned at ten to breakfast. At twelve sailed to Kilmun where the burying vaults of the Argyle family are situate, this is a most delightful and romantic spot at the head of the Holy Loch and entrance to the picturesque Glen Echaig. At 7pm returned to Gourock, drank tea in Mrs Adam's - sauntered about the shore until 10 - then retired to bed.

21 Dennistown and I determined on a ramble amongst the Cowal glens. Out of town Gourock escorted a part of the way by the Misses Craig Scott and handsome endearing Miss Brocky who beguiled a few miles of our journey by their bewitching presence, and visited en passant the ruins of Laven Castle [Levan], situated on a rising ground commanding a view of the firth and opposite romantic village of Dunoon and surrounding mountains. After resting for a short time under the mouldering walls of the petit castle, adjourned with the endearing fair ones to the Cloch ferry house and regaled them with bread and milk the best the house could afford. With sobbing hearts we bade the dear angels adieu and in passing the ferry cast still a lingering look on the fair ones as they distanced from our view, seeing them at times peeping across the glistening firth at the lessening back of their two wandering swains. Now vanishing from our gazing eyes as we neared the Cowal shore we landed at Dunoon and without stopping continued our romantic ramble alongst the pictured banks of the Holy Loch towards the entrance to Glen Lean when before us lay the wandering path at foot of the towering Cliffs and beheld the sylvan Strath Echaig with its sportive rills meandering through its bieldy [sheltered] dells giving beauty to the landscape and refreshing the gazing traveller e'er he dives amidst the solitude of the Highland glen. Turning our backs for a time on the cheering scenery of Glen Echaig, entered the peaceful Glen, where nothing appeared to delight the eye but towering mountains whose summits were hid amongst dense clouds rolling across the rugged dells and the solemn stillness at times broke by the bleating of the fleecy tribe, bewailing as it were the doleful like appearance of the wandering traveller who when hunger perishes casts a joyful look on the smoke rising from a solitary cot or two at the bottom of the hills, where thither we deviated our steps and were refreshed by the homely offerings of the hospitable mountaineers - making up for the paucity of Inns in this district. Nothing in appearance of a house of entertainment either for Man or beast appeared from Dunoon to Loch Strivenshead, where there was a miserable hovel with nothing but whisky and a small piece of badly baked oaten bread. At 5 pm we passed the head of Loch

Striven a beautiful saltwater inlet, where the scene changed from mountainic barrenness to a delightful valley interspersed with gentlemen's seats, meandering streams and bieldy hills. On leaving Loch Striven-head, the road takes a diversion over a rising ground which gives the traveller a fine view of the opposite side of the loch, and the Strath which he had just before passed, making indeed a very fine picture. About half past Six pm reached the head of Loch Reduin [Riddon], the pleasant Glendaruel - driving from our recollection the gloom of the dreary Glen Lean. Nothing can surpass the beauties of this cheering spot. A broad strath of two miles in length, a neat Church manse and Inn, with Campbell of Ormidale's mansion and pleasure ground, watered by a beautiful spouting stream meandering amongst the wooded hills yielding to the gazing traveller when he sits down on the summit of the Alpine road much joy and delight when he casts from his towering seat a longing look across this pictured dell. Being highly pleased with the scenic grandeur of Glendaruel we renewed our wandering steps and after traversing a barren heath of about three miles reached the ferry of Otter on Loch fine about nine o'clock pm where we took up our lodgings for the night.

22 About Six in the morning sallied forth with only my shirt on, and bathed in Loch Fine, a precaution which strangers ought to adopt in the highlands as a preventative for the itch, a disease very prevalent amongst the lower class and consequently in ferry houses where they are usually passing, one is apt without the caution of getting clean bed cloths, lying naked, and bathing in the morning to catch this loathsome disease. After bathing it rained hard till nine when clearing up crossed the Loch at 3d each and reached the opposite side in about half an hour, the distance nearly three miles. Walked about four miles to Lochgilphead, a neat looking village at the southern extremity of the Crinan Canal, inhabited mostly by shopkeepers and tradesmen of different crafts, and promises at some future period to be a flourishing place by the intercourse with the lowlands and western Isles saving the tedious and dangerous navigation round the Mull of Cantyre. After breakfast strolled for about two miles along the canal a stupendous work of about 12 to 14 feet deep cut mostly through the solid rock - and promises to be of great advantage to the Western highlands and firth of Clyde. Being satisfied with our morning perambulation, had a most romantic and delightful walk for about fifteen miles to the village of Tarbert down the banks of Loch fine which we reached about 7 o'clock pm. This road is romantic to the highest degree, lofty mountains towering over you whose sides are covered with refreshing shrubbery, sending forth a fragrant smell of honey suckle and other wild flowers which the bieldy road abounds with. The many Vessels passing to and fro, huge rocks blown asunder to admit of a passage for

the road - Gentlemen's seats here and there interspersed, render the journey from Lochgilphead to Tarbert delightfully grand. Supping on tea with some excellent Caller Herrings went to bed at nine being a little fatigued after our day's walk.

23 Sprung from my bed at six of the morning to pursue our homeward bound journey, but was prevented by the violence of the storm and rain as no boat could be large enough to carry us across the Loch. Crept into bed again until the storm would subside and snor'd away until nine am. When sallied out and bathed the weather having now cleared up a little, but the wind too strong for the small craft at this side of the Loch to venture out. Luckily the ferry boat from opposite side hove in sight, but owing to a strong head wind could not make Tarbert by two miles. At ten we breakfasted, then walked down to the boat, and after a remarkably quiet though rough passage of seven miles which we ran in twenty five minutes landed in safety on the opposite side. Drinking a little whisky in the miserable hovel mentioned [. . .] in one of my former perambulations to these parts, continued our route to the Kerry Ferry[15] at which we were to appearance likely to be detained. The ferryman being confined to bed by sickness, there was none but a boy to manage the boat which being a rowing one, and still a considerable sea, saw no possibility of getting over till an old man who happened at the time to be passing was prevailed upon by the aid of two gills of whisky to assist at the Oar, which he handled by the aid of the potent beverage with animated skill and landed us safe on Bute but not without our receiving a wet jacket by the splashing of the still agitated water. Paying 2d each for our passage, wandered on for about ten miles to Rothesay which we reached about seven o'clock. Being one of their periodical fair days, a sight of bustling confusion not altogether agreeable to an uninterested stranger who sets out on his peregrination in search of the calm solitude of mountain scenery and with a determination of shunning the haunts of dissipation and vice, such being our humour, we went to the quay to enquire for a conveyance to Greenock in order to get rid of the motley and dangerous attendants of a fair, but as there was no vessel to part until the next day, had to content ourselves with the accommodation the place would allow, which was not altogether to our wish. The horrid and confused mode of dancing, bawling, singing and other miscellaneous accompaniments of a highland fair kept us awake for the greatest part of the night.

24 The morning being very wet did not stir out of doors till eleven, but indeed from the fatigue of the preceding evening there was none stirring in the house till this late hour, when we got breakfast then sallied forth and perambulated the Country till One pm when we left Rothesay in one of the

---

15 Kerry is the most southerly division of the parish of Kilfinan, from which a ferry ran across to Bute.

packets for Greenock, a quiet sailing wherry, in which small boat there were about sixty passengers stowed, and these mostly the common attendants on a fair, fiddlers, Ravy [loud-talking] showmen, swindlers, etc. etc. who disgusted us with their low slang and dissolute manners, that we embraced the opportunity of the nearest landing place on the opposite side of the firth to escape from the infernal gang. Landing at Cloch ferry walked onwards to Gourock where we remained all night.

July 25 At six of the morning walked to Greenock to transmit some business, after which returned to Gourock and breakfasted in Main's public house for eight pence - sauntered about till two when dined in Mr Craig's - sallied forth again and seemed to be so far contaminated with the example that our messmates set before us in our preceding day's cruise as to pass an hour or two in playing at <u>pitch</u> and <u>toast,</u> [*sic*] but which had no further impression on us than a sacrifice of that portion of our time taken up with the gambling pastime, which in all probability might have passed in dissipation at the board of Bacchus or some other as unprofitable pursuit. At six we drank tea in Miss Scots and sauntered with the fair ones until ten - when supped in Mrs Craig's Inn - and thus closed another day of our perambulating excursion which if unprofitably spent was so far harmless as to avoid giving offence to others.

26 But this day we cannot be so far excusable for our conduct for being that portion of the week (Sunday) devoted to sacred and religious purposes, was passed as is usual at the Sea coast in idly sauntering alongst the pebbled shore or climbing amongst the heatherie heights but ceremonial no further we hope than probably differing a little from the views of Sectarians how this sacred day should be kept, for in our saunter amongst the sweets of nature our minds were occupied in meditations on the sublimity of the surrounding scenery the commanding effects of which is sufficient to divert the mind from an idle vicious propensity, and lulls it into pleasant contemplation of the grand and awful ways of Creation and Providence, a state of mind as much adapted for entering on the devotional exercises of Religion as many who sit on Church more Ceremonial than devout intention. Having thus calmly sauntered in and about the Village till ten at night, retired to bed.

27 Anxious now to see how our native city was jogging on we set sail from Greenock at four o'clock morning with the wind right a head. After beating about for nearly four hours in a crowded opon boat found we had only made Port Glasgow which we had attributed to the boisterous and profane conduct of a drunken sailor one of our passengers - whilst others thought that our adverse fate was owing to the presence of a black coat which another of our shipmates wore under the sanctified garb of a Clerical Presbyterian, minister of a Cowal

parish, which the superstitions of the country generally bestows on them when at sea the displeasure of Iolus [?Æolus[16]] and which renders them rather unwelcome guests on board a Vessel. However whatever was the cause of our tawdry progress all of us were anxious to get on shore, and landed at the Port, as much fatigued as on the arrival of Botany Bay convicts at their destined haven. Repairing to the Inn for breakfast astonished the inmates with our voracious appetites - we kept a waiter running to and fro the bakers shop, that at last with ringing of the bell for more of everything so confounded the good hostess of the Inn, and not a little abashed ourselves, that we gave in although against our still craving stomachs, and allowed them to set down if they thought proper in their diary the miracle of a Boat's crew after almost famishing the good town of Pt Glasgow still rising from their breakfast table unsatisfied. The gale still continuing accompanied with a torrent of rain we agreed to give up the idea of embarking again on the boat, and to hire a covered waggon, but the waggoner's demand being so extravagant, we also gave up the thought of that extravagance, and resolved to encounter the blast on foot rather as venture again on water. Therefore Dennistown and I, accompanied with Mr Gown and Lumsden, two Glasgow stationers, left the rest of our gormandizing crew and with the most indefatigable perseverance sauntered on through a deluge of rain to Bishoptown from where some of us were for having a Post Chaise, but as others of our group (for saving motives) were determined still to walk and not choosing to separate we again set off in a body and deviated our steps for Paisley which we reached about 3 o'clock pm, heartily sick of walking and drenched with rain, but our ills soon vanished with a good dinner and hearty glass, but still again afraid of encountering the blast we left Paisley in a more certain conveyance than a passage boat heaved to and fro at the mercy of the incessant wind. At five o'clock step into the Stage Coach and were agreeably surpassed at meeting two of our female aquatic travellers whom we had left at Pt Glasgow and getting the opportunity of a caravan had reached Paisley in a more comfortable state than us. Our hardships were now forgot at the material joy of the meeting and jogged on in a jovial manner to Glasgow where we arrived at 6 o'clock, thus ending an agreeable and variegated ramble of ten days.

Expences of above excursion[17]

Total expence £1-15-11.

---

16  In Greek mythology, as in Homer, Aeolus or Aiolus was the 'god of the winds'.

17  Bald here inserts in three tightly packed columns, miniscule and partially indecipherable, the costs of the excursion; lodgings, passage, food and drink. The list begins with a penknife and a stick (sixpence each), continues with passage to Greenock (one shilling and sixpence) and includes breakfast at Tarbet (tenpence), whisky (one penny) and bed at Bar Inn (one shilling).

## AN EIGHT DAY RAMBLE TO INVERAIRY ETC., AUGUST 1799 WITH JOHN MURE, AND STEPHEN ROWAN.

1st day. On a most dismal afternoon with wind and rain in the month of August, Rowan, Mure and Bald, after regaling themselves with a good dinner in the Crown & Thistle Tavern (Strathearn) alongst with a few of their companions, set off in the stage Coach for Dumbarton in search of adventures amongst the heath covered mountains of Caledonia. Being suitably equipped with jacket and trousers, and a plentiful supply of tobacco and snuff, articles which at all times assures travellers of a welcome reception from the inhabitants of these sterile regions. Thus accoutered they jogged on with light hearts, determined to banish care from their minds and to laugh for a few days at the plodding beings of the world. Convinced that a too rigid ceremonious behaviour does not suit those who wish to find out the dispositions of mankind, made them not over nice in their observance of the modern rules of politeness, nor in adopting the usual tacit affectation of finding out the weak point of their fellow travellers. Being assured that the descendents of Highland chieftains are at all times certain of a warm reception from their Gaelic friends, made them adopt the deceitful experiment of changing their names for a time from Rowan to Smollet, Muir to Cameron, and Bald to Campbell, expecting by this transnomination a more friendly reception from the mountaineers than appearing amongst them in their lowland Character. In this Quixotic Like spirit they were slowly carried forward in a crowded coach, acting up to the principles they laid down to laugh and be merry made them not very particular about the subjects of conversation, but with song and story, about Church and State, married or unmarried, all mingled together with much ceremony soon set to work the risible organs of their fellow passengers, with the exception of a stiff care worn out little dame who seemed to have had her flesh consumed from her bones by weeping at the world, and her tongue by railing at it, incapable of joining the jocular propensity of her joyous travellers but sat like the monument of Despair taking her life in silent rancour at their thoughtless merriment. Another of their female travellers, (Mrs McCormick) evincing by her ongoing and polite manners to have seen more of the world than the other splenetic damsel, and wishing to obliterate the unfavourable impression which her choleric temper had made the jovial trio form of the female character, joined them in all their eccentric stories, and which made her absence much regretted, parting from them about three miles from Dumbarton. Still convinced that Momus was hovering around them, continued their merry propensity till they came to Dumbarton, the end of the first day's journey which they reached about 8 o'clock pm.

This being one of the periodical fair days of this place offered them an opportunity of acting up to the object of their excursion. After a little refreshment they sallied forth in search of adventures, paraded the streets under a torrent of rain, and passing several dancing parties, arrived near the Jail, where having a fiddle in one of the apartments, they considered it a more fit place for exerting their Quixotian spirit than any other of the light fantastic toe assemblies. Dashing without hesitation into the midst of the skipping throng, joined them in all their rude manoeuvres, and after a few reels, Smollet and Campbell left Cameron, paying his devoirs and pouring out his effusions to a fat country wench, till her admirer, a stout country clown growing jealous of the rude behaviour of Cameron, was about to revenge the daring insult, when a son of Mars, commiserating the ticklish situation of the daring Cameron, rescued him from the motley crew, and coming to the inn, where Smollet and Campbell were enjoying the pleasures of the table, appeared by his agitated frame and ghastly look to have got by his amorous intrigue a complete fright. Sympathising for the disappointed and love struck youth, and to appease his desire for another interview with the Dumbarton goddesses, the waiter introduced the Cook, Chambermaid and Bairn's woman, in order to gratify his inordinate propensity for love adventures. Still bewitched with the Prison scene, his eyes rolled around on the three menials but seemed to linger a little on the Cook, a fat clumsy wench, appearing as they imagined to his yet unsettled imagination, as a prototype of his first love in the Prison Hall. Hesitating a little by the effect of the former adventure, he gazed with an idiotical like vacancy on his greasy charmer. Instantaneously arousing from his lethargic reverie and no longer dreading the interference of Jealousy, he flew on his melting fair one and after bestowing on her buttered lips a thousand kisses allowed her without any other molestation to retire to her sooty dominions. Smollet being also seized with the temporary mania of Cameron, was smote with the Bairn woman, a handsome girl, but his bluffy physiognomy seeming not to have the same engaging influence over his charmer as the sly blinks of Cameron had over his broiled nymph for flying from his Cold embrace with a frowning and disdainful look made the features of disappointment start prominent on his blushing countenance and turned the laugh against the chopfallen Smollet, Campbell being taken up with the Chambermaid a peaceable sort of a woman whose demure countenance extinguished in the beast of the philosophical Campbell the touch of Love and was glad without any restraint to allow her to attend the summons of her master, but not without giving her orders to prepare comfortable and well aired beds for them which having accordingly done, she sent a little girl to conduct them. Being afraid to trust herself with so amorous a group. Cameron having they supposed made an assignation with his charmer the Cook and to conceal his design from his two dispassionate comrades, took possession of a single bedded room, whilst they were shewn to a double one. Scarcely were their heads laid on the refreshing pillow when they were disturbed by a strange noise occasioned they understood by Cameron, having been discovered by the waiter whilst endeavoring to find out the apartment of his greasy charmer which made him quickly retreat to his bedroom, afraid of an immediate attack by the jealous waiter, and the noise made by his barricading his door with tables, chairs etc, disturbed the slumbers of his two contented companions, but who did not enjoy much rest, till Cameron was worn out, and disgusted with his many disappointments, at last embraced his cold pillow instead of his broiling Charmer, and allowed all to retire into the refreshing arms of sleep.

2nd Day. Next morning about 8 o'clock, Smollet and Campbell forced open the door of the disappointed Amoroso, and found him still tossing and trembling with fear, dreading a challenge no doubt from his charming foe the waiter. Assisting him in raising his agitated frame from its Couch, and washing themselves with Whisky which the affrighted waiter brought instead of water, so much had the adventure of Cameron confused him that he seemed unconscious what he was about. All things being amicably adjusted, and after a hearty breakfast, pursued their excursion about the banks of the Leven, where Industry seems to have fixed its chief abode, for every turn of the river presents to the astonished and delighted traveller such stupendous works where the Calico Printing and Bleaching trades are carried on to the highest perfection, as to fill the mind with astonishment at the enterprising spirit of the Sons of Caledonia. Having reached the banks of Loch Lomond about mid day, they called for a refreshment at a small Alehouse, where meeting with a descendant of the Camerons, a hoary headed Carl, made the glass go quickly round, which soon roused the native fire of their aged landlord and seeing the bent of their youthful march as to assure them that if the mountain goddesses would condescend to an interview with Lowland strangers he would do the utmost in his power to introduce them to his youthful friends. With the full precaution that our intentions were entirely Platonic he sallied forth to perform the object of his promise and soon returned leading in one of the mountain sylphs in form of a buxom country wench, which instantly aroused again the passion of Cameron, imagining her to be his pervious tormentor still hovering around his progressive steps. Flying to her with amorous joy, endangered the fair one falling a prey to his romantic passions had it not been for our aged Sire. Perceiving in her a strong resemblance to the features of his amorous Spark, made him relinquish his Quixotic madness afraid of her being a descendent of the family and him falling prey to the resentment of the Caledonian Clan.

Leaving the astonished rustics to their own conjectures, proceeded in search of fresh adventures, and arriving at Luss, reduced the fare of a rascally boatman one half. Embarked in his boat for the Rowardennan at the foot of Ben Lomond which they reached in safety without any other injury than a well-soaked jacket by a torrent of rain which accompanied them during the voyage. Rowdenan is a romantic spot on the banks of this Loch and at the foot of a towering Ben, the seat often in summer of bustle, confusion and disappointment from the crowds of visitors from different parts of the world of different ranks and degrees huddled together in a small and but indifferent plenished inn. Here Cameron expected again to meet with his favourite Dulcinea and was supported in his expectations by the appearance of a number of carriages surrounding the door of the Inn, which promised a source of rare adventures. Dashing sans ceremony into the kitchen amidst Coachmen, Carriers, etc. passed the glass briskly amongst them in order to gain friends for Cameron's intended attempt to regain his bewitching nymph which he soon recognised in the form of a flaxen haired woman, possessing all the meekness of the veiled sisterhood, and so gentle as did not require the assistance of the motley crew, to recover his lost prize as she promised to become his queen, provided they put up with the Hayloft for their night's lodging as the house was overcrowded. Smollet and Campbell seeing the credulous simplicity of the love smote Cameron, and afraid if his romantic passion was carried further of their falling a prey to the resentment of the Coaches and Carriers who would have been huddled together in the same loft with them, did not chose to accept of the Goddess' offer - which refusal was the harbinger of more joyful tidings - Observing three beautiful young ladies coming in from their journey to the top of Ben, drenched to the skin with rain, made them form the bold attempt of introducing themselves to the engaging damsels but was prevented from this scheme by a Spark from another company, informing them of the testy temper of an old fellow their Guardian, and letting them a little into the knowledge of the Group. They were, it seems, from Cornwall and apparently of a genteel cast and had posted without almost noticing the beauties of England in order to enjoy the sublime scenery of Scotland and such was the reception they met with from the dripping climate that whilst the fair ones with their tutor was nearly lost on the misty mountains, their aged Sire was distractedly roaming about the House and roads lamenting the absence of his dear children afraid of their being drowned in the deluge and bewildered among the mountain wilds. But his sorrows were soon forgot by exhibiting a capering joy at the sight of his drookit bairns. However the mirth making trio did not think proper to approach the Cornwall sufferers but allowed them to enjoy themselves and their gentility as they thought proper, and accepted of the kind invitation of the other spark to join his party. On entering the room where they were waiting for their dinner, the trio were agreeably surprised at the appearance of a number of beautiful damsels more bewitching than the three drookit Ben Lomond sylphs. After being regaled with a dinner of Herrings etc Smollet in his turn became enamoured with one of them, which he gave symptoms of by the many awkward blunders he committed, such as handing to the object of his fancy an old blistering plaster which he found laying on the casement of the window, instead of a piece of tobacco to a Gentleman who had asked it from him, which foolish or love smote mistake was the cause of many others. Cameron's convulsed frame betraying a similar position to that of Smollet, but which was hitherto stifled by the many disappointments he had already met with, now began to assume a more serious aspect but prevented from breaking out into his usual Romantic jargon by Campbell moving that it was time to proceed on their journey, which was gladly seconded by the blushing Smollet, well pleased to be freed from his love roused blunders.

Parting from their Ben Lomond adventurers with the smiles and good wishes of the fair ones, embarked in their boat for the other side of the Loch, which having reached in safety renewed their wandering steps. The road taking a direction over a steep hill, fell in with a Tinker endeavouring with his horse and cart to reach the summit of it but the Cart was so heavily loaded that the poor animal could scarcely pull it, till out of commiseration not for the tinker but for his ill used horse and beautiful wife, Smollet and Cameron shoved behind the cart whilst Campbell spirited on the horse and suffering female who was carrying a child on her back, and by their exertions brought with some difficulty the poor animal with its oppressive load to the top of the hill, and as a recompense for their exertions, the wretched Tinker offered them his wife to be their companion during their Quixotian wander. Laughing with disdain at the depravity of the diabolical fellow left this gypsy family to the freedom of their own pursuits, and jogged on their way towards Arrochar, which they reached two hours, after bright Phoebus had sunk behind the tremendous mountains which hung over them. The scene however was truly sublime. The lochs placid surface reflecting the light of the moon, the towering Ben Lomond, the murmuring of waters tumbling from the inaccessible heights, with the bleating of sheep lamenting the absence of all cheering sun, threw a damp on their spirits, till arrived at the Inn where seating themselves beside a good fire, and with smiling bumpers of the mountain spirit, soon roused them to their wonted madness and stirred up in the breast of Smollet his usual penchant for love adventures, dashing into the kitchen with his Clashmaclaver [idle tales] which he at all times thought was a favour fit to ensure him a reception either above or below stairs, but here he was blushingly again disappointed forby the abrupt and jeering retribution of the old Matron of the House and her jealous husband, caused poor Smollet to return looking more foolish than the fleecy inhabitants of the surrounding wilds. It was now Cameron's turn for some of his romantic manoeuvres, and imagined a single bed room would yield him some of his much wished for sport but in this he was once more disappointed, which afforded infinite sport to Campbell who was convulsed with laughter at the awkward and sheepish countenance of the two forward and now Chop fallen youngsters who were glad without any further molestations to retire to their solitary pillows in a double bedded room.

3rd Day. By break of day, Smollet and Campbell rousing Cameron from his love racking slumbers, they left the sequestered Arrochar to renew their romantic wander, and on their progress round the head of Loch Long, were in a manner stupefied with delight, whilst casting a lingering look across to the place of their night's rest, surrounded with woods and rugged cloud capped mountains. Directing their steps through Glen Croe were struck with astonishment at the place of horrific gloom, the soaring and rugged mountains threatening destruction to the gazing traveller, the wimpling rills down the surface of the wrinkled heights forming a small rivulet which meanders through the Glen with the thinly scattered huts of the shepherds renders Glen Croe the peak of romantic splendour. Entering some of the wretched like hovels which are seldom cheered by the rays of the Sun, found their inmates more fruitful than the soil around for in each hut they entered, crowds of stout brawling brats were stowed amongst cattle and filth without distinction of Sex or age and seemingly contented with their beast like lot - arriving at <u>Rest and be Thankful</u>, a seat on the top of a rising part of the road, formed by the soldiers in the Rebellion of 1745 - seated themselves down, and with silent contemplation viewed the horrid Glen which discovered to their inexperienced eyes scenes of life which till now they did not know to exist, and exhibited striking examples that contentment is to be found in the hovels of poverty amidst filthy attire, as well as in the ermine robed pageantry of the palace, and shows the wisdom of Providence in endowing the mind of man with that accommodating propensity as to produce happiness from whatever may be his lot in the world.

Leaving the place of mountain grandeur, pursued their walk towards the banks of Loch Fine which they reached at 12 o'clock both tired and hungry, having not yet breakfasted, but were soon gratified with a good breakfast with some excellent fresh herrings for which Loch fine is celebrated for producing. After breakfast crossed the Loch in a crazy boat belonging to a Son of Vulcan commiserating their fatigued legs, supplied the place of the stubborn ferryman who lived on the opposite side of the Loch and seemed to pay no attention to the many signals made for his boat. On reaching to the other side they meandered down the banks of the Loch, Cameron much distressed by not falling in with since he left Arrochar one single nymph resembling in the smallest degree the goddess of his heart, for the few robust damsels they met with in their progress through the glen by their peat reeked aspects bore too much the resemblance of the Gypsy tribe as to banish all desire of a close union from the love sick swain, hobbling onwards in desponding reverie. Cameron to his inexpressible joy casting his eyes athwart the mountains, observed as he thought something at a considerable height on the hills resembling his favourite nymph, at the sight of this phantom, Smollet and Cameron's drooping spirits were at once reanimated and springing at one bounce over a thorny fence striving with each other for a first interview with the Dulcinea, whilst Campbell sat at the bottom of the hills convulsed with laughter at their amorous pursuit, waiting the result of the impassioned adventure, which ended rather to the disadvantage of the two Amorosos for when they were within a few paces of the deceiver she took unto herself the form of a monstrous eagle, and with a screaming voice rose with extended wings rousing the feathered tribe to revenge the intended and daring assault on the queen of the mountain. Words cannot describe the consternation of the disappointed youths who left the outraged tribe with hasty steps and joining Campbell who scarcely could rise with laughter at the Don Quixote like attack on the Eagle pursued their journey for a few miles further, when they fell in with a group of Highland shearers, eating gooseberries at a gardener's door which the affrighted imagination of Cameron by his unsuccessful attack on the mountain Spirit represented a daemon of the wild, laying in wait to punish the daring disturbers of their pinioned neighbours. Standing at some distance from the third sisterhood whilst Smollet and Campbell dashing into the midst of them, soon found them to be game in human form and were about having some fun with them when an old withered Hag, with Broom stick, and other witch like missiles dispersed the motley crew and leaving them to the guidance of their own will, the three youngsters pushed forward to Inverary which they reached about 4 o'clock and after dinner decked in their gayest apparel which was an addition to their former dress of only a little powder to their hair and a fresh scraped chin.

Sallying from the Inn in search of adventures and perambulating the town, heard a fiddle in one of the houses which offered an opportunity for gratifying their frolicsome humour. Entering the house where sat an old hero playing the fiddle by himself. On striking up some merry tunes were soon visited by a number of buxome wenches, with whom and several highland servants, who came to pay their respects to their supposed countrymen and strangers as they imagined them to be, were highly amused till near midnight. However were about being discovered to be lowland imposters by two of the damsels whilst the circling glass was passing, drinking to the healths of Rowan and Bald instead of Smollet & Campbell, this unexpected discovery by tipping them the wink was laughed over, and sending round the trusted plentiful supplies of Tobacco and Snuff with frequent bumpers of Strong Whisky Punch the trio's pretended Gaelic extraction was soon confirmed amongst the mountaineers, and every one strived who would entertain them the most with their highland flings. The whisky now beginning to operate, the rustics were rather indecent in some of their capering pranks, and not very mindful about the subject of their Songs either man or woman which disgusting the three Lowland sparks found it was now time to depart from so whimsical a party. Paying the expence of the night's entertainment, the trio were about leaving the house, with the three nymphs whom they had persuaded them to accompany them to the Inn, when a Son of Neptune with some of his accomplices snatched the girls from their arms and carried them back to the temple of Belial for this and other similar rebuffs the trio had sustained during their pilgrimage were determined to think more of themselves hereafter and endeavour to engage the affections of the nymphs by either a pretended stoical behaviour towards them or a determined spirit to reserve their airs of affectation.

Retiring to their lodgings were all three shewn shown into a double bedded room which Cameron for this night seemed satisfied with, being now nearly convinced of his inability for love adventures. Campbell seeing the coast now clear in his turn tried the experiment of finding out his Dulcinea. Traversing the long passages of the Inn with candle in hand and opening the first room he came to - lo! To his inexpressible astonishment a beautiful face peeped out from behind the curtain of a bed, and with a heavenly voice cried out who's there? Fired with the mingled sensations of Joy and fear at this unexpected sight, Campbell insensibly let fall the Candlestick which caused a reverberating noise along the passages of the house, so as to rouse Smollet who imagined some disaster had befallen his friend Campbell came running with only his shirt on to his assistance and no sooner understood the cause of the disturbance, and getting a glimpse of the trembling fair one who was almost speechless at the frightful appearance of her bold intruder, strived with Campbell for a private view of the Goddess. In the midst of this struggle the arrival of carriages at the door of the Inn reanimated the expiring spirits of the fair incognito which caused such a bustle amongst the waiters as to make the two daring Sparks retreat with trembling fear to their apartment and barricading the door crept into their beds which made Cameron now in his turn treat with derision the failure of the mad-like prank of his two companions. No sooner had they retired to bed than they were alarmed by a loud knocking at their room door occasioned by the offended damsel with some of the household searching for the daring disturbers of her repose. Smollet & Campbell now as the fit of the adventure had partly subsided resumed their wonted courage and with presence of mind, pretended ignorance of the cause of the disturbance and that it must entirely proceed from the effects of a dream on her vain conceit, which belief beginning now to operate on the minds of her attendants the two stirring youths were allowed for remainder of the night to enjoy their rest undisturbed.

4th Day. The day was pretty far advanced ere the three lowland wanderers left their bed. After breakfast they paid a visit to the Princely mansion of the Duke of Argyle where traversing the stately apartments of the Castle, mounted to the top of it, and on their way thither, met a number of beautiful and bewitching nymphs, passing from one part of the Castle to the other which again heated the romantic imagination of the three lowlanders as to perceive in these goddesses strong resemblance to their favourite girls and were about saluting them when their Guide assured them that they all belonged to the family of Argyle, and to take care in not rousing by rudeness the resentment of the Clans who were attached to adoration to their venerable Chief; a hint was all that was necessary in subduing the love smote fancy of the three Glotianas,[18] the appellation here for Smollet, Cameron & Campbell. The youths being thus satisfied left the Castle ashamed at their humour and trembling with dread for the consequences of their foolish and forward pranks, amongst the romantic and high minded highlanders.

Left Inverary with precipitation, and crossed to St Catherine's on the opposite side of the Loch under a heavy rain. Eating a hearty dinner in the ferry house, with more than a sufficient quantum of mountain dew soon made them forget the awkward effects of their former Quixotian like attacks on the Highland Queens, and thinking themselves now safe from the resentment of the Highland clans, soon resumed their former penchant for an interview with the fair ones, when to their inexpressible joy, each discovered in the beautiful countenance of the landlady an imagined likeness to their respective favourites which no doubt every young man at their time of life have, and when form and physiognomy or at all times hovering before his imagination and oft occasions to his love struck vacancy many an awkward blunder. They were about inviting the Captivating hostess to join them in their banquet when by chance observing sixty stout Highlanders descending from the mountains with large cudgels in their hands, imagined by their still heated imagination to be the Clans in search of

---

18 *Glotiana Valla* translates as 'sons of the Clyde'.

them for their late transfinick [i.e. Loch Fine] misdemeanors and remembering the old saying 'One pair of heels are worth two pairs of hands in times of trouble' made good use of the former and ran with rapidity up the heath clad mountains, where meeting two men were surprised from their perturbation by being informed that the warlike group were Volunteers assembling for Drill. Thus once more ashamed at their credulous fears, which exhibited a striking example of the means which Providence uses in discovering transgressions and altho nothing Criminal in the romantic pranks of the Glotianas, their disturbed conscience presented in every wavering bush some one laying in wait to chastise them for some of their youthful frolics. They would now with pleasure have returned to St Catherine's to make atonement for their suspicion but were persuaded to continue their route by the two rustics who promised faithfully to conduct them to Loch Goil head, the place of their destination for that night, as thither they were likewise bent. Following them therefore alongst a Sheep track over a high mountain, in frequent danger of breaking their necks in jumping over dreadful chasms, which the incessant rains of the climate had worn in the rocks, and the day being very wet, made the deep heather they were wading amongst very slippery which occasioned to the Glotianas many awkward stumbles, in one of which were near to losing poor Cameron, who in attempting to bounce over a small rivulet, which tumbled into a deep glen, missed a foot and was nigh falling into the dreadful abyss, where he might have laid to the end of time, had he not providentially caught hold of a large stone and secured his feet with no injury than a bruised haunch, which caused him however to hobble onwards till coming to a river much swollen with the heavy rain where there was no bridge across it. Following their guides through the streams up to their middle in water and with their Cloaths on, which they did not think proper to take off, being already so well soaked with rain, they all got safely through the flood, and reached Loch Goilhead Inn about 6 p.m. Sun.[19]

It bore more the resemblance of an ordinary Ale House than an Inn, but the accommodation in these sequestered parts of the highlands, are not of the most elegant appearance, nor comfortable and substantial livery. As the Glotianas were determined to find fault rather with a lack of objects for fun, than of objects for the palate, they put up for the seeming scarcity in each of these luxuries. Satisfying their faithful guides with a bumper of whisky, and drying themselves at the Kitchen fire, were conducted upstairs to a large room which a funeral party had just left, all seemingly intoxicated by making rather a free use of the gill stoup, a common custom of Highland burials. Observing the landlord a

19  This should be Saturday; perhaps a mistake in the copying out?

whimsical looking old Carl ripe for fun, the Glotianas invited him to their banquet and were soon roused by his eccentricities to their wonted animation, and gradually excited their risible organ to such a pitch that Smollet fell insensible from his chair and with difficulty was recovered by some nostrums administered by the old Chieftain, and his favourite servant maid who conducted this seeming expiring youth to her bedroom where he soon recovered from his stupefaction more it was presumed from the appearance of the damsel than from the quackery of her aged sire. His mind notwithstanding his apparent recovery, seemed still bent upon some frolic, for he came running into Cameron & Campbell's apartment with only his shirt on, and throwing himself down on their beds, swore he would not stop in the room allotted him, as it was certainly haunted by some invisible agent, which disturbed him by an uncommon noise. Calling the servant to have the matter explained, assured him it was only the scratching of a few harmless mice, which his deranged imagination had represented as hobgoblins. Not altogether satisfied and apparently abashed at his childish fears, he sprung up and snatching a large bowl of punch from the table which Cameron & Campbell were still sipping at, threw its contents on their bed cloths then hastily retreated to his haunted apartment, carrying alongst with him the servant girl, whom his heated intellect had represented as his favourite fair, but was soon brought to his sense and convinced of his mistake by the rustic nymph throwing him headlong on the floor and ran with disheveled hair to the bedroom of Cameron and Campbell, who were by this time sitting at the fireside almost naked. No sooner did she observe the nude State of the two seeming sedate Glotianas, than she retreated in confusion, oversetting everything on her way, till she was met at the door by Smollet, who carried her off again in triumph, left Cameron & Campbell to enjoy their rest undisturbed for the remainder of the night but indeed the now seeming philosophers were glad to leave them to their romantic frolic, and crept into their beds in a state of exhaustion with laughing at the whimsical scene.

5th Day. Early in the morning Cameron & Campbell were roused from a sound sleep by Smollet, capering and bawling in their rooms, seemingly displeased at some part of his last night's frolic. After breakfast went to look out for a boat to carry them to Ardentinny. Altho a calm pleasant day, yet afraid of these sudden squalls peculiar to these mountain regions, wished some ballast in the small boat they had engaged but being Sunday the boatmen would not touch a stone for the purpose wanted, without permission from the Provost. Sending for the Provost with their compliments, a hoary headed Carl with a broad blue bonnet soon was introduced resembling more the appearance of a Cowherd, than the dignified character of a magistrate. Introducing themselves to his worship and presenting him with a bumper of whisky, their request was immediately granted. Then leaving the Reverend Sage, who enquired at their departure if they knew Archy Campbell the great Charleston merchant in Glasgow answering him in the affirmative, he replied that he was uncle to that celebrated man, and that Lochgoilhead was the honoured place of his nativity. Leaving him puffed up in the affected conceit of his friend's prosperity the Glotianas had a pleasant sail down Loch Goil and part of Loch Long transported with delight at the magnificent scenery of Loch Goil surrounded by towering rugged mountains some of them being almost perpendicular above the Loch, which renders at times the navigation in small boats dangerous by the sudden squalls from these Alpine regions being fortunately a calm sunshine day the Glotianas reached Ardentinny in safety about 12 o'clock. Cameron & Campbell having got their cloaths washed the previous night the time that Smollet was taken up with his love smote gambols, made him now look rather shabby and more so as he was about appearing amongst the beaux monde in Gourock, was determined to be as spruce as his companions. Getting a basin of water scrubbed his vest in the best manner he could, as the people in the Ferry house (being Sunday) refused doing it. Having not time to dry it, being anxious to get on their way, he put his Vest over his Coat and setting sail from these regions of romantic grandeur, had a smart scud across to Gourock (the wind having sprung up) which they reached at 4 o'clock pm, and dined in a relation of Campbell's.

After tea they walked to Greenock and leaving Smollet in Faichnies' Inn Cameron & Campbell sallied forth in search of adventures, amongst the plebian race as usual, and their whims were soon amply satisfied with a hotchpotch of absurdities, for falling in with groups of Soldiers, Sailors with their doxys all jovially pacing their respective ways, and accompanying them to their haunts had an opportunity of witnessing some of the jealous and deep rooted disquietude which exists between the Sons of Neptune and Mars especially in that petite Seaport, and which at times nearly breaking out into open rupture, but was always subdued by the interference of the two Glotianas over the honest hearts of the jolly tars. This preventative service however did not seem altogether to please the keepers of this temple of discord for a fierce black looking ragamuffin making up to Campbell who had wandered to some retired corner of the House, was endeavouring to provoke him to a quarrel, which being observed by the sons of Mars who knew the character of this sink of pollution came running with Cameron to his assistance and rescued him from the snare of infamy. Rewarding the services of the Red coats, Cameron & Campbell bent their course for the Inn, and were nearly enticed again from their path of returning repentance by two amorous queens who endeavoured unsolicited to persuade them to accompany them to their lodgings but resisting with scorn their vile schemes of ensnarement, left them to their midnight pursuits and joined their friend Smollet when after gratifying with a good supper his frowning aspect at their long absence, retired to their respective pillows.

6th Day. Walked down to Gourock early in the morning and after breakfasting there, had a pleasant sail to Helensburgh, where arriving about 12 o'clock called on several female acquaintances sojourners in that marine retreat, and after a tete a tete with them the Glotianas passed up the Gairloch on a fishing excursion where they remained till the absence of bright Phoebus put an end to their aquatic amusement, pleased with their pastime and highly delighted with the surrounding scenery. Landing about two miles from Helensburgh, each carrying their string of fish approached the Village joyfully proud at their progress till coming to the house of an aunt of Cameron, where he said he intended to take up his night's lodgings, and left Smollet and Campbell to enjoy themselves as they thought proper, claiming it more for his interest to please his old aunt than his two travelling companions. Smollet & Campbell, being sensible of his selfish nature did not altogether wonder at him leaving them but wandered further through the village and coming to the abode of two female cousins of Smollet, he acted the same unfeeling part which Cameron had done and left Campbell without any seeming concern for his fate, to wander in quest of some kind mortal to give him a night's lodgings being nearly two miles from any Inn. In his saunter he observed by the seaside, of a group of females old and young, meditating on the beauties of marine scenery. Having often heard of the kind and sympathising treatment of the fair sex towards forlorn strangers, and not yet abashed by his many rebuffs, that he and his comrades had met with from the damsels in their mountain saunter, caused his disponding spirits to be again reanimated, and dashing into the midst of them, offered his string of fish to any who would give him shelter for the night. In place of being alarmed at the bold intruder, every one with looks of benignity displayed their angelic nature by kindly inviting him to partake of their village cheer, and not observing by the twilight any known faces among the group, and by this disguise and weather beaten appearance of Campbell, his physiognomy at first was not recognised by the fair assembly till his voice betraying his native Cast was eagerly eyed by two or three of them and was saluted by his name by Lady Clanranald and her amiable daughter, who invited him to supper, which he cheerfully accepted of. After which accompanied them with another young lady to an entertainment in the village, consisting of Slight of Hand, Magic Lantern, and other drolleries. In their way fell in with Smollet who joined the party to the temple of Buffoonery where after laughing a full hour at the tricks of the jester, sallied forth when Smollet steered for his cousins in whose house he expected to be accommodated for the night, and Campbell now deserted by his two companions did not know where to lay his head that night, till two young ladies commiserating his situation, kindly procured him an elegant apartment, for which returning his grateful acknowledgements and parting from the angelic group laid himself down for rest. But that was soon disturbed by Smollet who could not be accommodated in his cousins and was glad at last to throw himself on the mercy of the commiserating Campbell who readily granted him the prayer of his petition and both enjoyed a comfortable night's repose.

7th day. By morning sun Smollet & Campbell rising from their slumbers, sent for the unfriendly Cameron who did not think proper to enquire the preceding evening how they were to be accommodated but selfishly contented himself with his old aunt and young cousins, being afraid of offending them if his snakish disposition would alienate them from its usual bent by a too courteous behaviour towards his comrades. Forgetting however all by-pasts, the Glotianas left Helensburgh about seven o'clock morning and after a pleasant walk of nine miles to Dumbarton seemed to have lost the bottom of their stomachs, by the amazing breakfast they devoured which caused astonishment to the whole house for by their voracious appetites they seemed to ahead been in a state of starvation which no doubt was the case having got no substantial meal for two days. Leaving Dumbarton at 12 o'clock they walked about three miles to Dumglass, where fortunately at the nick of time a fly boat was passing from Greenock to Glasgow. Getting on board with difficulty got a berth, having about forty passengers stowed fore and aft more than the boat would conveniently hold, and which allowed ample scope to the Glotianas for creating their Quixotian spirit and returning in the same mood, they set out in laughing away care, and joining in all the eccentric humours of the plebeian race. Amongst such a motley assemblage of aquatic adventurers, promised them their heart's delight. Being now pretty well accustomed to the ups and downs of a passage boat and its squeamish effects amongst fresh water sailors, the Glotianas were highly amused at all the horrid grimaces which some of the passengers assumed when the boat chanced to heave from one side to the other. 'Lord have mercy on us', cries one, 'I wish I was on shore', cried another. 'Fool that I was to venture on water', said a third. In short it appeared to be a second Babel by the confusion of tongues which the Glotianas availed themselves of, and getting among a group of nymphs who were sitting at the prow of the boat, discovered by their wanton and giggling behaviour to be fond of fun. Cameron screwing his mouth and moving his eye brows in his usual manner, when excited by the presence of the fair sex, shewed he had discovered in someone of this lustrous group a resemblance to his favourite lass, and poured out his usual love effusions, and was rising into exultant raptures which being observed by Smollet & Campbell endeavoured to divert him from the object of his increasing passion until coming near Govan but there appearing no abatement of his romantic manner, and afraid of the consequences from such a mixed group if he came to closer quarters with this imagined goddess, Smollet prevailed on him with petulance to accompany him to his father's domain. Landing at three at Haughhead the paternal residence of Smollets, when after eating and drinking a sober glass bent their course for Glasgow, where they spent the remainder of the day in social harmony in the Crown & Thistle Tavern from whence they had set out on their rambles, and retailed some of their whimsical adventures, to a few choice spirits who witnessed their departure.

# ANON:
# Tours to the Highlands, 1817 and 1818

## Introduction

Both of these tour accounts – the one entitled 'The First Tour to the Highlands, 1817' and the second untitled tour of 1818 – are by the same writer, a youngish man, who is unfortunately nowhere named in the text. There is nothing in the provenance or from any associated papers to assist in his identification. We know only that the family surname began with a 'P'; that he was English, that he had a brother named Edward and that his father (who may have been of senior rank in the customs service, and was certainly someone of standing) and mother were living in Edinburgh. They were people of some means, wealthy enough to be able to afford to hire a carriage and driver for their first tour, but not sufficiently grand to have owned their own. It can be inferred from the opening to his second tour, where his departure north is delayed by a requirement to attend a Mr Fitchett at the Lancaster Assizes that he himself was in the legal world. His writing shows a clarity of thought and of expression, suggestive of a good education.

The volume, acquired by the Mitchell Library in 1979,[1] starts with a tour to the Lakes, and also includes the plan of a venture to the Isle of Wight. The first tour described is an eight-day pre-planned circuit in early September 1817 from Edinburgh to Lanark and the Falls of Clyde, up to Glasgow, then to Loch Lomond, the Trossachs and Dunkeld returning home to Edinburgh by way of Perth. Although there is an awareness shown of Walter Scott, generally very important in Scottish tourism at this period[2] with Rob Roy's cave a place that they visit, the search for the 'picturesque' was the dominant factor in shaping their schedule. Scenic attractions, such as rivers, lochs, hills and crags, are high on the travellers' agenda. Waterfalls and cascades were a particular enthusiasm which they made every effort to see. But they also admired man-made attractions such as the hermitages at Taymouth and at Dunkeld and made good use of a morning in Glasgow. The party

---

1 Glasgow City Archives, TD 637.
2 A.J. Durie, "'Scotland is Scott-land': Scott and the Development of Tourism', in M. Pittock, (ed.), *The Reception of Sir Walter Scott in Europe* (London, 2006), 313–22. *Rob Roy* was published in 1817.

was a mixture of men and ladies, young and old, and the core group were the writer, his brother Edward, his father and mother, aunt and cousins Hesketh. They took a carriage that could carry six, and the younger males quite often walked their way by a different route. By the writer's tally at the end of the tour, more than half of his 236 miles had been done on foot, rather than riding in the carriage.

The shape of the second tour in the following year, also in September, was rather different. He was to meet up with his parents (and brother Edward) once more, his father having planned a tour of the Highlands, but because he was delayed by an unexpected commitment, they had already gone on ahead to Inveraray. He made his way there, either alone or with a companion – his account moves back and forth between 'I' and 'we' – using the very newly established steamboat service to Loch Fyne from the Broomielaw on the *Dumbarton Castle*, which had just been switched from the Rothesay run.[3] He caught up with his parents at the mansion of Minard, where they all stayed as guests of 'Mr Campbell' for a week, enjoying fishing and other outdoor sporting activities. His brother Edward appears to have been particularly keen on field sports: there is a nice aside towards the end of the second account about his gratitude for being given a day's shooting near Greenock. The stay at Minard and the subsequent visit to Inverary (as he spells it, rather than Inveraray) seem to have been the fixed points in the family vacation, with what they did next open to discussion. The writer had wanted to go on to visit Staffa, but deterred by the weather and the lateness of the season, the group opted instead for Loch Lomond-side. The trip concludes with them reaching Greenock, after some unnerving experiences in the Clyde estuary, embarking and, after running aground, disembarking in open water, rather than at a pier head of which there were few.

The way in which the steamboat, a very recent arrival on the scene, in combination with the growing number of coaching services, was helping to shape where and when visitors could travel, is apparent from the 1818 tour. The first paddle steamer, the *Comet*, had begun commercial service only a few years previously in 1812. Yet such was the development of this new form of transport that our writer, only six years later, was able to comment on the 'vast numbers of Steam Boats that are seen continually on the Clyde'. Slow as they were, they nevertheless allowed a better use of time, with regular sailings and what amounted almost to a taxi service in the firths. The boats had a distinct and immediate influence on the kind of tourist to be found in and around the firths and lochs of Western Scotland. A steam boat proprietor told Thomas Cook in 1860 that during his lifetime he had seen a great change in type of visitor on his boats from just the

3   Kenneth Davies, *The Clyde Passenger Steamers* (Ayr, 1980), 49. The *Dumbarton Castle* had been launched in 1815 by McLachlan of Dumbarton.

few, who were wealthy, to large numbers 'of the middle and humbler classes of society'.[4] There is a very revealing passage in the 1818 account when he arrives from Glasgow at Inverary, where he gets a distinctly off-hand reception at the local inn. Steamboat passengers are clearly regarded as inferior and much less welcome than those visitors 'who brought their families, their servants, their chariots and their horses' . . . and tipped better. Tourism was changing, and transport was playing a significant role in this.

## Note

This is a forty-four-page notebook held in Glasgow City Archives, TD 637. It is reproduced in full with original spelling, underlining and paragraph breaks retained. On occasion, punctuation has been modernised for ease of reading. The places and dates of the entries have standardised.

# Journal

## First Tour to the Highlands, 1817

### EDINBURGH

The short though agreeable visit which my companion and myself paid to the English lakes had given us such a taste for the <u>sublime and beautiful</u> that we had not been long resident in this City before we mutually expressed our eager desire to visit those scenes which had been the admiration of every Traveller and the theme of almost every Poet. I shall never forget the chagrin and displeasure with which the communication of our extended scheme was received by the members of this house; suffice it to say that the result had ultimately a beneficial effect by producing an almost immediate convocation of the Members of the House for the purpose of taking into their serious consideration what route of a Tour it would be most advisable to adopt and what would be the most economical as well as the most commodious mode of conveyance. At a subsequent meeting of the said inhabitants held at their house on Saturday the 30th day of August 1817 It was resolved that the plan proposed to this meeting by Mr West, a Surveyor of considerable eminence should be carried into effect and that a commodious carriage capable of containing six persons should be procured and

---

4  Cited from the Introduction to Cook's *Tourist Official Directory and Guide* (London, 1861) in A.J. Durie, *Scotland for the Holidays* (East Linton, 2003), 146.

be in readiness to convey such Persons on Tuesday the 2nd of Septr by nine of the clock in the Forenoon. Every preliminary preparation being settled by Mr Niven their secretary my Father and Edward set forward as the advanced guard of our Party while the rest of the Company on the day and at the hour above mentioned took their seats in the vehicle provided for their accommodation. This is an easy and commodious carriage and with a tolerable pair of hacks which to say the least of them were not vicious we pursued the road to Little Vantage[5] the first stage on the Lanark road. Our party consisting of my Aunt and Cousins Hesketh my mother & myself occupied every seat in the carriage and the clearness of the sky and the extreme cheerfulness of every countenance rendered our outset peculiarly propitious. The road to Little vantage and indeed we may say the whole way to Lanark is flat dull and uninteresting. We arrive at the latter place at 5 o'clock and having with difficulty secured tolerable acco[mmodation] and having issued the necessary orders to the Cook and Chambermaid we sally forth to visit the celebrated Falls of the Clyde. We could not help observing in our walk to this sequestered spot the striking contrast which existed between the bleak and dismal scenery we had quitted to the beauty and luxuriance of that which surrounded us. After pursuing the high road for about a mile you descend a deep declivity on your right towards the banks of the Clyde, which is occasionally seen through the rich thick foliage which adorns its banks. At the bottom of this declivity you enter the well ordered grounds or rather Policies of the Lady Ross which are ornamented with thickly sheltered walks through an extensive shrubbery. The celebrity of the Falls of the Clyde, the most magnificent perhaps from their peculiarly picturesque situation in the three Kingdoms, had naturally raised our expectations and the loud and thundering sounds in the hitherto silent glen gave us warning of our approach and of the nature of the scene we might expect to behold. The fall which was first shewn to us by our guide was that of Cora Linn consisting of two distinct Falls or sheets of water which discharge themselves into two immense basins at the distance of about 60 feet from each other. To convey to the mind of a stranger the sublimity and grandeur which distinguished this spot would baffle the efforts of the most enthusiastic Poet or the most experienced Artist it is utterly impossible to draw a faithful picture of so sublime a scene. The steep and rugged precipices clothed with thick brushwood and with the mountain Ash overhang the celebrated falls and barren promontories which here and there jut out from the Parent Rock afforded us the opportunity of viewing more distinctly the beauties of this enchanting spot. By adopting this latter mode you may approach much closer to

5   On the Edinburgh to Carluke road in West Lothian where there was an inn, later called the Cross Keys.

the Fall and while you are enveloped in the gulph beneath by the foaming and sparkling spray you find yourself as it were buried between towering heights of at least 200 feet which here and there threaten to close in upon you and exclude you from the light of heaven. We also visited the second fall in the same grounds which in point of scenery greatly resembles the first though the fall of water is not so strikingly grand. Having enjoyed but a hurried view of these scenes we returned to the Inn much delighted with our walk. Dinner having been announced and the arrangements for the following days plans being settled the party retired to their respective apartment while my Brother and myself were balloted [*sic*, ?billeted] upon one of the inhabitants in the village.

## LANARK, WEDNESDAY MORNING [3 SEPTEMBER]

The light infantry division of our party rose at an early hour this morning for the purpose of revisiting these charming Falls and of contemplating more at leisure upon the beauties which nature has so richly lavished on this delightful spot. Pursuing our walk through the thick and well grown shrubbery which we had yesterday passed through we gained the promontory from which the second fall is seen to advantage. This is called Boniton Linn which though inferior as a cascade yet in point of majestic boldness and sublime grandeur of the Rocks and Scenery which surround it stands prominent and is altogether equally interesting and magnificent.

On our return through her Ladyship's Policies we visited the Summerhouse where as was the custom for Tourists we set down our names in a book. We were also very much inclined to have paid a visit to the extensive works of the renowned Mr Owen[6] which are situate in the neighbourhood and from the space of ground they occupy give rise to the name of 'The Lower Lanark' our time however was too limited and we hastened with what speed we could to the Inn where we [were] not a little pleased to find our breakfast on the table. After breakfast was over we set forward with our full complement accompanied by a guide to visit the romantic cartland craigs which are within a few minutes walk of this town and which have been so ably and accurately described by Miss Porter in her beautiful novel called 'The Scottish Chiefs'.[7] After leaving the Town of Lanark behind you and ascending the opposite bank through the land and garden of a Mr Lockhart of Brownhill your course is suddenly interrupted by an extensive and terrific range of Precipices and Craigs which on the other side present themselves.

6   See Ian Donnachie, *Robert Owen. Owen of New Lanark and New Harmony* (East Linton, 2000).
7   Jane Porter's successful novel of Wallace and the Wars of Independence, *The Scottish Chiefs*, had been published in 1810.

From the almost impervious path through which you are conducted you are struck by the deep dark and awful chasm which lies before you and when from the gleam of sunshine or from the uninterrupted projection of the rocks, you look down these dismal and almost perpendicular heights into the abyss below, you may behold the Clyde pursuing its rapid and rugged course, presents a scene awfully grand and imposing. These Craigs are clothed from their foundation to their summit with thick and lofty trees except here and there perhaps where the barren sterility of the rock was such as not to afford a grain of Earth to nourish or support them. It was wonderful to observe the coolness and dexterity with which our guide bounded or rather hopped like a bird from one promontory to another without the slightest emotion of feat, particularly when you consider that one false step might have plunged him headlong into <u>bottomless perdition</u>. After performing several of these bold feats with which I must confess I was by no means entertained he conducted us by a circuitous path through the thick brushwood to the bottom of the glen for the purpose of visiting the cave of the renowned Wallace which is in the recess of the rock and though now by no means difficulty of access was formerly considered the most secure place of concealment. After passing what is called the vale of Brig Earn you approach the road to Hamilton at the distance of about two miles from Lanark where we were met by the carriage into which the senior members of our party deposited themselves while my brother, Loveday and myself pursued our journey on foot. We had not proceeded more than two miles when we invited to diverge from the road and the falls of Stonibyres whose thundering Torrents are heard rolling down the Craigs from the roadside. Immediately on leaving the road you descend into a thick and intricate wood abounding with holes and precipices and are guided towards the Fall more by the noise of the cascade than by any path which you may attempt to pursue. We found it however well worth our notice and by no means grudged the occasional scratches in the face or falls on the ground occasioned by being entangled in the briars which procured us a sight of Stonebyres. As we approached we found it divided into 3 distinct and stupendous falls of about 70 feet in height & though perhaps somewhat inferior to the 2nd view of the Corra Linn it equalled if not exceeded either of the others in its romantic scenery and in the extreme boldness and majesty of the Precipices above it. On returning to the high road the Sky appeared to bear every indication of rain which so far from damping our spirits only renewed our vigour and afforded us the best opportunity of viewing this most rich fertile and luxuriant country to the greatest advantage by the alternate changes of light and shade. The whole road from Lanark to Hamilton is adorned on the right by the most prolific orchards while the opposite banks were thickly clothed by the abundant crops of the Golden Acres and between these two pleasing and agreeable [? sights] ran the Clyde whose glassy surface was occasionally ruffled by the breeze which prevailed. On the banks of this river you may see the seat of the Marquis of Hyndford called Malmedy Castle. As we danced towards Hamilton the rain began to descend but conceiving that it was merely a partial shower and would soon blow over we took shelter under an adjoining wood but finding our conjectures upon this point proved false we issued from our retreat and entered Hamilton under a heavy shower. Upon joining our party at the Inn at this place we learned that a division of our party had preceded us on their way to Glasgow and had left directions for us to follow as soon as we came up being determined on reaching Glasgow that evening. We accordingly hastened to change the most material parts of our dress and to dry the rest at the Kitchen Fire. On leaving Hamilton we had only to regret that our short stay did not allow us time to visit the Palace though if the interior decorations be not more worthy a strangers observations than those on the outside we could not lose much by the disappointment. The weather during our drive to Glasgow became thick gloomy and wet so that we were obliged to close the Carriage and during the drive I could only indistinctly hear our driver communicating to his companion that we were passing the well-known Bothwell brig and that the castle of that name was to be seen at a distance on the left. We arrived at Glasgow at a late hour of the day and drove to the Star kept by Mrs Younghusband where we engaged our accommodation for the night.

## GLASGOW, THURSDAY 4 SEPTEMBER

My father and myself amused ourselves early this morning by sauntering through the principal streets of this populous city which enabled us to form a very imperfect idea of the beauties of the Town. We were able however to obtain a general outline sufficiently so at least to observe that in point of beauty of situation and in the grandeur of public buildings it must ever rank inferior to the Northern Metropolis. The principal street is spacious, extensive and regular and that through which the Clyde flows is very commanding. The principal public buildings are the Cathedral which as a place of great antiquity, the only monument which escaped the fury of the bigoted Knox and as a place rendered immortal by being designated the Laigh Kirk in the Novel of Rob Roy is well worthy the notice of the Traveller. Next in order is the College, and the College Museum, the lunatic Asylum, the Infirmary, The Roman catholic Chapel and though last not least the Tontine Coffee room where the stranger may pass a dry hour without the fear of interruption or intrusion. To the farmer and Country Gentlemen the celebrated Cow house may be an object of curiosity. We returned to the Inn to breakfast which being concluded my Father and Wm Hesketh pursued their walk to the

Broomielaw where they were to embark on board the Steam Boat for Dumbarton while the rest of the party ordered their carriage and proceeded to the same destination. The morning was unfortunately very unpropitious and the drizzling rain or rather Scotch Mist which prevailed during the greater part of the day prevented our enjoying the drive. The road from Glasgow to Dumbarton is by no means uninteresting being accompanied the greater part of the way by the soft flowing Clyde which runs at no great distance from the road and is here navigable for ships of great burthen. The Scene becomes particularly enlivening as you approach what is called Bowling Bay where you abruptly come upon the banks of the Clyde which is here interspersed with numerous vessel of different dimensions and is seen gradually expanding itself for many miles. Erskine House and the grounds which are seen on the opposite side of the river, the residence of Lord Blantyre, tend considerably to add to the richness and beauty of this charming landscape, and the Traveller will be well repaid by mounting what is called Dunotter hill to view this extensive and variegated scene. Dumbarton Castle is also here seen in the distance projecting itself into the agitated Frith which nearly <u>insulates</u> the steep and rugged rock upon which it is built. It conveys to the mind of a stranger an appearance of great strength from its situation though the Fort itself seems very inconsiderable. The Governor's House and the old Watch Tower on its summit being the only objects discernable from the road. On visiting the interior however the stranger will find that it contains some very commodious and capacious barracks and that there are several batteries mounted with numerous pieces of cannon of different sizes. We loitered around the streets of Dumbarton and refreshed ourselves at the Inn with a tolerable luncheon while the horses were baited though we observed nothing particularly worthy of notice. On our return to the Inn we found our <u>merry hacks</u> only waiting our pleasure to convey us on the <u>long trot</u> to Luss a stage in which we expected to behold more beautiful and greater variety of scenery than we had before visited. The morning's rain had ceased and the clouds had dispersed though not disappeared and as we abruptly approached the unrivalled shores of Loch Lomond the variegated rainbow was seen in the distant heaven extending from shore to shore - Surely Travellers were never so blessed in their visit to this favoured spot. The residence of Sir James Colquhoun is the first object of your attention and while the rich and darkening wood which adorns this mansions [?grounds] and shelters this part of the lake you may observe its surface gently agitated by the breeze. In our ride along the shores of this lake we were gratified with every kind of scenery which Hill and Dale Wood and Water could present until we arrived at the Inn at Luss which is within a stone's throw of the water and though a paltry shabby looking house we were soon reconciled to it from its romantic situation. It is nearly opposite the lofty Ben Lomond over whose summit might be seen the deep coloured blushes of the setting sun and whilst here the mountains appear to rise gradually above the lake the bold Cliff and Promontories stretch forth their rugged sides over its banks & form dark shaded bay in the deep cavities and recesses beneath. While dinner was preparing we took a short walk along the pebbly banks of this elegant lake and were gratified with the most elegant coup d'oeil combining all the romantic beauty, taste, and richness which cultivation and Improvement could exhibit while in the black and barren chain of mountains towering irregularly in the distance beyond is drawn a grand and formidable outline to the highly finished picture. Before we returned to the Inn we paid a short visit to one of the Cottages or rather Hovels which as we expected we found very uncomfortable and wretchedly dirty. We made Luss our head quarters for the night and it was determined that the Light Infantry Division should proceed further up the Country and by crossing a Ferry near Inversnaid visit the far famed Loch Catrine whilst the other members were to return by the way that they came and cross by Drymen to Callander where we agreed the following day to join our forces.

### FRIDAY MORNING [5 SEPTEMBER]

We were again favoured with another fine day and in pursuance of our previous arrangement W.H. L.R. FP Ed P[8] and myself under the command of major M set forward on our road to Tarbet which is situated 8 miles further up the Lake. This short stage extends the whole way along the left bank of the Lake which you keep in view the whole time except here and there where the thick wood intervened between the brink of the Lake and the road. Amongst the great variety of Scenery in which new beauties are every moment displayed there was a scene about three miles from Luss nearly opposite what is called The Row of Dennan which surprised me exceedingly; the range of mountains which bound the lower part of the Lake and the great expanse of Water in length and breadth in your front, the wooded promontories appearing almost to recline on the glassy surface of the Lake and the naked peak of the Proud Ben Lomond towering in majestic grandeur to the Hills. On our arrival at Tarbet, which we found far cleaner and more comfortable than most of the Scotch Inns where we had bivouacked, we partook of a hasty luncheon and I took a dip in the Lake. It is from this place that strangers usually sally forth to visit the top of Ben Lomond and where you are furnished with a Boat, Guide, and other requisites but when we were informed that this arduous undertaking could not be accomplished with tolerable comfort under

---

8   Perhaps, therefore, the male members of the party were William Hesketh, Loveday R[****], [?Father] P, Edward P and the author with Major M[****].

a day we found our time too limited to admit of the delay. On entering the room however into which I was shown I observed the following lines written on a pane of glass which as they were written for the benefit of posterity and as describing the obstacles which a Traveller must encounter in mounting this formidable mountain & possess some merit I have deemed them worthy of insertion,

> Stranger if ever this pane of glass perchance
> Thy roving eye should cast a casual glance
> If taste for grandeur and the dread sublime
> Prompt thee Ben Lomond's fearful height to climb
> Here gaze attentive nor with scorn refuse
> The friendly rhymings of a Tavern Muse
> For thee that muse this rude inscription planned
> Prompted for thee to raise her humbler poet's hand
> Heed thou the Poet he thy steps must lead
> Safe o'er yon towering Hills aspiring head
> Attentive then to this informing lay
> Mark how he dictates as he points the way
> Trust not at first a too adventurous pace
> Six miles its top points gradual from the base
> [****] rise with panting haste I passed
> And gained the long laborious steep at last
> More prudent thou when once you pass the deep
> With measured steps and slow ascent the steep
> Off stay thy steps off taste the Cordial Drop
> And rest of rest, long long upon the top
> So shall the eye behold with one survey
> Vales, Lakes, Woods, mountains, islands rocks
> Huge Hills that thus and Sea in crowded order stand
> Stretched over the northern & the western land
> Vast lumpy groups which Ben who often shrouds
> This lofty summit in a bed of clouds
> High o'er the rest displays superior state
> In proud pre-eminence sublimely great
> One side all awful to the gazing eye
> Presents a steep 300 fathoms high
> All this and more shalt thou transported see
> And own a faithful monitor in me.
>> Thos Russell
>> 5th October 1771

The boat being ready to convey us to Inversnaid which is about 5 miles further up the Lake we all embarked in high spirits the weather being remarkably clear and the scenery in every direction either wild and romantic or assuming an appearance of the richest cultivation. As you advance towards Inversnaid you are suddenly introduced into an amphitheatre formed by the projecting Rocks and stupendous Mountains exhibiting not the smallest vestige of verdure or cultivation. We all safely embarked at the creak of Inversnaid composed only of one solitary Hut and having procured a guide we proceeded by a forced march to Loch Catrine a distance of 7 miles. We immediately ascended a very steep hill and losing sight of this Lake which had afforded such delight and gratification passed through a bleak dreary and uninteresting range of hills which intersect the rival lakes of Loch Lomond and Loch Catrine. Nothing occurred to attract our observation or arrest our attention during this dull and laborious walk though our progress was occasionally impeded by a swampy morass or the intense thickness of the Heather and Brushwood. It must have afforded considerable amusement to our Highland guide to observe the difficulty and labour with which we surmounted these difficulties and the repeated cries for quarter or rather for breath evidently showed that we had not been much accustomed to such a mountainous country. We at length came in sight of that Lake which had been so long the object of our curiosity and which had occasioned all our toil and only conceive the disappointment we must have experienced when we beheld nothing but a tame sheet of water without a stick or a tree to adorn it. Having discharged our obligations to our [guide] with a pretty liberal donation we embarked on board one of the Highland wherries which we had observed moored to the banks and directed our course towards the upper part of the Lake to Stewart House where we intended to bivouack for the night. In our progress up the Lake we were sorry to observe that it still continued to observe the same tameness until we had passed the lonely Isle when we certainly did enjoy a scene indescribably sublime - The majestic Rocks and rugged cliffs & Precipices which jut out on both sides enclose you in a small solitary bay and while the overhanging Woods gave grandeur and darkness to the Scene above the rays of the setting sun displayed the enlivening features of the Silvery Lake beneath. You soon appeared buried in the extended chain of the lofty Trossachs luxuriantly wooded to their very summit and scattered in chaotic confusion along the banks of this part of the Lake where the bold and conical Peak of the renowned Ben Ledi stands conspicuously grand and forms upon the whole a very different picture from what we had hitherto seen. The evening now began to close and as we walked from the lake to the house of our guide I could not help contemplating upon the Beauty and magnificence of Nature's Works which I had this day beheld. From the almost unprecedented favourable circumstances under which it unfolded to us this morning it may naturally be supposed that I should give a decided preference to this lake over its neighbouring rival and so I certainly did but not for the reasons above stated but because I conceived it exhibited a greater uniformity of splendid scenery upon a much grander scale and in much greater variety than the renowned Loch Catrine appeared to possess. From the unfriendly reception which we had met with on a previous occasion from the owner of the House we were to occupy for the night I must confess my hopes of admission into his inhospitable hovel at this late hour of the evening for it was nearly 8 o'clock were but very faint but we were agreeably surprised on our arrival to find that the <u>Gentleman</u> had enlarged his premises and that he was disposed not only to give us a courteous but a civil reception. We accordingly feasted upon some cold mutton and cheese and as was usual when we had taken violent exercise we terminated our evening in a plentiful libation to Bacchus. We then retired to our respective apartments consisting of two miserable rooms the one occupied by the ladies the other by the gentlemen. My father and Hesketh deposited themselves in one crib while Edward and myself occupied the other. In this way we passed the evening without changing our dress and were awake at an early hour in the morning by the clattering of the rain against our windows.

## SATURDAY MORNING, [6 SEPTEMBER]

On looking out of our bed chambers we perceived that the atmosphere was in every direction enveloped in a thick and drizzly mist and having in vain waited for a fair blast we set forward on our road to Callander (12 miles). We found that we had been sleeping near the brink of Loch Venachar which flanks the road to Callander for about 3 miles and which from its contiguity to the Trossachs forms a very pretty landscape. After passing the Brig of Turk where you cross the Teith our view became greatly obscured and the rain descended in such torrents as to leave us little opportunity for observation. The vale of Glenfinlass to the your left and the tame insipid lake of Achray on your right are the only remaining objects of notice. As we approached Callander we observed from the lights immediately above the Town that it was composed of one irregular street with a very tolerable Inn where we had the pleasure of joining our party. The good old Ladies with <u>that prudence</u> which such alone possess had prepared breakfast and had aired by the fireside a change of dress which was by no means unwelcome. About one o'clock we all sallied forth to view the celebrated cataract at Brackland Bridge distant about two miles from the village. Ascending the hill behind you are placed in a situation commanding a very grand and extensive prospect and amongst the most interesting objects are Stirling Castle and the

<u>gigantic group</u> of Trossachs. The sudden descent & burst upon Brackland Bridge is somewhat appalling and to a timid or nervous traveller the passage across from its peculiar construction and antiquity is a very dangerous experiment when you consider that a trifling diversion either to the right or left would hurl you into the deep and boiling chasm which lies beneath from a height of at least 80 feet. The bridge consists of a Few old Planks rudely put together of a breadth of about 3 yards and having for its base on either side a bold and rugged rock its breadth may be considered about 2 feet and a half or 3 feet without battlements or supports of any kind and in addition to these formidable disadvantages it is from its situation generally covered with a wet and slimy moisture which renders it extremely slippery. We all contrived to pass over and entered into the wood on the opposite side and on turning to the right you are conducted by a path to the Promontory from which you have a most delicious view of this grand fall of water. Nothing could exceed our wonder and admiration at this truly awful sight which nothing but some horrible convulsion of nature could have created. The fall commences its course between two huge towering rocks covered from their base to their summit with the most luxuriant brush wood except here and there where thick patches of the Purple Heather give additional beauty and variety to the scene and rolling with considerable impetuosity against every piece of rock which attempts to check its progress it throws up the dark and foaming spray and agitates the rugged bed of water for a considerable distance. While we were meditating an attempt to scramble down to the waters edge my Brother and myself received orders to form the advanced guard and to proceed by a forced march to Lochearnhead 14 miles. This was no pleasant intelligence to keen travellers who were exploring new beauties in this sequestered spot and who had already walked on that morning 12 miles to breakfast. We quitted Callander and proceed in quick time as it was now 3 o'clock along the road. When we had walked for about 4 miles we heard a soaring rumbling noise very much like that of a waterfall and being determined to satisfy our curiosity we descended the precipice until an opening of the wood presented us with a view of a very pleasing cascade the name however we were unable to learn and soon came to the margin of Loch Lubnaig which extends about 3 miles. The country in this neighbourhood is wild and dreary and the mountains over which you pass are bare and naked. After climbing up one of very steep ascent we were gratified by the sight of the romantic village of Lochearn Head situated on the verge of the Lake under the brow of a hill and the confined cultivated spots about it when contrasted with the cold bleak and mountainous part of this stage was pleasing and agreeable. When within a few yards of our place of destination we were struck with the rumbling noise of our vehicle which just came up in time to

witness its defeat. It may be though worthy of remark that although the carriage left Callander half an hour after us we arrived before it having accomplished the stage in three hours. We were most agreeably surprised to find most comfortable accommodation in so remote and retired a part of the country and we were regaled with better cheer than any we yet had met with.

## SUNDAY MORNING, [7 SEPTEMBER]

Having heard that there was a Fall to be seen at no great distance from our headquarters called the Fall of Edinample we rose early this morning and having continued our course for about a mile on the right banks of the Lake we came within hearing of the object of our search. Pursuing a path through a well grown wood we shortly found ourselves placed immediately under its influence and though greatly inferior to those we had seen we still found it well worthy of our attention. Breakfast being over we pursued the road to Killin through a bleak barren and uninteresting country and over a range of mountains enveloped in mist until you abruptly descend upon the charming little village of Killin sheltered by hills and bounded on the East by the Dochart. While our horses were baiting we strolled about the village and crossing the well built bridge were conducted to the mausoleum of the ancient family of McNabs called Kinnell. We found nothing remarkable curious except one of the Tombstones representing the exact and perfect outline of a man in armour which by tradition reports was placed there by one of the clan who discovered it among the hills and appropriated it for the purpose of covering the mouth of a vault. The story I must confess appeared to savour much of the marvellous particularly when I was informed that it required four men of the present generation to remove it. Our horses being ready to start we proceeded towards Kenmore but the atmosphere became thick and hazy and we lost much of the beautiful scenery which Loch Tay affords. When we had driven about 8 miles we stopped at a small solitary hut to procure some water for our horses and were met by a large concourse of the Highland Peasantry clad in the various tartans by which their clans were represented and who seemed to have been collected from distant parts of the country. We soon afterwards discovered a small neat kirk in the hollow of the valley and were no longer at a loss to account for this extraordinary sight. The population of two very extensive parishes had assembled upon this spot to receive the Sacrament which I believe in this remote part of the Highlands is not administered more than once a year. It is however very much to the credit of this hardy and warlike race that though the residence of the greater proportion of this congregation is at the distance of 15 nay in some instances 20 miles from the Kirk they uniformly make appoint of attending by some means or other upon their solemn occasion. The remainder of the road to Kenmore was covered with these rustic stragglers who were returning to their homes some on foot, some on horseback and others in carts. As you approach the village the road lies beautifully situated between the wood which towers above you on the left and the Lake which flanks your right. The country around this part of the Lake exhibits almost as great a variety of scenery as can well be imagined; Kenmore with its Church and bridge thrown over the Tay at the extremity of the village and the distant view of the Hermitage on the opposite bank form one of the most cheerful & enlivening landscapes I ever beheld. The situation of Kenmore is most enchanting being built upon an eminence commanding a very extensive view of the Lake on the Lorne side and surrounded by the luxuriant grounds of Taymouth. The Inn at that place resembles that of Luss the rooms we occupied being dirty cold and damp and beds hard and uncomfortable. As we did not reach the Inn until 7 o'clock in consequence of the bad state of the roads we postponed visiting the neighbouring scenery until the following morning.

## MONDAY MORNING, [8 SEPTEMBER]

The more active of our party rose at an early hour this morning to visit the celebrated falls of Achearn situate near a hermitage in Lord Breadalbane's grounds. We walked along the road which I believe leads to Crieff and which extends on the opposite banks of the Lake from that which we had travelled yesterday and after pursuing it for about a mile and a half were conducted by our guide up a steep and rugged path. Just as we reached the summit we paused for a moment to recover our wind and on turning round were struck with a wonder and amazement at the magnificent landscape which lay before us. The rays of the Sun were shining in all their splendour upon the sparkling lake which reflected the nearer objects like a brilliant mirror and while the proud and lofty Ben Lawers raised his stately head at one extremity of the Lake you may observe at the other the interesting objects of the Church, Village and Bridge of Kenmore with Taymouth Castle in the distance. After viewing this prospect we followed our guide though a wood and after shewing us two very inferior falls one of which is called the Devil's Punch Bowl he led the way through a dark and subterranean passage and suddenly opening the door of the Hermitage exhibited to us in all its splendour the famous fall of Achearn. This cascade is more renowned for its great height than for the weight of Water which it throws up. The perpendicular fall of Water when the burn is well supplied being 209 feet of one continuous sheet. The Hermitage itself was built by Lady Glenorchy and is rural & romantic being commodiously fitted up in the rustic style with seats covered with the skins of foxes, roe Deer and other animals. We returned to the

Inn by the way that we came and after breakfast was concluded and we had
procured a guide we proceeded to visit the Grounds of Taymouth. Immediately
on entering the gate you are introduced into a spacious green walk shared on
either side with rich and well grown timber. We were shewn into a neat
summerhouse on a little eminence from which you may enjoy a very pleasing
view of the Church and Lake at Kenmore. At the extreme of this delightful walk
you catch a view of Taymouth castle a fine noble building the centre of which is
of more modern architecture and its order I believe "Florid Gothic" surmounted
with a sort of glassy turret or Lanthorn [lantern]. The only remains of the
ancient structure are the two wings which we understood were shortly to be
pulled down a circumstance we were glad to hear as they were vastly ugly and at
present only tend to deface the beauty and destroy the uniformity of the
Building. We were very much tempted to visit the interior of the building but
our time was too precious and we could merely indulge ourselves with a lounge
through these spacious and well kept grounds. There is a pretty little battery
placed nearly opposite the house mounted with one and twenty guns which are
discharged upon the usual Holidays. At the extremity of the grounds we found
our vehicle in readiness to convey us forward and while the rest of our party took
their seats in the carriage myself & E[dward] pursued our journey on foot to
Aberfeldy. The walk from this point to Aberfeldy is distant about six miles and it
extends for the greater part of the way along the rich and fertile banks of the Tay
and through the luxuriant Glen of Strath Earn it is peculiarly interesting and
cheerful. When we reached the village of Aberfeldy we observed the carriage
waiting for the rest of our party who had not yet returned from visiting the Falls,
but who we met on our way thither and from their account of what they had
seen our expectations were somewhat raised. We accordingly engaged a guide
who conducted us through a narrow winding path thickly shaded on either side
by a well grown shrubbery and here and there might be seen the smooth
mountain ash or the ruddy Birch overhanging with his extended boughs the Path
which we walked. The first fall which is called the Fall of Moness soon presented
itself to our view while we observed directly the two other Falls distinguished by
the name of "The Birks of Aberfeldy". The first of these runs with considerable
impetuosity down a steep and perpendicular staircase of many 100 feet and
though the scarcity of Water from the Burn above prevents it discharging a very
great water yet it pattered down the steps with an infinite velocity. The breadth
of these cascades is not more than 6 or 7 feet and as the Falls must rank certainly
inferior to those of the Clyde though they certainly have a fair claim to the notice
of the Traveller and will reward the exertion he may make to view them. We
crossed the [?Breda] Burn over a rudely constructed bridge which from the spray

constantly falling is rendered extremely slippery and after pursuing our course for about a mile were brought in view of another cascade also called the Burn of Moness. This we found to be greatly superior to the others we had seen the depth from the summit of the rock to the basin below being no less than 370 feet and we <u>were given to understand</u> that when the Burn was <u>large</u> that the Water fell in one continued sheet the whole depth of 370 feet. On our return to the road through the same romantic and picturesque walk we could not help observing the lofty Chehallion [Schiehallion] raising his proud and naked summit above the mountains and Craigs which surrounded him and at the same time enjoyed another very pleasing though more distant view of Taymouth and its scenery. Having descended into the high road we proceeded to Balnaguarde a small village about 4 miles off where we found the carriage waiting to take up the rear guard consisting of myself and my companion and having taken advantage of this conveyance we were driven towards the sweetly smiling vale of Dunkeld. When you approach within a mile of this place the scenery around becomes beyond description grand. Figure to yourself a rich and beautiful valley extending itself for several miles and yielding almost spontaneously the various productions of the Earth enriched and enlightened by the streams of a large and magnificent river circled by a zone of mountains through whose fissures thousands of young trees are seen struggling for existence among the aged and lofty pines which already adorn their sides. The mighty and barren Craigs which overtop these forests of Pine were no less the objects of our attention and astonishment and the magnificent Bridge which has been erected over the Tay and the ruins of the ancient Cathedral which adorn the opposite Banks of the river form a most pleasing and truly beautiful landscape. Having crossed a small bridge at Inver over the rapid and rugged bed of the Bruar which flows into the Tay we soon reached Dunkeld which as we expected we found filled with strangers. Our Host gave us however a very civil reception and offered us the best accommodation in his power.

## DUNKELD, TUESDAY MORNING [9 SEPTEMBER]

The town of Dunkeld is remarkably neat and is situated in a most rich and luxuriant valley bounded by the Tay over which is thrown a very handsome stone bridge. The Old Cathedral which forms a most pleasing object and was the first subject of our attention is at the extremity of the town on the margin of the river and still made use of as the Parish church. In the interior there is a large and spacious vault the burying place of the Athol family in which is a Table of almost illegible characters said to contain the Arms of all their relatives. It is composed of a mixture of Gothic and Saxon Architecture. Having procured a guide we all sallied forth to visit the celebrated beauties of the neighbourhood and were first conducted by him across the bridge at Inver and along the left bank of the agitated Braan towards what is called the Hermitage. In our way thither he pointed out to us the obscure birthplace of the Fiddler Neil Gow. As you approach the Hermitage, you come in sight of a very pretty cascade which to say the least of it may boast both of wildness and grandeur. You are first shewn into a small handsome vestibule adorned with a Portrait of Ossian which in fact forms a sort of doorway and which being removed introduced you into a most superb room elegantly fitted up with all the taste of a modern Drawing Room and decorated with three large windows commanding a full view of the Fall. The roof and walls are elegantly painted and richly embossed with Mirrors of all sorts of coloured glass which produce a very curious and singular effect in exhibiting several Cascades of various coloured liquids. In our walk through the grounds of his Grace we could not help observing the stately timber which every where adorns them and were particularly struck with the beauty and neatness of what is denominated Ossian's Cave. When we had satisfied our curiosity in this quarter our guide conducted us to the Rumbling Bridge which is at a short distance from the town and the scenery in that neighbourhood resembling very much that of Branklin Bridge but the rocks are more broken and scattered and the Fall much greater. The Cascade at this place like that of the Hermitage is supplied with water from the rocky bed of the Bran which when swollen with rain rushes with immense impetuosity till it approached the Bridge when defusing its spray a considerable distance in all directions it passes with a thundering noise into a deep dark chasm and conceals itself under a large ponderous stone which appears suspended between the rocks which support the Bridge. The view of the Town of Dunkeld from this point is strikingly picturesque and in our return to it we varied the scene by walking on the opposite side of the Tay through a fine well grown wood and we at length came in sight of the Duke of Athol's residence which is close to the town and which to the eye of a stranger appears rather to form part of it than the residence of a Nobleman and but for its situation would not deserve notice. As we quitted the Grounds we observed a very handsome stone cottage which has been lately erected of the order of Florid Gothic and we understood it to be His Grace's intention to build a Mansion to correspond. We returned to our Inn highly gratified with what we had seen and determined to remain the greater part of the day in this enchanting little spot.

## DUNKELD, WEDNESDAY 10 SEPTEMBER

We set off this morning after breakfast to view the Craigs on the north side of the Town - the beauty and luxuriance of the wood which cap the very summit of these Craigs is truly wonderful and you gradually ascend in a zigzag direction here and there catching a glimpse of the sweet vale of Dunkeld and on ascending the highest part of the rock you are placed in one of the most commanding situations that you can conceive. You may at one moment see a tract of country extending for 30 miles and the proud range of Grampians and Birnam Wood and Dunsinane immortalised by Shakespeare are distinctly pointed out to you by your guide. We left Dunkeld about one o'clock and proceeded on our way to Perth a distance of 15 miles. The road winds at the foot of the Grampian Hills for many miles until you come in sight of Scone Palace a large red looking building set on the left of the road within about 5 miles of Perth on a rising plain and celebrated as being the Place for the Coronation of the Scottish Kings and surrounded by some of the largest and finest Timber in the Kingdom and beautiful with shrubs and rising plantations. A little further in the same road is the renowned plain of Loncarty [Luncarty] on which the Danes received a most signal defeat from the Scots - in 976 when a Peasant by the name of Hay distinguished himself whose family were afterwards ennobled and bear the motto 'sub Jugs' [sic]. We soon reached Perth which we found lay at the foot of richly wooded cliff called Kinnoull Hill and bounded on one side by the Tay. The Town itself is neat and handsome and there is a noble Bridge erected across the Tay. We put up at the Salutation which is a most extravagant Inn and our Tour being nearly accomplished we determined upon reaching Edinburgh on the following day as the road from this place to Edinburgh contains nothing worthy of remark. Our vehicle being not sufficiently capacious to hold us all four of the party secured seats to Edinburgh by the Perth coach whilst the rest of the company proceeded at a more sober pace and we arrived in Edinburgh on Thursday the 11th of September after an absence of only 8 days.

## EDINBURGH, THURSDAY EVENING, [11 SEPTEMBER]

We all assembled once more round a cheerful fireside each attempting to express his feelings on the scenes he had witnessed. And while the grand and noble cataracts of the Clyde engaged the attention and pleased the taste of some others appeared captivated with the more lively and animating features of the Lakes. Upon the whole it may be said that few Tourists could have derived more pleasure from their excursion none could have seen more in the time we were absent and none could have been more grateful for a participation in this agreeable Tour.

| Edinburgh to | Rode | Walked |
|---|---|---|
| Little vantage | 11½ | |
| Carnwarth | | 13 |
| Lanark | 8 | |
| Hamilton | | 18 |
| Glasgow | 13 | |
| Dumbarton | 15 | |
| Luss | 11 | |
| Tarbet | | 8 |
| Loch Katrine | | 7 |
| Stewart's House | | 4 |
| Callander | | 12 |
| Loch earn Head | | 14 |
| Killin | 8 | |
| Kenmore | 8 | 8 |
| Aberfeldy | | 8 |
| Balnaguard | | 6 |
| Dunkeld | 10 | |
| Perth | | 15 |
| Queensferry | 30 | |
| Edinburgh | | 9 |
| | 114 | 122 |
| [Total] | | 236 |

# [Second Tour to the Highlands,] 1818

## WARRINGTON, THURSDAY 20 AUGUST

The usual period for recreation being returned I obtain a month's leave of absence with the intention of visiting my family in Edinburgh but while making arrangements for my departure I was unexpectedly requested to attend Mr Fitchett at the Lancaster Assizes where I was detained six days and during my confinement there had the mortification of receiving a letter from my father informing me that he had left Edinburgh on a Tour of The Highlands and requesting me to join him as early as I could at the Town of Inverary in Argyleshire.

## LANCASTER, SATURDAY 29 AUGUST

Immediately upon being released I secured a seat in the Carlisle Mail at which place I arrived at ½ past nine in the Evening.

## SUNDAY MORNING [30 AUGUST]

Having attended Divine Service in the Cathedral and learned that there was no Conveyance but the Mail on Sundays to Carlisle I procured an outside seat and left Carlisle at 3 o'clock. The road from Carlisle to Glasgow is most uninteresting and after passing through Gretna Green alias Springfield near to which place is the boundary of England and Scotland and the scene of many a hard fought battle we successively arrived at the Towns of Ecclefechan Moffat Kirkdale Moor and Hamilton and reached Glasgow at 6 o'clock the following morning a distance of 103 miles.

## GLASGOW, MONDAY [31 AUGUST]

My first enquiries upon my arrival in this populous city was to ascertain the earliest packet which would sail for Inverary and I am directed to the Broomielaw for the information I wanted. It was rather difficult for an Englishman to discover what this place was or from what it derived its name. It appears however to be the Harbour or Quay from which vessels sail and the day and hour at which they start is placed on a conspicuous part of the Wall upon a red or yellow board. After attentively examining these for some time I discovered that the first vessel which was the 'Dumbarton Castle' Steam Boat would not sail until the following day. This circumstance induced me to return to the Tontine and after breakfast I determined on employing my leisure hours in visiting the objects most worthy of notice. We first proceeded up the ancient and dirty High Street at the top of which is situated the Old Cathedral on your right and the Infirmary directly before you. The Former building we determined to explore and having occasioned some disturbance in wishing to make a forcible entry we were soon hailed by the Wife of the Sexton who was seen approaching with the massive Keys of the outer Gates. She immediately unlocked the gates and conducted us across the Church Yard. She introduced us into this stately Edifice which is now called the High Kirk and is used as a Place of Worship. We were informed by our loquacious conductress that this building was erected in the sixth century and was one of very few religious Monuments which escaped the fury of the bigoted Reformer Knox. We were shewn some very ancient monuments and the prodigious massive columns which support the roof of this building gave us no reason to doubt the authenticity of our guide's statement as to its antiquity and the allusion made to the Laigh Kirk in

Rob Roy[9] which is pointed out to you proves that it cannot be a modern erection. We next went to visit the College Museum which both to the Antiquary and the Tourist is alike an object deserving his notice and attention. We passed through two of the College quadrangles which are remarkable for nothing but their dirty and antique appearance and at the extremity of these is placed a modern brick building neat and plain in its exterior and which we were informed contained the celebrated Hunterian Museum. At the Entry of the Museum we were about to pay our admission money when one of the Professors who happened to be passing at the time and who observed that we were strangers very politely invited us to accompany the party he was attending. An extensive collection of Paintings and Drawings by the most celebrated Masters and a very rich and valuable Library of rare works are contained in an upper room of very peculiar shape and construction while the lower is occupied with an endless variety of interesting curiosities in the Animal Vegetable and Mineral World. It is here also that you are shewn the very valuable collection of Anatomical and Surgical curiosities bequeathed to the University by the celebrated Dr Hunter and in which the gradual progress of Generation a *semine usque foetus* is curiously and wonderfully displayed. There are also several specimens of Egyptian mummies in a high state of Preservation which with some large and well-stuffed animals occupy the space below. We spent the greater part of the day very agreeably in this place and went afterwards to visit the Exchange which was immediately below the Tontine and where we read the Newspapers until dinner time. I did not feel disposed to accompany my friend in his evening stroll having travelled the preceding night on the Mail and having ordered my tea I retired early to rest.

## GLASGOW, TUESDAY [1 SEPTEMBER]

I was called this morning according to appointment and proceeded immediately to the Broomielaw or Quay where I found the Packet preparing to clear out. It was long before we were afloat and proceeded along the deep and narrow part of the Clyde which here assumes only the appearance of a moderate sized river. The banks of this river between Glasgow & Dumbarton are on both sides richly cultivated and are ornamented with Gentlemen's villas - Mr Oswald of Scotstown, Mr Spears of Inch and Mr Campbell of Blyth are amongst the most conspicuous. After sailing for about 12 miles down the river you suddenly come in sight of Dumbarton Castle which is situated upon a steep and rugged

9   Walter Scott's *Rob Roy*, to which further reference is made later in this account, had been published at the end of the previous year, 1817.

Promontory bold projecting itself into the Clyde which at this point was so rough and expanded as to resemble a Frith or narrow sea. We stopped for 5 minutes at the town of Port Glasgow which is still further down on the left bank of the Clyde and likewise at Greenock but as we were not permitted to land we could form no opinion of the size or opulence of either. The customhouse at the latter place is a large messy Building and is situated on the brink of the river.

On the opposite shore you may perceive the sweet little village of Helensburgh so famous for its Baths[10] and on the same side still further up is Roseneath Castle the property of the Duke of Argyle which forms a very beautiful object from the river. The present building was begun by the late Duke upon a most magnificent scale but owing to the pecuniary embarrassments into which he involved himself he has been unable to complete it and it now remains in an unfinished state. Near this point is the entrance to Loch Long. The atmosphere about midday became extremely thick and hazy and the showers which fell were so heavy that we were obliged to retire below and to remain satisfied with being told that we were [**** ?passing] the towns of Rothesay and Port Bannatyne and also Kames Castle the residence of the Marquis of Bute. We shortly after our arrival at this point took a farewell leave of the Clyde and entered into the narrow necks of Sea which run between the Islands of Bute and Arran and are called the Coils of Bute and at length entered Loch Fine at a place called Tarbet a beautiful little bay on the left of Loch Gilp Head. The scenery on the banks of Loch Fine is far less luxuriant and interesting than on most of the Scottish lakes and you may sail for many miles without meeting with either a <u>Clump</u> of trees or a Gentleman's residence to diversify or adorn the prospect on all sides seems but thinly inhabited and you only occasionally meet with patches of ground that appear capable of cultivation. In fact the only mansions I met with worthy of notice in this long sail were those of Mr McLachlan Mr Campbell and a General Campbell. When we approached within 12 miles of Inverary the surface of the Lake was covered in every direction as far as the eye could see with the nets and Wherries of the Highland fishermen employed in the Herring Fishery which in Scotland forms an article of great consumption and the Fisheries in this Lake claim a decided superiority over those caught in any other part of the kingdom. The profits arising from the Sale of these fish are laid up by the frugal Highlanders against the time of need and the immense number of Barrels which you see piled up in heaps would lead a stranger to

---

10 This is a reference to the 'hot and cold' baths establishment run by Henry Bell, the steamboat pioneer, and his wife at the Bath Hotel which they had purchased in 1808. She was in charge of what were described as 'public baths', lodgings and reading room.

suppose that the profits must be something considerable. At a late hour this evening we reached the capital of the Western Highlands where owing (it is said) to the despotic and arbitrary disposition of the Duke of Argyle there is only one Inn and that very uncomfortable and very dirty. It was not much to be wondered at that in a house of this description Steam Boat Passengers should not receive a very cordial reception, or that those visitors only should be welcome who brought their families, their servants their chariots and their Horses. Labouring under the disadvantages which I in common with some others did, it was some time before our Host would condescend to inform us whether we could be accommodated and at length he was pleased to huddle us all into one sitting room and to oblige me with a 4 bedded room. Finding there was no alternative I reluctantly submitted but should I again visit Inverary under similar circumstances I'll pay my respects to some one of the inhabitants who will entertain you civilly and be grateful to you for your company. I made immediate enquiries after my family but as these were regarded by the haughty waiters with rather less attention than my wants I was compelled to retire to my lofty apartments without learning any tidings of my friends.

## INVERARY, WEDNESDAY 2 SEPTEMBER 1818

We rose at an early hour this morning and found ourselves close on the shores of Loch Fine which here forms a most beautiful sort of Bay and closely hemmed in on all sides by the mountains which surrounded us. To the Inverary Castle His Grace's residence which is within 10 minutes walk of the town we first bent our steps and were struck with the grand and stately row of Majestic Pines which line the road from the Entrance Gate to the Castle and were not a little pleased with the neatness and order in which the grounds [are]. The Castle itself is indeed a most noble structure and bears every external mark of being the residence of a Nobleman. It is modern Gothic and adorned with four handsome Turrets. We ventured to ring the Bell of the outer door when the old housekeeper soon made her appearance and as the Family were not down a little silver key soon procured us admittance. The Saloon and Cupola which form the grand entrance are very magnificent and the former is fitted up with a variety of Highland Arms such as claymores Lochaber Axes and Musquets which were taken from the rebels in 45. The entertaining rooms are very magnificent and are ornamented with some rich tapestry and the subjects which are worked upon them. A Dutch Fair is very amusing. The Paintings and landscapes are also very numerous and the greater number of the latter are Performances of Nasmyth; upon the whole we were very much struck with the peculiar neatness and cleanliness which pervaded the whole house and the extreme comfort yet magnificence which it appears to combine. I indulged myself with a solitary walk through his Grace's Policies for the remainder of the day and nothing was wanting but a companion to complete my enjoyment of the scene. I returned to the Inn and found every place occupied but a sort of Travellers' Room where I was compelled to listen to the harsh and unintelligible language of the Celtic race few of whom could speak English and those who could speak English appeared to prefer the Gaelic. I determined therefore upon leaving this barbarous spot and endeavour the following morning to find my family, who I afterwards recollected were to pay a visit to Mr Campbell of Minard at about 12 miles from Inverary.

## THURSDAY 3 SEPTEMBER

At an early hour this morning I took the road to Minard which I found lay the whole way along the banks of Loch Fine and was bounded on both sides for the first 8 miles with the Policies and Plantations of the Duke of Argyle and whose Keepers Lodges at a mile asunder mark the road for that distance. I bolted into a Hut on the right hand side of the road where I made my breakfast upon Bannocks Cheese Butter Milk and Eggs. I at length reached the long wished for Mansion[11] and the fatigue trouble and disappointment I had experienced was more than counterbalanced by our happy meeting at Minard and the kind and hospitable manner with which the Laird received me. Here we remained for the space of a week experiencing the greatest attention and civility from our Host and participating in all the rural and <u>wholesome</u> sports of Shooting Fishing and Hunting. In the two former we were particularly successful as the Fish in the Lake are very plentiful. The Roe Deer are also numerous and are found in the woods upon the Lake. On the 8th of September in the evening we left Minard with regret and were rowed to the Steam Boat by some of his sturdy Highland dependents. We arrived at Inverary at about 10 o'clock and as I suspected neither Mr Hislop the Agent my Father employed to secure us a tolerable sitting room nor the fascinating manners of the good man himself could procure for us any thing more comfortable than a dark back parlour which looked into the stable yard.

## INVERARY, WEDNESDAY 9 SEPTEMBER

We found Mr Hislop a very intelligent serviceable person and gladly availed ourselves of his kindness in shewing us the beauties of the place. My father and mother not having seen the Duke's residence I paid a second visit with them to

---

11 Knockbuie House, later Minard Castle, is where they stay for five days, as house guests of Campbell of Minard, which is confirmation of the standing in society of the writer's father.

that place and the remainder of that day was occupied in loitering through his Grace's grounds and viewing the scenery from the most advantageous situations. Nothing can equal the beauty of the landscape which is exhibited from the 2nd station. Well ordered walks are cut through a rich thick Plantation from which you every now and again catch a glimpse of the Castle and Town of Inverary with Loch Fine in the distance. That part of his Grace's policies with which I was most pleased was the sweetly sequestered Lake and vale of Glensheid the entrance to which is through a beautiful and extensive row of climbing Beaches [*sic*] where an immense herd of deer are seen sportively playing over these apparently boundless regions. They extend 18 miles in length and two in breadth. The Hill of Dunquoich bounds this part of the Lake and is capped with an ancient Tower from which it derives its Gaelic name and which [I] determined to ascend the following morning with Mr Hislop.

INVERARY, THURSDAY [10 SEPTEMBER]

In consequence of the severe exercise I had taken the previous day Morpheus laid violent hands upon me and could I believe have exercised his powerful influence upon me for the greater part of the morning if we had not been roused by my friend Mr Hislop who in a satirical tone enquired whether that was the way I meant to gang to the top of Dunquoich. I rose immediately and having dressed myself went downstairs when I found my guide had deserted me. Resolving not to be disappointed I scrambled up the Precipice as well as I could having lost all trace of the Path by which Travellers usually ascend. Upon reaching the summit however I was well rewarded for my labour by one of the most enchanting and extensive views I ever beheld. An immense range of barren and uncultivated Mountains on one side the huge Forests of well grown timber slightly marked with the autumnal tinge which lower above and all around the Castle which lies immediately below you and the glassy Lake before you with the town of Inverary in the distance conspire to render this the most beautiful and diversified prospect that ever was exhibited. In our descent through the grounds to the Town we saw several species of Game as Black Cock Partridge and Roe Deer. The day now becoming very wet we were confined in the house the greater part of the day and were employed in planning our departure and the Future route we should take. For my own part I wished to visit the far famed Staffa from which we were only 14 miles distant but my motion was negatived without a division in consequence of the advanced state of the season whilst the motion that we should proceed to the shores of Loch Lomond was received with shouts of applause and carried nem. con. The next difficulty which occurred was the procuring a conveyance for our persons and luggage for it is a circumstance worthy of remark that when you once enter the Highlands you find it difficult to procure a public or private conveyance either for love or money. Our Host at length said he thought he could provide us a gig and with this promise we were all satisfied. My Father and Mother left Inverary this evening for Cairndow while my Brother and myself were left to bring up the rear guard and baggage on the following morning.

## FRIDAY [11] SEPTEMBER

At an early hour this morning our vehicle was ordered to the door which to be sure was but a cumbrous machine and having with difficulty first stowed in our luggage and afterwards our bodies politic our youthful driver who was not a very expert Whip set forward on his way to Cairndow. The road for the first 3 miles winds along the banks of Loch Fine and is remarkable for being a military road cut in the year [...]. The date and name of the Regiment are effaced from the milestone by age. The distance from Inverary to Cairndow is only nine miles but as our Driver was not inclined to shew off his horse's paces we took advantage of a ferry which brought us immediately across to the comfortable inn at Cairndow. We found breakfast ready provided for us and we had no sooner finished this meal than we received orders to march to Arroquhar distant about 14 miles. At a short distance from Cairndow you pass Arkinglas the residence of Colonel Callander and after mounting the very steep hill on the left arrived at the awful and romantic vale of Glencoe. Nothing remarkable was to be observed in this walk but the huge gigantic mountains which enclose you on all sides and whose lofty summits seem towering to the Clouds. The wild black sheep and stots lie scattered here and there while the Hovel of the Shepherd may be seen reclining as it were at the base of the Hill and the pretty little cataracts which are seen gushing down the deep ravines of these mighty mountains add to the beauty and sublimity of the scene. It is upon this road also about the middle of one of these steep tedious and winding mountains which so frequently impede your progress that the Stone with the inscription 'Rest and be thankful' is situated and we can give credit to the author for having spoken feelingly when he penned these emphatic words.[12] Having passed through 10 miles of country of this bold and romantic description we suddenly came upon the banks of Loch Long [when] first burst upon which is really very grand. After pursuing our

---

12   If the inscription is to be believed, the stone which commemorates the work of the 93rd regiment in 1768 had only recently (1814) been transferred to this spot. For a discussion of other travellers at this place, including of course the Wordsworths in 1803, see Carol Kyros Walker (ed.), *Dorothy Wordsworth, Recollections of a Tour Made in Scotland* (New Haven, CT, 1997), 168.

course for 3 miles along the left banks of this Lake you turn a road to your left which brings you to the picturesque village of Arroquhar and two miles further to that of Tarbet on the shores of Loch Lomond. While we were in the yard of the Inn at this place I was suddenly accosted by a Gentleman who I afterwards recognised to be Mr Turner of Liverpool and who I afterwards learned had in company with Mr Littledale been scaling the lofty Ben Lomond. It seemed they had procured their carriage at Glasgow and were come like ourselves to have a Peep at the Highlands. We made this place our headquarters for the Evening.

## TARBET, SATURDAY 12 [SEPTEMBER]

The former part of this day being very wet were some hours before we could decide whether we should proceed on this day by the Steam Boat to Dumbarton or remain at Tarbet. We at length determined to remain as we thought it would afford us an opportunity both of seeing Rob Roy's cave and also of ascending the lofty Ben Lomond. The evening proving fine we walked to Arroquhar upon the banks of Loch Long and fished afterwards in Loch Lomond but without success. Upon our return to the Inn we were greatly surprised by the unexpected arrival of Mr McNair and his friend Dr Gregory and upon hearing that we had ordered our dinner and secured the best room in the house they requested leave to join us and we accordingly spent the Evening together.

## SUNDAY MORNING, [13 SEPTEMBER]

My brother and myself after breakfast this morning walked together to visit the cave of Rob Roy which was situated at the distance of about 3 miles further up the Lake and being informed that we should have no difficulty whatever in crossing the Lake as there was a regular Ferry we declined taking a boat from Tarbet which though perhaps not the most usual is certainly the most secure mode of proceeding. On arriving at the spot where we wished to cross we found that we must either have been misled by our informants or that the religious notions of these enlightened Highlanders would not permit them to ply their oars on the Sabbath a day most scrupulously observed all over Scotland. In vain did we look for the inmates of the deserted ferry, in vain did we hold up our Handkerchiefs and hoist them on Poles to attract the observation of the boatmen on the opposite shore and in vain did we exert our utmost efforts to be heard by our shouts and cries across the Lake which at this point was not more than 3 quarters of a mile broad.

Having exhausted all our breath and nearly wasted all our time we were upon the point of despairing of success when some of the inhabitants who were passing informed us that we must light a fire or the men would never cross. We immediately took advantage of this hint and having laid the sticks in order we procured a light from a neighbouring farm house and having set fire to them we had shortly the pleasure of seeing the two jolly fellows coming across and in less than a quarter of an hour we were on board their boat and the space of time brought us to our place of destination. This celebrated cave where it is said Walter Scott composed part of his Tale called Rob Roy is situated about the middle a huge cleft of rocks extending from the brink of the Lake to a considerable height & the aperture by which you entered was so exceedingly small that we with difficulty crawled in even on our hands and feet. The hasty manner with which the Boatmen answered our signal prevented their bringing a candle a very necessary and very useful article in visiting this deep dark Den. From the faint glimmer of light which passed through the cracks in the rock we could scarcely judge of the convenience of the interior which was very spacious but the tremendous deep holes in the cavities of the rock rendered a long visit rather dangerous. We therefore soon returned and descended with difficulty the declivity of the Cliffs and were rowed to the Fall at Inversnead. Having loitered about here for some time we at length gladly availed ourselves of the share of a Boat in which two Englishmen were about to cross the Lake. On our return to Tarbet we were very much struck with the handsome dress and majestic gait of the Highlanders returning from the Kirk that of the Elder ones was strikingly picturesque & dignified. Upon our return to the Inn we found that Mr McNair and his friend Dr Gregory had just arrived from their excursion to Inverary and were very much amused with the relation of their adventures.

## MONDAY 14 SEPTEMBER

This morning proving very dull and the atmosphere on all sides being excessively thick and hazy it was resolved we should not prosecute our journey further into the Highlands but return <u>via</u> Greenock & Glasgow to Edinburgh. Mr McNair having secured a boat to convey him to Dumbarton we determined to accompany him and accordingly at 10 o'clock we all embarked, my brother and myself taking the two first oars. Had the weather been tolerable such an excursion could not have been otherwise than agreeable but it was so thick and gloomy that we could scarcely discern the banks of the Lake. We regretted this the more as we had visited this enchanting spot under such peculiarly favourable circumstances and as we had anticipated so much pleasure from our sail down the Lake we were the more sensible of our misfortune. It continued fair however until we had passed the village of Luss when the rain began to descend and continued without intermission until we reached Balloch which is at the extremity of the Lake. It was at this point also that the oar which I was using either from the unskilfulness of the Rower or from the rottenness of the material that it suddenly snapped and we were consequently deprived of two hands, a circumstance which tended very materially to impede our progress. We had now performed 13 miles out of 20 of this tedious voyage and 7 more remained to be passed over the narrow rapid and rugged bed of the Leven into which the Lake at this point discharged itself. The boatmen appeared perfectly ignorant of the navigation of this stream and came quite unprepared to meet the difficulty and dangers which we had to encounter from the extreme shallowness and impetuosity of the stream. From the former circumstance we were frequently aground and from the latter we were under considerable apprehension of being sucked under by the rapidity of the current and the numerous Dams or Leads which issue from this river. We passed several manufactories and the workmen seemed to look with astonishment at our novel and bold undertaking. At about 7 o'clock in the evening we reached our long wished for Port completely drenched and hastened with hurried steps to the inviting blazes of a Kitchen Fire. We partook of a comfortable dinner at the Inn and reluctantly parted with our fellow travellers who had taken their places for Glasgow.

## DUMBARTON, 15 SEPTEMBER

The few intervals of sunshine which we were allowed to enjoy this morning were employed in visiting the Castle and Church of this town, the only objects that are deserving of notice. The Castle of Dumbarton is situated on a narrow projecting rock and surrounded almost by the Frith of Clyde. The Fort itself though small and inconsiderable is generally occupied by a Garrison and is capable of containing 100 men. It is mounted with 21 pieces of Cannon and is commanded by a Governor General and was occupied by a Company of 60 men. The view from the summit of the Castle is very extensive and the Towns of Glasgow Port Glasgow and Greenock may be distinctly seen from this point. Upon my [**** ?returning] from my visit to the Castle I found that my Father had decided upon going this day to Greenock which we expected to accomplish without any difficulty from the vast number of Steam Boats which are seen continually upon the Clyde and which we had every reason to believe would call for Passengers at Dumbarton. We were very much disappointed to find that that Steam Boats did not call at Dumbarton and that it would be necessary to procure an open boat to convey us into the middle of the Frith which by this time had become extremely agitated. After having with some difficulty procured a Boat we continued for more than half an hour under the shelter of Dumbarton Castle in the expectation that a Steam Boat would shortly appear in sight. The storm raged most violently and we all secretly wished to return to Dumbarton and avoid the danger but at this moment we observed a Steam Boat in sight and being assured by our boatmen that there was no great cause for alarm we launched out into the Deep and giving made the usual signal to the Master to stop his engine we rowed along side and were not a little terrified to find that the Engineer had neglected his orders and that we were every moment in danger of being swamped by the quantity of spray thrown up by the wheels of the Engine. One of the men broke his oar in bringing to and we with the greatest difficulty were rescued from a watery grave.

Our joy upon finding ourselves once more in security may be more readily conceived than described though it was destined not to be of very long duration for the Steam Vessel which had all the time continued in motion had no sooner passed the Town of Port Glasgow than she got aground & stuck so fast that it was impossible to get her off. We were at this time about half a mile from land & notwithstanding the storm continued unabated we were compelled to trust ourselves to a cockshell of a Boat which was launched for the Conveyance of Passengers and were disembarked at a quarter of a mile distance from dry land, Rocks and Seaweed which the Tide had just quitted occupying the intervening space. It was about 6 o'clock in the Evening when we landed & about two miles from Greenock where we had the satisfaction after all our disasters of meeting with one of the most comfortable Inns in Scotland kept by Mr Parke.

## GREENOCK, 16 SEPTEMBER

The Town of Greenock being one of the most important Ports in Scotland the communication between the customhouses of this place is constant & frequent & this circumstance induced many persons connected with the Establishment to shew my father every attention. We were therefore called upon early this morning by Mr Johnston the Collector to introduce us to the Town and after accompanying him to the different places worthy of notice we dined with him at his house in the country on venison & other rarities. His house was situated upon rising ground immediately above the Town he had invited a large party to meet us & had two very agreeable girls for Daughters which upon the whole rendered our visit exceedingly pleasant. Amongst the number of visitors was a Gentleman of the name of Stuart but who seemed known to the rest of the Company only by the familiar name of Baillie from his being Steward to Sir Carmichael Shaw Stuart whose grounds are in the immediate vicinity of the Town. This individual treated [**** ?us] during our stay with the greatest hospitality and kindness and quite won Edward's heart by giving him a day's shooting in the neighbourhood where the Game is very abundant. Greenock though a very improving town appears at present to possess no very great attractions there being but one Street and Square of consequence and the Customhouse the Chief Ornament of the Town. It appeared to us to be quite the Liverpool of England, though of course very inferior in its public buildings.

# THOMAS ADAM:

## Journal of an Excursion to Loch Maree, 24 June to 13 July 1857

## Introduction

The journal, which is in private hands and has been kindly lent for this edition, is in a small green notebook, with the writing clear, if a little faded. It is an account of a three-week tour taken in the early summer of 1857 by rail, foot and coach to Loch Maree in the north-west of Scotland, starting from St Andrews on Wednesday 24 June, and concluding with the writer's arrival back at Greenock on 13 July. On the way north he moves at pace from Blairgowrie on to Ballater and Braemar, reaching Aberdeen on the Saturday. Sunday is spent quietly there, but Monday after a long day of travel finds him at Dingwall. Wednesday 31st sees him arrived at the foot of Loch Maree, staying at Kinlochewe for a few days before working his way south. A lengthy walk in the rain on the Tuesday is made even longer – 46 miles he claims! – by an incompetent guide, leading to a necessary rest over at Corpach. The final leg is by steamer to Greenock.

The assumption of the present owners of this journal is that the writer was Thomas Adam, a forebear of theirs, who died at the age of 74 in October 1913. Born on 15 July 1839, the second child of John Adams and Catherine Thornton of Forfar, Thomas entered the service of the Clyde Navigation Trust in 1862. He was an accountant, or so his occupation is entered in the 1881 census, when he and his family[1] were living at North Kilmarnock Road, Fife Place, Eastwood, in Renfrewshire. He later (c. 1890) became treasurer of the Trust and retired in May 1901 after sixty years of service. He was a keen fisherman and made good use of his free time: on Saturday 19 April 1902, after 1½ hours' struggle, he caught a record 36 pound salmon in Loch Lomond, as recorded in a photograph still held by the family. There is another photograph from Dingwall of him with three cheerful cronies.

There is a pleasing symmetry to the publication of this account by the Scottish History Society as Thomas Adam was himself a member. But there are some

---

1   According to the 1881 census, Thomas Adam, then aged 41, accountant, had been born at Forfar. His wife, Mary Lyle Jeffrey was aged 38, born at Paisley, and there were three children: Jane L. aged seven and Robert L. aged five, both born at Crosshill, Renfrewshire, and Thomas aged two, born at Shawlands.

niggling loose ends. The first is that Thomas Adam at the time of this tour in 1857 would have been only 18, yet the admittedly not infallible impression given by this account is of someone more mature and older, who is financially on a firm footing. More worryingly, there is a reference in the journal when he is at Glen Shiel, of having been there for the first time 'just about 16 years ago' and having often since then dreamt of the scene, which would be a remarkable legacy for a two-year-old child! So is this really Thomas's work, or if not, who else in the family wrote it? There is nothing that enables us to clarify this conundrum, or to get a better fix on the writer from internal clues other than a suggestion of a mercantile background at Liverpool. He refers to the experience of students at St Andrews but there is no listing of Thomas Adam in the matriculation registers of the period.

What matters here, of course, is the calibre of the account, the writer's eye for behaviour and his ability to describe scenes, such as the quack doctor in action at Aberdeen, the Blairgowrie excursionists, or the dismal sermon at Kinlochewe. His attention to detail, the names of the staff, the furniture and decoration, the listing of the books in the remote inn at Torridon, is remarkable. While scenery interests him, and he makes great efforts to identify each significant feature of the landscape through which he is travelling, people matter more; the ice cream seller, the photographer, the one-eyed coach driver, the slattern landlady.

But most distinctive of all, is his ear. Thomas Adam, if it is he, listens. To music, language and speech, how people speak and what they have to say. He takes down what the locals tell him – guides, drivers, waiters – in their voices. It is not often in tourist accounts that the visited get so much room.

## Note

The account, which Mrs Jean Macdonald has kindly lent, is written out very neatly in a small green 80-page volume, mostly only on the right hand side, but occasionally spilling across both sides. Thomas does write very clearly, and underlines in places for emphasis. One descriptive – and tedious – part of the account from 2 July 1857 has been omitted. Proper names are rendered as in the original with modern equivalents [thus]. The underlining in the original is reproduced, but punctuation and dating for the journal entries has been standardised for ease of reading.

# *Journal*

## WEDNESDAY 24 JUNE, TO BLAIRGOWRIE

Left St Andrews at 12 for Dundee and after calling on Mr Thomson (a burning walk it was) left Dundee by the Newtyle Railway for Blairgowrie.

Mr Thomson, who is about 84 or 85, when I congratulated him upon a capital calotype, (which really makes him look younger than he does) was evidently much disappointed. "That", said he, "That! It might be my grandfather."

I was rather disappointed with the view today from the old Castle immediately above Newtyle. It is the only fine view upon the route however and probably that made me admire it so much on a former occasion. It was a misty day in the distance too at this visit.

Disappointed also at Blairgowrie in finding there was no coach, as yet, to Braemar. It is not set agoing until July, and even then, the charges are high. I must therefore return to the railroad, and go to Dunkeld - thence to Pitlochrie (to see the scenery of Loch Tummell which is praised so highly by Dr McCulloch and Black's guide[2]) and then get to Rothiemurchus and Aviemore by the mail.

That weary moor where Dalwhinnie and Dalnacardoch lie seems to dodge me. This will be the third time I have past [*sic*] through it, most unintentionally, I can surely see something of that central mass of Scottish mountains from Rothiemurchus. It has the advantage, I suppose, of being an unfrequented way of approaching the Cairngorm range. Loch an Eilan, I see lies near it, and there are some fine old woods, it is said in the neighbourhood - rather skeletons of woods; well, I can surely make something of the route and see the Ben MacDhui range without going to Braemar after all. I grudge that long useless drive by Dalwhinnie however.

What a wretched <u>Manuscript book</u>! It is nearly as bad as Blotsheet. It is worse in one way, because it is more dishonest. Blotsheet does not pretend to be writing paper, but this does. The pen picks up hairs, bits of cotton and something else unknown every now and then. This is the way that the poor students at St Andrews are treated & cheated. Anything good enough for a student's notebook! Merchants manage booksellers better as my old Liverpool notebooks witness.

A very comfortable inn at Blairgowrie, Queens Hotel. I suppose Her Majesty has something to do with it as her portrait is on the landlord's bills. I got a

---

2    Dr John MacCulloch, *The Highlands and Western Isles of Scotland, containing descriptions of their scenery and antiquities* (London, 1824). Black's *Picturesque Tourist of Scotland* was in its 12th edition by 1856. While strong on Invernesshire and the north-east of Scotland, it carried only a brief notice of the country to the north and west of Dingwall, including Strathpeffer, with nothing on Loch Maree.

private parlour, (as there are a number of commercial gentlemen in the house) and after a very fairly served dinner am inclined to benevolent views of things in general. There is little to be seen here so I shall get up early, be off to Dunkeld by 8.20 minutes & see how to get on afterwards. A gig to Spittal of Glenshee from this place would cost about £1 and from that to Braemar 15/- more, rather a serious item to begin with. Tomorrow at Dunkeld, Friday Pitlochrie, Saturday to Rothiemurchus and Saturday, Sunday and Monday there - and Tuesday for Inverness and the far north. This may possibly do.

Had a serenade in the evening from some gentleman in the adjoining room, a stranger who arrived a little while ago with a lady. There's an old, jingling, out of tune piano there it seems, and he has really struck some sense and feeling out of it in accompanying himself. He sung two songs tastefully, pleasant to hear this; I never heard it before in similar circumstances. There seems to be a musicality about the house for in the bedroom adjoining mine there was a fiddler in the afternoon labouring away most valourously at the scomfishication [*sic*] of some Scotch reels & Strathspeys. He really seemed to be more in earnest about the squeals & jumps, the things that spoil music, than about any beauties in our dance music. However it is sometimes pleasant to hear even an ill played fiddle.

## BRAEMAR, THURSDAY 25 JUNE, 5 O'CLOCK

Scarcely slept last night for sweating. A most comfortable bed and room but overpowering summer heat - And to assist it a party of Blairgowrie teetotallers who had been on an Excursion to Cluny Castle gave me a serenade at one in the morning with trumpet and drums most villainously played and the rattling of two or three coaches, and some thunder at the door of the inn to get more drink. My landlord told me this morning that 'he banged out of bed' whenever he heard them and sent them about their business - which was to bang into their beds as soon as possible.

I was up at 6 and got a capital breakfast at 7. "You have changed your mind, sir", said the waiter. "Yes". Upon conversation & enquiry I thought it best to go on. Had I adopted yesterday's plan I could not have got to the Cairngorm range at all this trip.

So I hired a gig from Blairgowrie with a not very intelligent driver, a lad with but one eye though that was a piercer so far as to looking to the main chance was concerned. He's welcome to what he got however.

The drive to Spittal of Glenshee is by no means interesting on the whole. Craighall above Blairgowrie, the seat of Clarke Rattray (a colonel distinguished in the Creamy [Crimean] War as it is generally called in Scotland) is a fine object of its kind perched upon a wooded rock, on one of two fine turns in the wooded valley of the Ericht. A short glen above it, the Craigs of Leith, is also fine for depth of shadow and a sheer face of rock on one side but there is little or nothing else worth looking at until one reaches the end of Glen Shee where the Spittal is. Whether the inn bears that name, I know not, but it seems a good one. The room I was shown into was well furnished and on the walls were good engravings of Her Majesty and Prince Albert.

I left my one eyed charioteer here and got another to Braemar. The opening of Glen Beg in coming to the Spittal inn is rather striking. The shadows kept steady on the hills & I was able to make a sketch which I may colour but, whenever I had done, a rent in the clouds gave light upon one of the mountains in the background and (though the effect of the light itself was very beautiful) the whole charm of the previous picture vanished. It was quite a different scene & looked rather tame. So much does one touch of light or shade do in pictures.

The ascent at the upper end of Glen beg is very steep & at one part called the Devil's elbow, the abrupt zigzags of the road not very creditable to the engineer. The downward road after this is in Glen Cluny and Glen Cluny reaches to Braemar. Long drives both of them and though the country is mountainous (or Mountanious as it is generally termed) it's not very impressive. The forms of the hills are monotonous long elliptical curves occasionally rising into points promising grandeur but never exhibiting anything like it.

I noticed a remarkable quantity of juniper bushes on the upper hillside in Glen Beg. My driver told me there was a mineral spring having a salt taste and with red colour round it "up on the hill where they cast their peats". The name of the principal hill hereabout is the Kirnwell and her Majesty has travelled to Balmoral by this route. Such are all the memorabilia that I could gather of Glen Beg & Glen Cluny. In a nearer approach to Braemar, the distant mountain range was evidently much higher - larger in every way & with an amphitheatre form. The ridge had several abrupt lumps in it too which must be very large to be so prominent to the eye at such a distance. I found a tolerable inn and a tolerable dinner and am now ruminating how to proceed.

In approaching Braemar my Driver pointed out three things worth recording. The first was the prettiest man that wore the kilt in all this part of the Highlands. "Yes," said my Jehu, "I never saw a prettier man in a kilt. His legs are just like a horse's. But there's he's." On looking in the direction indicated, I saw a Sir John Falstaff sort of personage seated upon a wheelbarrow turned upside down - with a face like a cochineal-tinted cheese both as to form and colour - a grey jacket and kilt and a pair of knees and calves protruding - which were much more like an elephant's than a horse's. "That's him," said Jehu, "Aye, is that him?" said I. Jehu seemed pleased.

The second recordable thing was a bagpiper at a sheep shearing. Near Braemar we heard the skirl from the hillside, and Jehu, with a peculiarly jovial expression said, stopping the horse, "Do you hear that, sir?" "Yes, what is it?" "It's the pipes at a shearing. They're shearing the sheep; they'll maybe be three days at it there, & a fine time they'll have, they'll get their dinner & some drink & a dance at nicht." "Surely", I said, "the piper must have too hard work if he puffs and blows for three days and nights that way!" "Oh no", said Jehu, "it's what he likes well and when he's tired he can rest himself a wee." "And has the laird to pay the piper; and feast and dance the rest of them?" "Ou aye! They gather roun' frae a'about!" "Won't that be very expensive? Won't it be more expensive than regular wages to hired shearers?" "Ou aye! But it's the fashion of the country, just to keep up the old feeling."

And the third recordable thing was about a dozen stuffed foxskins hung up beside a gamekeeper's door. Very large animals they must have been. I asked my guide if they shot them hereabouts. "Yes, or trapped them; they couldna hunt them in a country like this." So *Punch* of last week is wrong in laughing at the story in the *Dumfries Courier* about a gamekeeper <u>shooting</u> a fox. But the English cannot conceive anyone doing otherwise than <u>they</u> do, for with all his great qualities John Bull has a few stupid self sufficiencies too.

After dinner took a walk to <u>Braemar Castle</u> as it is called, a white square tower with round projections at the corners and with the Dee flowing past it and large but shapeless masses of mountains all around. There is a tantalising peculiarity about the neighbourhood. One is always looking for some fine view but it has not yet, for me at least, made its appearance. On my going down I saw Dr Cook's brother and family at the other inn door; and on my return I met a fine little fellow who was at St Andrew's but whose name I cannot remember.

I am sorry to find that the grand mountain district here is a most bothersome affair. I got an old guide, Downie, to tell me all about it & first, there's <u>no</u> means of getting to Rothiemurchus with my luggage. Then if I go to see Cairngorm and Loch An and return hither, it will cost more than a pound, and hard work beside. I think I shall take the old man's hint and go and see the view from Morrer [Morrone] the hill opposite the hotel, the more especially that I fear the weather is breaking. Went to bed about ten, keeping to my rule of having only breakfast and dinner per day. Quite enough when one is travelling in warm weather.

## FRIDAY 26 JUNE

Rose at 6. Little sleep. Serenaded all night by the river at the side of my bedroom. I had rather it had, even in June all night long "sung its quiet song to the leafy woods" than to me. Perspired too freely and rose cold and uncomfortable but soon got fresh and made a hearty breakfast at 7. I then walked to old John Downie's by the Manse which seemed to be in a very primitive condition; the common ill-kept pasture up to the very door, no sign of anything approaching to taste or neatness, and the cows standing at the kitchen door, one of them half way in. Indeed, I lost my way owing to the slovenly direction of the <u>untidy</u> lass at the manse and found it by the obliging convoy of a little girl from Braemar who was driving her uncle's cows to the hill through the wood. John was preparing to come down as I entered his domain. He told me his was the highest inhabited house in Britain. (The Minister's house at Wanlockhead in Dumfriesshire certainly looks higher). We immediately went leisurely to the top of Morar & I was rewarded by a very comprehensive view of mountain ranges with their glens. That was all, however. The day was hazy, or as my guide said, "There's a good deal of gum in the sky", so that the sea and extreme distances were not visible but, though rather monotonous the view was unimpeded all round and the localities were interesting. North West lay the Ben Mich Dhuie [Ben Macdui] group. It comes in view a little below John's house immediately above Braemar & has rather disappointed me, both in its forms and indications of height. Cairn Toul to the west, Brae Riach in the middle and then Ben Mich Dhuie with Cairngorm lying lower between it and the spectator. Ben na Bhourd is to the east of Ben Mich Dhuie & Loch A'n lies between them but on the other side of the range.

To the west, nearly due west, appeared the long, cultivated and well wooded vale through which the Dee flows from Brae Riach. The course of it is visible for about seven miles and forms the only relief from the mountain monotony. Then, due west over glens and hills, appear the two distant summits of Ben y Gloe. And in front of them, Altanour, a decided looking chasm among the brown mounds in that quarter. Turning southward, the peak of the Kirnwell which I past yesterday between Glen Beg & Glen Cluny is seen, then due south, a still continued level but high range half way down which gleams Loch Callater & then, to the south east, careers away along the sky, the finest mountain mass & outline from this point of view Lochnagar. It rises gracefully & satisfies the expectation as to height and steepness much more than the Cairngorm range & in combination with Loch Callater & a smaller tarn higher up & nearer with prolonged mass of hill in front, forms a fine picture of its kind. That picture of its kind I have rarely seen on canvas however. Common, almost universally common as it is in Scotland & the lakes of England at least, I have as yet seen no type of it from any of our artists & that is the more remarkable because Colour and Form constitute the great characteristics of it. Detail is not required for the peculiar effect. Gradations of very finely varied grey blues from the farthest off summits and lines of mountain down through aerial greens and olives to rich velvet like browns with here and there streaky lines of as aerial reds and light greys, for channel'd courses or worn ridges of rock on the mountain slopes, appear to be nearly all required as to colours. As to form, none in nature can be easier to draw because in the particular case to be drawn, they never vary if taken from the same point of view. It is different with the human form and with trees and even with rivers and every other feature which usually enters into landscape.

After turning from Loch na Garr (with some reluctance) and looking eastward, there is only a more disappointing specimen of mountain monotony. No doubt Deeside goes down in that direction and Balmoral is there, and the ocean beyond it - and "you could see Balmoral with a spy glass, aye, and you could see further than Aberdeen", said John, but I have always thought that part of the scenery from a hilltop which requires a 'spyglass' to see it, was not intended to form the best part of the view; and so, therefore, I turned eastward notwithstanding my loyalty to the best of Queens that ever wore a crown.

North east was a long ridge of high blue mountain, like a wall, with several odd, abrupt, nodule looking stuck up bits of rock. This was Ben An - "the line of abrupt lumps" - which I noticed in approaching Braemar last night. And then, before coming again to the Cairngorm and Ben Mich Dhuie group, was Ben na Bourd a stately mass, but having the usual level outline to which there is unfortunately, so prevailing a tendency in the whole of this central mountain district of Scotland - with the exception of Loch na Garr. Cairntoul & Cairngorm may be similar to Loch na Garr from other points of view in gracefulness of outline, but not from this quarter. My guide was a very "ancient mariner" as to appearance of age. I thought him 65 at least. He said he was "about coming near to 55". I most impolitely asked him if these fine children's father was at home. "They're my children" said he. I did not say that I thought he was their grandfather. But although his face and hair indicated old age, his form and activity intimated plainly enough that he was by no means as old as he looked. He is a shrewd Highlander and a Highlander can be shrewd on many matters beside mere pocket money as a guide.

Here are a few of John Downie's scraps of intelligence.

1. "This poor law, sir, is doing no good to the country. There's no Charity now-a-days. It's all Law and little Justice. And then, although our men agree very well, I mean our three ministers (we've a Free ane and the Established ane, and a Roman Catholic) yet there's a great deal too much division, and I've always found the most ignorant, vulgar man was the man that talked the loudest and longest about their controversies. It just sets people by the ears like dogs. By the good luck it was a rare true thing that the Sheriff said when he asked me many

questions about the Highlanders and I told him a hantle [great deal] (but I did not know then that he was the Sheriff or I would have told him more) - says he, 'well, John, I'm glad to see Faith and Hope in the Highlands still, but I fear', says he, 'that Charity has gone for ever!'"

2. "Brae Riach is a word I don't know the meaning of. I call it 'Bry-yae' the head of the river Dee. I could put you to a good way of seeing Ben Mich Dhuie and Ben An & the rest of it, if you go to the keeper's lodge and stay there. I know him: you could tak' your leisure & see it all. Tak' a pound of tea & things with you, and little to the keeper for his trouble!" <u>This is evidently the way & I may try it next summer.</u> Not now!

3. "See there!" I saw two white sticks out of a peat moss looking hollow and then a beautiful roe's head and eyes looked up. John 'shu'd' and flung a stone, but the roe would not stir till we were within a yard of her when she suddenly seemed to see us and then made a noble spring & bounded out of the hole, turned to look at us, and then bounded off down hill, though not as quickly as I expected. "They get frichted and stupid for a wee when ye come upon them of a sudden", said John, "A-a-ch!

4. Though, they're nae guid to this country. Up the Glen Cluny there, where ye cam' down yesterday, sir, I have ken't there were 80 cows where there'e now but four. There were twenty farmers, and about maybe 8 in each family and now - when everything's in sheep - there'll maybe be only 6 shepherds required; and where there's deer forests (& the shepherds and sheep must then go away) there's maybe only 6 foresters for the same extent of district required. To be sure they use gillies, but that is only for two months in the year & people canna starve the other ten. But it'll be seen if you live six years - this depopulation of the Highlands will be seen one way or another." "How do you mean?" I asked, "What do you think will be the danger?" "Why, sir, the danger is where'll ye get men for war?" Then suddenly changing his tone, he said, "But sir, a gentleman that was up the hill with me ae day tried to make me see the richts o't this way! Says he to me, 'War's not now what it used to be when Highland men were required. It's now the gun. And if a man is just strong enough to draw a trigger, it is all that's wanted. When it was the sword and the bayonet and hand to hand, and a fair fecht between man and man, then the ould way micht do for keepin' up your Highlanders,' says he, 'But now the gun does it and if a man has but strength enough to draw a trigger, he can do as well for the army.' "Now," added John, "That's the way they don't need strong good men. They get weavers and broken down lads and poor manufacturing creatures frae the large towns, and the Army is not recruited as it formerly was."

Here however John took a start back to some region between Culloden and

Waterloo which he seemed to think the time of perfect recruiting. In conclusion upon this subject he lamented that the morality of the Highlanders was fast degenerating. The strangest instance he gave me was singular enough. "Formerly a young man that misbehaved had to walk on Sunday barefooted to the church for a twelvemonth; and then they smeared his face with ashes while he sat drest in a white sheet and he had to appear this way before the whole people! But nobody would submit to that now, sir", said John with something like with a sigh - (I began to suspect he was a papist) - "nobody would submit to that now, & Free Kirk & Establishment & Roman Catholic and all must just do as the people will have their own way! But I'll tell you what it is, sir", he added emphatically, "The best of us go away from the country & the worst of the Highlanders remain and the lads in bothies and farms are far waur than they used to be; and the Masters give a bad example to the servants and what wi' that & the deer forests & the sheep, the Highlanders are clean changed altogether."

"Did you never think of going to Canada?" I asked. "Na. Na." "Don't you think the Highlanders that emigrate will by and by perhaps lose all affection for their native hills & fight against us in an American war for instance?" John said most decidedly, "No, sir, for if I had been twenty years away and just cam' and lookit doun on yon farm (ye see't doun yonder) I was born there, I wad be just as fond o't as if I had never been away - for my grandfather lived there, sir, and his father for maybe two hundred years back!" "But," I rejoined, "supposing you left this country for Canada and a grandson of yours was in America when a war broke out with Britain, do you think your grandson might not enter the American army and fight against the Mother Country as some sailors did in American ships during the old war?" "No, sir! Because I have known a grandson of a man that lived away over yonder in a farm just behind yon hill, and he had been long away abroad but he came to see the place and travelled all the way and I believe every Highlander would do the same!" This clinched that part of the argument! Then said I, "John, may not the best part of the Highlander be better after all in Canada and elsewhere than contending with wealthy lairds about deer forests & sheep farms, if they still retain their good old qualities there and their remembrance of home and their loyalty and are getting on better than they could do here?"

John's answer was to this effect (though he had changed his ground a little) - "Well sir, if you want men to defend a country, the men must be in the country & born & bred up in it, and if this country is left without men, the enemy will soon find it out, and if you'll live six years ye'll see something aboot it!" Here ended the Socratic part of our Dialogue.

In asking him about the remains of national music about this part of the country, I found him ignorant of any. Very likely there are none. Any national music is fast disappearing in Scotland. Any taste for it seems to exist only in two bad extremes, the one for the lowest bagpipe rants, the other for the so called fashionable Fantasia & polka & mazourka music of some of the London publishers.

But I was amused at his account of the real reason (as he said) why a bagpiper was employed at a sheep shearing in this part of the country. I told him that I heard one in coming down Glen Cluny last night. "Ah", he said, "do you ken what that's for?" "To amuse them and have a dance afterwards!" "Well", said he, "it amuses them and they often dance afterwards, but the principal raison is that, when a large party is shearin', and there's a number of women, the women by themselves get into talking of nonsense and things amang themselves & they don't get on with their wark - so the bagpiper strikes up and it <u>bumbaazes</u> [bamboozles] them. They can't hear one another speakin' for the sound of the pipes and it <u>bumbaazes</u> them, you understand, sir."

This was a little different from my Jehu's account about "keeping up the old feeling" but there are always two sides to a story and sometimes indeed more than half a dozen. I have often heard of the bagpipes rousing the men, but I never heard before of them bumbaazing the women.

I found on the hillside when returning many of the leaves and but two flowers of the <u>Rubas Chamoemorus</u>, the cloudberry, the "averins" as Downie called it. He said it was very plentiful formerly but not of late and was esteemed wholesome but not <u>preserved</u> here.

We found a fragment of a deer's horn. He said that after shedding their horns every year the deer generally "gnaw and crunch them" so that comparatively few shed horns are found in their walks. It was cool and pleasant on the hill but scorchingly hot in the descent, and after giving John his 4/- for the guideship, I came home from Morar at 2 and dined at five and wrote till 6.

I have been thinking about that Keeper's house in the wilderness for Saturday & Sunday night and am still hesitating. If it were only a little nearer Loch A'an! But - No! It would, I see, be two pounds at least of itself, going & staying & returning. I must not think of it at present. So let me see about Aberdeen tomorrow morning and the far north immediately.

Expenses (of going & coming) from Braemar and Ben McDhuie & Loch Aan.

| *Going* | *Staying* | *Returning* |
|---|---|---|
| 10/- to guide | 1 lb tea | 7/- for gig |
| 7/- for gig | 1 leg mutton | 2/6 for driver &c &c &c |
| 2/6 for driver | gratuity | |

In the evening I went to the other inn to enquire concerning the conveyance to Ballater tomorrow. The conveyance is by a mail gig carrying six, which goes at 4 in the morning. A coach however begins to run on Wednesday first. The landlord of this inn, an intelligent & blunt but obliging fellow, told me that two ladies had come to his house yesterday from Aviemore by Ben MacDhuie, and gave me a specimen of how comfortable a night's lodging may be had occasionally at the celebrated Shelter Stone on Loch A'an side, by describing how a party of gentlemen (of whom he was one) had dinner there, "with champagne and toddy, playing at cards for sweethearts, with capital heather beds for sleeping on, a bath in the loch at morning, with scented soap, by George, & towels & all that, and salmon trout and eggs and tea to breakfast." An old wife (I was told by Downie) used to stay at it during a part of the summer & sell whisky, but "they drave her oot", he said, "for fear of spoilin' the deer, ye ken", whether by her whisky or her visitors, John did not say.

I took a walk in the woods of Invercauld at the suggestion of the landlord, but at the risk of being challenged by gamekeepers; I saw a fine view of Invercauld House but nothing else of consequence and got back about 9, to have a bowl of warm milk & cream, and got to bed at 10. Braemar has not come up to my expectations. There are some fine vistas along the river (Cluny) but the mountains, though large, are shapeless. Four or five of them surrounding the wide valley are more like stranded whales than anything else. They have hugeness of bulk certainly but neither the grandeur nor the grace necessary to make mountains interesting.

## SATURDAY 27 JUNE

Slept little, almost none, & rose at twenty minutes past 3. A most lovely morning. Shouldered my knapsack & walked to the other inn amid the singing of birds, the pleasant noise of waters, the scent of birches & wild flowers, and the glory of spring at its full maturity. For spring is late here, but none the less beautiful for that, and I think that beyond all question, the finest time of the whole year is just when spring is passing into summer. Autumn cannot compare with it. "Youth is full of pleasaunce, Age is full of care." And even the boasted hues of autumnal woods are to my eye gaudy & glaring compared with the exquisitely tender & wonderfully varied colours of spring.

We got away about half past four, three of us in front of the Mail cart & three behind. I had the privilege of being smoked nearly as fully as a Welsh ham or a Finnan haddock, by the driver and seemingly a drover in front; both of them were using very bad tobacco too. However, the drover left us soon and I stept into his place immediately.

It is a fine drive all the way to Ballater. I was rather disappointed with Balmoral as seen from the road. It stands too staringly out in the middle of the valley, and the number of outhouses & detached buildings of various kinds gives the palace somewhat of the appearance of a large church tower in the centre of a considerable village. The woods as yet are young or at least small and low, and in this respect the place has less seclusion & dignity than I thought it had. But the situation, as regards the river, is fine & they say that no one can form an idea of the beauty of the place till you are at it. "I had a vision of my own" - of Balmoral however, decidedly finer than what I saw today.

Abergeldie, the Duchess of Kent's residence is further down the Dee, plain & unpretending, and the Prince of Wales' estate, Birkhill, still further down, near Ballater, & still more unpretending.

But the great glory of this morning's drive was the view of Loch-na-gar and of Balloch Buie (which is the name, I was told, of the extensive pine forest around the base of the mountain & skirting the river) Perhaps the best point of view is on the bridge of Invercauld, about 3 miles below Braemar. There is a fine view from the bridge up the river with the high blue ridge of Ben A'n in the distance; but it is nothing in comparison with the splendid amphitheatre of dark pine woods rising, tier above tier (like those which hung above the dethroned Saturn in Keats' wonderful fragment of Hyperion), the grand foreground of the river, with its characteristic rocks & rapids, & the majestic masses of Loch na Garr more graceful in their outlines than ever, receding far over all, as if away into a region so truly pure & beautiful as to deserve indeed the name of heaven. I have seen nothing so fine in its way before. The range of wood especially was quite new to me; seen from the road a little way below the bridge, it conveyed the impression of depth, closeness and extent to a degree unequalled in my remembrance. And from both points of view, grand size of objects, vastness of space, beauty of form, grandeur of arrangement, & mingled fineness & force of colour, presented the noblest picture of one good mountain I have ever met with, I deeply regret that I had not known of it before. I hope I may be able to spend a day or two at it next year. The morning, to be sure, was remarkably fine, and I may have seen it to unusual advantage but, if the objects themselves - mountain, wood and river are only visible - I can scarcely conceive a sky under which they could not be most impressive.

The drive by Deeside is fine, all the way to Ballater and for several miles below it. We had to wait at Ballater from 7 till 1, & an ill served breakfast & an ill tempered girl who served it, do not sweeten the remembrance of the inn. But the neighbourhood is pleasing. The view from the bridge adjoining the inn is good both up and down. The former view including Birkhill, the Prince of Wales' estate, & the latter Moutraltrie [Monaltrie] house belonging to Invercauld, and a long reach of the Dee with a good <u>Corrie</u> in the hills above it.

Invercauld's property extends (along the route I have come) from above Blairgowrie to below Ballater. I was pleased to hear the genuine old Aberdonian accent once more, which I did all the way from Braemar during this day's drive. Among the people generally, it is much the same. The richer and poorer speaking it pretty nearly alike. To my ear there's something musical in it though it is not nearly as sweet as the pure Highland accent in speaking English as I have heard it about Inverness and the Highlands generally. The vulgar drawls of my own dear Calf Country the <u>tones</u> (as we used to call them by way of compliment I presume) the tones or <u>twangs</u> either of Greenock, Paisley and Glasgow are an <u>abomination</u> in comparison. Today, at Ballater, I was amused by a very pure bit of Aberdeenshire Doric. The coach had arrived from Banchory and after the passengers had departed the guard was searching the boot as it is called, "Here's twaa thingies sin last nicht!" said he, handing out a travelling bag and an old rope). "Aye" said the clerk who was standing beside the coach, "An' there's a wee laddie's clokkietee but a donna kin faa's eest." As nearly as I can tell, that was the sentence. I could scarcely help laughing. The meaning was "Aye, and there's a little boy's cloak too but I don't know whose it is." The tones of the sentence were as Aberdeen as was the pronounciation. They might very nearly be indicated thus:-[Treble clef drawn in text here][3]

It is from kindliness I think that the Aberdeenshire people are so addicted to diminutives in description - a roady, a hillie, a housie, and a hundred and fifty more, are common expressions. The "wee laadie's clokkietee" had something touching in it. The clerk was a gigantic young man six feet six inches. He said he was that height (when a fellow passenger asked him) & he looked it: but he evidently felt that the unknown little boy might be needing his clokkietee for there was an accent of regret in the "donna kin faa's eest!"

It was after Ballater I think that the coachmen pointed out the farmhouse where Lord Byron passed part of his childhood. He said the bed was still preserved in which Byron slept and some, not very interesting, anecdotes of his childhood are current in the neighbourhood.

Long before reaching Aboyne the country became almost dreary. Morven a very large looking mountain, was the only redeeming feature of the district. Aboyne itself is a remarkably neat and clean looking place. So were all the towns we passed - Banchory in particular. But there we found the railroad and got into

---

3    Stave of music drawn in text here, with the notes showing the rise and fall of the voice to the sentences "Aye. An' there's a wee laddie's clothie tae. But I dinna ken faa's eest."

Aberdeen and into the Douglas Hotel close by the station, and after dinner at 7 o'clock here we are at this present writing. I took a walk through the <u>two streets</u> of this metropolis of the North East of Scotland. It seemed to be a more than usually idle evening for the pavements were crowded with lads chiefly of the working classes and about the Market Cross there were several booths for the sale of confectionaries, <u>two sellers of ice cream</u> and one quack doctor, in addition to about a dozen women, each at her own "receipt of custom" - selling haddocks and <u>seaweed or Dulce</u> as it is sometimes called, and something else about which I missed the opportunity of enquiring.

The most popular merchant was the man who sold <u>Ice Creams</u> with a tin jar full of ice, among which he was continually rumbling, another jar full of some creamy composition - he stood on a stool beside a small table with spoons and very small glasses and a great number of pence and half pence displayed to view. His appeal was by no means as clever as an English hawker's or an Irishman's like the Quack, but he had an astonishing number of customers. It was amusing to watch their faces upon what was evidently their first taste of Ice Cream. Some screwed their mouths but most were rather pleased and a number seemed determined to show no emotion but to retire and meditate upon the new sensation.

The quack is plainly enough <u>Irish</u> to the backbone, tho' he has a German coat and a French moustache. He attempts practice it seems in town and takes this way of courting it. He exhibited a <u>cashew nut</u> upon the point of a skewer (presuming I suppose that none of his audience ever saw such a thing before) and burnt it at a tallow candle (which he had great difficulty in sticking upon the top of a board) telling us while doing so that he was now showing the great problem "how to find the centre of gravity" - and as the nut jetted out its oil in flame he told us that this was a "most wonderful and mysterious production of an inscrutable providence. This nut was known to the Ancients, to Galen, to Socrates, to Hippocrates & to Lennyus (Linnaeus, I presume). Its most wonderful virtue is to cure the toothache and if any man, woman child here has the toothache, I'll cure them instantly with a drop of this nut oil, or I'll forfeit - <u>the City of Aberdeen.</u>"

Whether this meant that he would immediately be off from the city or whether he meant to impress us with some vague notion of his extraordinary wealth I know not but it was received with a hum of applause from some and a laugh of derision from others. The nut, however, was evidently a novelty to them all and they seemed to respect it.

He then handed round some white stuff saying it was a cure for - <u>everything</u>! I tried it and found it insipid enough, but it made me sneeze. A tall consumptive looking lad beside me took some also and after sneezing held his handkerchief to his nose with a perplexed air. He took the handkerchief away for a moment and the blood came pouring down on it rather violently. With an oath he said to me, "he's made my nose bleed wi' his snuff!" "Apply to him then to cure you," I replied. He was shy about it but as we were speaking the quack caught our eyes and turned to the lad. "What's the matter?" "My nose is bleeding wi' your snuff!" "Oh, that's because you're of a delicate constitution, and that's the very way it should operate upon fellows like you! Come here! Come here, man! Hold up your head and let me catch your nose!" He then "catchit his nose", gently passed his forefinger and thumb up and down it, gave it a twist with a sort of knowing manner - though not at all violently - and said very confidently, "There now!" Go home at once and you'll find yourself better of that pinch of my snuff tomorrow than you have been for five years before. I see you are of a delicate constitution and that's just the thing for you!"

The above is, I believe, nearly <u>verbatim</u>. <u>Literatum</u> it could not be without the <u>brogue</u>. The poor fellow, with his nose still buried in his handkerchief and very pale, walked off immediately. I followed to advise him (as I thought I could do better than the quack) but he began to run and I lost sight of him in a side street where of course I could not follow in the circumstances.

Home at 10. A glass of toddy and to my bedroom where I now am in hope of a good sound sleep to make up for the want of <u>three</u> nights' rest.

## SUNDAY 28 JUNE

Lay long and was not in time for forenoon service. Attended church in the afternoon and then had a walk by Balgownie Brig and Donside. Saw a very fine view of the old cathedral and the Don from a bye road a good way beyond the Brig and leading down to a mill. Returned and had coffee which by no means agreed with me. I had indigestion and palpitation after it. Went to bed early.

## MONDAY 29 JUNE

At 8 on a drizzly morning, left Aberdeen for Inverness by railway. The railroad is completed only to Keith.[4] From thence to Nairn we had a coach. At Nairn we had to wait for an hour and a half as the engine had broken down in going to Inverness in the forenoon so that we did not get thither till half past six in the evening.

The day was so wet and misty that there was very little to be seen on the

---

4    The Inverness & Aberdeen Junction Railway had been authorised in July 1856 to complete the eighteen-mile link between Nairn and Keith, and work was underway, to be finished in August of 1858.

journey, and the weather seemed to have a saddening effect upon the passengers, for a more woebegone and taciturn set of travellers I have seldom met with. I saw Benochie [Bennachie] however once more & it looked larger than I expected. I saw Huntly Castle also, a fine looking ruin towering above some respectable looking wood, and situated apparently on the river which has the name of Bogie above Huntly, and Devron [Deveron] below.

After leaving Keith, (where I saw one of the very finest faces I think I have ever seen) we crost the hill of Fochabers, first a wide cold moor, with a great many cottars houses on it, and then some extensive woods and a large ravine, going down upon Fochabers. At Fochabers there is a splendid educational establishment - the building in good taste erected from the legacy of a Mr Mills and in which our driver told me "the whole parish has every sort of education for everybody, rich and poor, with books too and everything provided free and gratis for nothing."

I was very much pleased with the remains of "The Lamp of the North", Elgin Cathedral, which the Wolf of Badenoch on one occasion lighted up rather strongly. The ruins were smaller and indicated a less extensive building than I thought it had been - but all was very beautiful - of a more ornamental style than either Glasgow or St Andrews and nearer Melrose in elegance than any other of our Scottish cathedral churches. But I had merely a <u>Race View</u> of it and regretted much that I had no time to see the interior.

The only additional things of interest for me on the rest of the day's journey were the finely mingled woods skirting the road on both sides after leaving Elgin - a brief sight of the Spey and as brief a sight of that fierce flood maker, the Findhorn, with its handsome suspension bridge & the enormous mounds of gravel washed down by its spates. The woods, away into the interior beyond it, seemed to indicate deep channels and rapid descents but it was a mere glimpse which I got of them. In addition to these I had a noble view of parts of Sutherland, Ross and Caithness stretching away to the north east on the opposite side of the Moray Firth in a continuous line of mountain land. Coachee however knew nothing of the names of the hills and the rest of the party were preserving their consistency in being silent and sulky as they had been from the first. At Nairn where the railroad began again, of course, the scenery ended - and we were soon at Inverness.

After dinner in the Caledonian Hotel (served in a very offhand way by one of the most intolerable puppies in the shape of a waiter I have yet met with, effeminate, discourteous and <u>greedy</u> in the extreme) I went to the riverside and then to the Castle hill. The views from it both up and down the river are noble. The sun was setting in fine style behind the western shoulder of Ben Wyvis; and mountain, sky, river and city made a picture exactly suited for Turner alone to give permanence to.

On making enquiry I found I could get to Dingwall by mail at 12 the same night so, although the Loch Maree coach does not go from Dingwall until Wednesday, I thought I might as well take a day there and have the chance too, of having a less insufferable waiter to get my dinner from.

At 12 we started by coach. The night was mild at first and the sky tolerably clear. The lovely light of sunset never seemed to fade away. The stillness and mystery of the dewy midsummer night was delightful as ever. And a higher quality felt to be in it recalling to one's mind the Bible description of that better country concerning which it is said, "There shall be no <u>night</u> there, for God shall be the light of it." I could have gone onwards, although the cold was becoming sharp, but my destination was Dingwall where I found a comfortable Inn and a most obliging waiter and went to bed about three in the morning.

## TUESDAY 30 JUNE

Rose at nine after a most refreshing sleep and made an enormous breakfast. Walked about the town and found both it and the neighbourhood cleanly and pleasing. Took a look at Ben Wyvis from the heights above the town and then tried a sketch or two. Made up my accounts (which I find have been foolishly lavish) and then wrote up journal which brings me to the present half past four o'clock. So now for dinner, without the fear of a puppy before my eyes to hurt my digestion.

And an excellent well served dinner I had with a clever little obliging laddie of a waiter, Johnny by name whose father is dead and whom, Mrs Robertson, the landlady, has taken in hand. Johnny will never turn out a puppy flunky, I think. There's too much natural kindness and simplicity in him. I asked him, while standing at the door in the forenoon, whether there was anything in particular to be seen about Dingwall and the neighbourhood. "No, sir," said he, "not at present", but with a face of delight at the remembrance, "but there were two shows last week with tumblers and dancers and people taking pictures - likenesses of people".[5] Such was Johnny's notion of things worthy to be "seen in Dingwall". There seems little or nothing of the Lowland Scotch tongue here. All Gaelic and English, but there is a distinction which even in passing along the street the ear can catch between correct and incorrect teaching of English. I noticed it in several instances. The following is a specimen. Three or four little kilted boys

---

5    *The Inverness Advertiser* of 23 June 1857 records that a Mr Hay from Princes Street, Edinburgh was in Inverness taking photographic portraits 'in a few seconds'.

were poking with a long stick in a very narrow opening between the walls of the two houses. One of the boys, a rather aristocratic looking fellow, the other a true shock red-headed son of the hills! "What are you doing?" said I. "Have you lost a bonnet?" - No, sir," said shock head, "it's a pudgeon!" "A dove," said the other boy, <u>correctively</u> and <u>apologetically</u>.

There's a monument here in wretched taste, a tall obelisk leaning to one side as if Dingwall wishes to imitate Pisa and Saragossa by having a leaning tower too. I was surprised at what seemed either the shyness or the ignorance of the people about it. I asked four persons and they seemed unwilling or unable to tell me why and for whom it was built. One old man when I said, "Whose monument is that?" immediately began to jabber in Gaelic. On being made to understand that I had "no Gaelic" he said, "Oh! Well, they first beeried him and then they built it!" "Yes," I asked, "but who was buried there?" The answer was: "It was after he was beeried that they built the Monument." This being rather superfluous information I thanked him and came away - but all I could learn was that either an "Earl of Cromarty" or "somebody else", being afraid that some indignity would be perpetrated upon his grave (something of this kind having been threatened by an enemy) got his surviving friends to watch his grave until this monument was built to guard the spot from the profanation. They had been in such a hurry however that the crazy pile would not stand upright so they bolted and barred it with iron bars as well as they could and there it stands or rather leans to the great annoyance of Dingwall, and its people, and its visitors until this day.[6]

But enough of Dingwall. On Wednesday 1st July, I was called by Johnny most punctually at five o'clock in the morning and after paying a very moderate bill, set off for Loch Maree on the top of the mail. The morning was cloudless, clear and cold. There is nothing of interest between Dingwall and Strathpeffer except the evidences of <u>good farming</u> still more observable in other parts near the town. At Strathpeffer the invalids were walking about in considerable numbers and variety at such an early hour in the morning. Beyond this, the scenery was bleak-looking with a slight approach to wildness of character, but not decided enough, and the only object with anything of grandeur about it was Ben Wyvis which seemed to have walked after us, for it had very nearly the same look at 12 miles from Dingwall to which it had there. As we went on, there was a gradual change. Mountains of the true Highland type began to make their appearance

6   This obelisk was a memorial to the first Earl of Cromartie, and thrown lightly off the perpendicular by an earthquake in 1816, according to Francis H. Groome (ed.), *Ordnance Gazetteer of Scotland* 2 (London, 1894), 355.

suddenly standing up (from behind long sweeping hills and valleys) with sharp and steep outlines against the pale blue horizon sky. First came "Fannich", once a great sheep walk and celebrated for its mutton, according to the Driver's account, but now a deer forest and celebrated for its venison. Then and now equally respectable as a "Hielan Hill". Then came Scuir Vuillin [Sgurr a Mhuilinn] which plays a prominent part from every point of view in the scenery of the district & then we had a distant view of the Torridon hills & very abrupt and singularly coloured they were; & then came the beautiful Loch Cullen. From either end this is a fine loch, well wooded on the north side and with a pensive though noble beauty about it well worth a landscape painter's study. It is a scene which comes completely within the limits of his department in Art too, which many great and beautiful scenes do not - but we must, on, on, on and at length we were at Achnasheen.

Here the mail left me to go in another direction and I went onwards in a gig with a very obliging and well informed driver. We first came in view of two, and then three, of these Torridon and Loch Carron hills with singularly shaped peaks and ridges and still more mighty colours, fine reds and whites being most prominent and then a beautiful sheet of water clear and unruffled as the most perfect glass and reflecting the heaven and earth as only water can. This was Loch Rosque and of a simpler but grander character than Loch Cullen it had the same advantage of presenting fine views from either end; having the Torridon mountains to reflect on the west and Scuir Vuillin with its long blue mass and four fine peaks on the east end.

I should add that I think it was hereabouts twenty-four miles or so from Dingwall that at last on turning a corner we lost sight of the ubiquitous Ben Wyvis. I thought he was never to disappear. On looking back at any time during the whole twenty-four miles the old gentleman seemed still as if looking over your shoulder and became tiresome.

On leaving Loch Rosque we had still these fine Torridon mountains to gaze at until, after a long walk (to spare the horse) up a steep winding part of the road, a turn to the right and another climb brought us to the head of Glen Dochart. Here the gig came up, and in a minute or two - Lo - Loch Maree!

An intensely deep blue distant expanse in an immense hollow with aerial purples and browns and greys rising from it on all sides into mountain conveyed first the idea of Loch Corursk [Loch Coruisk or Coire Uisg] expanded into ten or twenty times its size and set before me at a great distance. But the scene almost instantly assumed a character of its own and one which it still keeps with me after a day's travel along its banks. No doubt this point of view owes much, perhaps most of its effect, to the change of form and colour from what is seen all along the previous part of the journey and to the suddenness with which it comes upon the spectator. (This may account for the comparative disappointment which it gives in a picture such as Fleming's. The picture, however good, does not seem to answer the enthusiastic description which accompanies it because the spectator of the picture has not been previously prepared like the Traveller). It is a grand sight however.

I found a plain but comfortable inn at Kinlochewe about a mile or two from the head of Loch Maree. In approaching the inn the scenery became truly magnificent. But of this I shall have occasion to speak afterwards. Having had no breakfast at Dingwall I had it here at 10 o'clock and an excellent breakfast it was and so well served that I have now forgotten everything about the puppy waiter, excepting his fast vanishing shadow into oblivion and forgiveness. After breakfast I walked down Loch Maree side 7 miles and back just in time for dinner at 6 o'clock and here I am after dining and dressing and making up my journal at half past 8 precisely.

On coming down Glen Dochart after the first view of the Loch, the traveller is beginning perhaps to think that the end next to him wants dignity as Glen Dochart has nothing to attract attention. But suddenly, a noble mountain towers into the sky upon the left as the valley widens - then another still more magnificent (and remarkable from the nearly pure white of its peaks and corries), then again another and another though more distant until four great and beautifully varied masses of Mountain Majesty stand rising into the blue air before him in a range so wide that slight turns of the head are necessary to enable the eye to command them as it were at once. These are reckoning from right to left hand Sleugach (or to the right Sleuach as they pronounce it here) [Slioch][7] and beneath him stretches away Loch Maree - then MeeEwes [Meall a'Ghuibhais] one of the outriders of Beinn Eigge [Beinn Eighe] (to the left) then Ben Ae [Beinn Eighe] or the File Hile (from its sharp outline like a file) & the final group of the Loch Carron hills. Beyond Sleugach too is Ben Arrichar [Beinn Airigh Charr] at the far end of Loch Maree though lower than the others and more distant, and nearer on the right is Benzieboonie [Beinn a'Mhuinidh] though his high rocky side is seen only in perspective. It is a glorious view though from its great range scarcely transferable to canvas.

The road down the lochside so far as I went today is delightful; everywhere commanding scenery of the finest kind whether as to loch, mountain or wood. In one respect Loch Maree is totally different from any that I have seen, and it is this - for 3 or 4 miles the mountain Sluach [*sic*] rises opposite you like an

---

7   Note that variant spellings used for Slioch are: Sleugach, Sluach, Sleuch, Sleuch.

enormous perpendicular wall - seen apparently without a break from top to bottom and rising into more sheer precipice-like attitude as you advance. When you are about half way down the lochside, the upper half, especially Sleuch, assumes this wall like appearance and seeming actually to come closer upon the eye in consequence conveys an impression of height most astounding. I question whether a mountain three times the height of Sleuch but retiring from the spectator could produce the same feeling of extraordinary tallness.

About 5 miles from the inn, the wooded part of the road ceases and the road itself turns from the loch to the moorland for a mile or two but as if to compensate for the loss of the fine old pines and graceful birches two conical blue mountains of new shapes and sharp outlines immediately appear on the left rising solitary from a wide deer forest and detached from any of the other mountains connected with the district. At this point I turned back to Linlochlewe & saw the upper part of Sleuch starting sharply from the high ridge on which it rests more abruptly than ever over the dark blue narrow expanse of the stern but still beautiful loch and I enjoyed the walk back so greatly that I am still in doubt whether it is preferable to approach this lovely region for the first time from the upper or lower end.

I am not disappointed with Loch Maree & that is saying a great deal. I had of course 'a vision of my own' and a really good one but it was far inferior to the reality. There is so deep a solemnity along with a pure beauty both so blended that I remember nothing in Scotland to equal it. The same remark is so often made of all mountain lochs, sternness and beauty mingled, forms indeed their characteristic description. But in none that I know is the description more true than in this one.

It still continues to possess one rare quality and I hope it long may do so. No villas adorn its banks, no *olla podridas*[8] of architecture crowning with their turreted abominations (as Chalmers would have said) the very finest features of the scenery - praise be blest it is too far from either Edinburgh or Glasgow. Neither Lords of Session nor fortunate merchants can conveniently build modern palaces here. The buttresses of Sluech have scarcely a shepherd's sheiling on them. The lofty pines and waving branches of MealEwes [Meall a'Ghuibhais] have plenty of tall heather (sometimes four feet high) among them but no bowling greens and closely shaven lawns around their Merchant Boxes. The very mention of the thing seems profanation here. All honour of course to the enterprise which increases wealth but it is an advantage that a true Highland loch can be seen in all its old, genuine sternness - yet 'beautiful exceedingly' with

8   A Spanish stew with many ingredients.

nothing of man's work except the road. And even the road is not obtrusive. In Loch Lomond, Loch Etive, Loch Katrine and Loch Tay we can trace human interference. Here all seems as God left it.

The evening was splendid. I took another walk after tea to a wooden bridge crossing the river and had an opportunity of seeing, in addition to a fine sunset, a double shadow. The sun was imaged in the water and the light from that image was so powerful as to throw my image on the bank in combination with the shadows in connection with the sun itself. It was in a different direction of course however and the two shadows presented the appearance or indication rather of two persons walking together but the one so much above the other that his feet seemed on the level of the other's knees. I mention this among other incidents of Loch and mountain scenery because it is in such localities that these things are most to be seen.

I found a snug clean bedroom and had a sound rest but only after an hour or two as in the room next to mine some of the neighbours were having a gill and were most eloquent in Gaelic, probably about wool and the prospects of the sheep market. However silence came at last, and with it, sleep.

## THURSDAY 2 JULY

I rose at six with the determination to ascend Sleuach and after breakfast, my landlord, Mr McRae, provided a guide for me. On asking McRae what would be a fair remuneration for the guideship, I was most agreeably surprised to hear him say, "Oh! Two shillings will be quite enough." At Ben Nevis a guide charges <u>ten.</u> On going to the door to look at Sleuach I found a tall gentlemanly looking fellow with a basket slung round his shoulders. Thinking he was some youth upon a fishing excursion, I addressed him accordingly, when I found that he was my guide & that the basket contained our provision. "How can I offer that chap two shillings?" thought I. He was very obliging and a most capital guide as to the mode of climbing and descending a steep hill. He quietly led me along - up crags and down precipices which, by myself, I should never have dreamt of venturing. Insuperable difficulties seemed to vanish before him. One steady step to a side or one sudden turn round a corner transformed toil into ease, and danger into safety. We had a long walk to the base of the Mountain, & then a very hard pull up the eastern shoulder of it. "How do we go now?" I asked, as the rocky rampart rose above us, and so abruptly that it looked as it would tumble upon us. "Right up", quoth John Murchison. Right Up!! The only way to do this seemed to be to get feet like flies, that can walk upon a ceiling, with their heads downwards. However, right up we did go, & just when I was beginning to feel very queer in looking up, and still more queer in looking down, one of John's quiet turns to the right landed us on level ground, more than half way up the whole mountain. And with the grand sight before and around us of the <u>Corrie of Sleuach</u>.

After this (with the exception of one rocky bit on a higher shoulder) the ascent was quite easy, & over fine soft green turf. We found a small tarn of fine clear water just beneath, and saw a smaller one very near the top. At twelve exactly we stood on the summit having been just four hours in accomplishing the journey. The ridge of Sleuach forms a huge curve, very nearly semi-circular. At one end of the curve is the boulder like mass, over which we climbed. At the other extremity there is a high sharp pointed peak, called Ben Tarsling or the Spirehill. In the middle bend of the curve is the peak of Sleuach proper. All around on the outside of the semicircle are perpendicular precipices and buttresses of rock; all within the curve is an immense hollow, in which the slope of the ground is comparatively gradual, & covered with grass and heather. Any mode of ascending the hill must be either in the way we did so, or up the hollow. The view from the summit amply repaid the labour of getting to it. I have not seen a finer mountain view indeed I never saw a mountain view at all to be compared to it. My guide unfortunately knew next to nothing about the objects in sight but it was not difficult from my own knowledge of locality to make out a tolerable list. Loch Maree with its many islands at the lower end, Meal Ewes, & the File Mountain, while beyond them, we saw Skye from Dunvegan on to the Sound of Sleat.[9] [. . .]

After remaining about an hour, we began our descent and arrived at the inn about 5 o'clock having been away about 9 hours. I was never so much pleased & so little fatigued upon any such excursion. After having more than satisfied my gentlemanly & gentle guide who, though rather taciturn & uninformed & a great smoker, was invaluable as a leader in climbing - remarkably so. I took a walk to the churchyard, a lonely spot at the head of the loch with a fine large old tree in the centre & some others round it. The wall was broken down, however, the ground open to cattle & utterly neglected. Whatever may the reason, such a sight is a disgrace to the people. What should be an ornament is a reproach at Loch Maree. On enquiring afterwards I was told it was a flood in the river which had broken down the walls and overswept it. This might be prevented by a bank however and at any rate the rough stone wall would not take a day's work for two men to rebuild it. "Canna be fashed [Can't be bothered]", is the explanation.

## FRIDAY 3 JULY

Rose at nine having another dose, not of sleep but of Gaelic, after going to bed, the next room being again occupied by three or four Celts who were either

---

9   Section omitted: about two pages of description of the view from the summit.

swearing at the whisky or trying extempore philippics against excisemen. At length one began to sing, but it was such a horrible howl accompanied with such a splutter and hotch potch of unpronounceable consonants, that even his companions seemed disgusted, for the party immediately broke up telling their Apollo as I understood them to "hould his tongue and be-something to him." And so they clattered with their heavy brogues like a cataract of rocks down the wooden stairs and after a short hullabaloo at the front door, off they went and silence and sleep once more succeeded.

Oddly enough I felt rather amused instead of being annoyed at this nightly palaver so I said nothing about it to my worthy landlord and he, honest man, said nothing about it to me.

The morning was cloudy and I felt a strong presentiment of rain but landlord and two weather-wise and certainly weather-worn personages declared confidently that "there wad be nae rain the day yet!" So after breakfast, with my stick and sketch book, I set off for Loch Torridon at ten and notwithstanding the falsification of the prophesy of the ancients aforesaid I have had another delightful day's excursion.

The road to Torridon is eleven miles and a half long so my walk has been twenty three but surely Highland miles have been greatly shorn of their old glory.

Just when I was writing that last word, about 10 o'clock, in stalked a portly personage saying it was of no consequence whether there was a gentleman in the room or not. A good looking frank man about 35 or so whom I took for a commercial traveller. After some general conversation he most kindly offered me a drive to Dingwall in his gig if I were going that way and though his remarks on the Highlands and Highlanders in general were besprinkled with some rather wild flowers of speech (d---g and infernalising them all at no allowance for a pack of cowardly, lazy, want of pluck, set of degenerates), he was so obliging and gave me so much information as to neutralise all that, so after some talk, I left him at his toddy and went off to bed. I had a <u>third</u> palaver this night, as well as the other two, but it was a mumbo jumbo sort of concern and had so little character about it that I must have fallen asleep in the middle of it for I don't recollect the termination.

## SATURDAY 4 JULY

To continue my route to Torridon, the Highland miles appear to be now as remarkably short, as formerly they were remarkably long. I certainly <u>felt</u> as if I walked only fifteen instead of twenty two. Highland landlords must have no objection to the change for their gig hires increase accordingly at a shilling a mile.

The walk to Torridon from Kinlochewe is first up the base of Ben Ae [Beinn Eighe] for 5 or 6 miles and then down by the side of Ben Ae and Liagach

[Liathach] another tremendous mountain which continues to <u>wall</u> the glen until Torridon. Ben Ae is remarkable for its spire like peaks & large corries which look as if washed from top to bottom with <u>white sand</u> so that the lines on the mountain are all more or less sloping from summit to base. Liagach on the other hand is still more remarkable, first for its <u>dark</u> hue as contrasted with the white slopes of Ben Ae, secondly for its singular outlines (for which I cannot find an illustration at present) & thirdly for its terraced like appearance so that the lines on the mountain are all more or less <u>horizontal</u> from summit to base. The contrast (in colour, form & what I may call bodylines) between these two hills is very striking and, rising so closely together as they do, it is the more so. In some of the upper masses of rock upon the ridge of Liagach (when near the end of the glen) I noticed similar resemblances to the rocks of Sinai and Petra as given in the common pictures of them which I noticed on the side of Benzeboonie.

Loch Torridon soon gleamed before me a tolerably wide expanse of water bounded by low blue hills. A wide moor with peat stacks, a lonely white washed slated house in the very centre of the desolation and 7 or 8 women and lads weeding a corn or potato field, I could not tell which in the distance, for the field was small and the crop whatever it was, small indeed apparently.

Mrs Stuart however was in a quandary. Such a host of visitors she had not had for nobody knew how long. There were some wool gatherers and there were a party of four from Gairloch and she could only give me - ham and eggs of course - and it must be taken immediately for her house it seemed was not an <u>inn</u> (though called so on the map) and how to manage her visitors she knew not. She was very willing however and so I got my <u>ham and eggs</u> in a bedroom with the other party's bonnets and philabegs [kilts] on the bed and chairs around - and after a crack with Murdoch Stuart, the landlady's boy, and paying my bill, according to the Highland fashion of "It's just at your own pleasure, sir!", I retraced my steps towards Kinlochewe in the beginning of a shower of rain which continued with little intermission, blotting out everything from view except the road, and drenching me to the skin until I reached my comfortable <u>howf</u> here again and exchanged wet clothes for dry, and hunger for - ham and egg - with <u>tea</u> however this time.

The mountains of Loch Torridon (as far as I could see them and learn their names today) are (on the left and looking toward the <u>head</u> of the loch) Ben Aligan & then Liagach already mentioned. In front of the loch head there is a range of separate heights the names of which Mrs Stuart could not tell me; to the right are Kirkhill [Beinn na h'Eaglaise] & Ben Damph [Beinn Damh] and so endeth Torridon list.

In this remote and lonely house, I found on a table in the parlour the following little library: The Ettrick Shepherd's Tales, 3 vols., Johnson's Chemistry of Common Life, 2 vols., Millar's Testimony of the Rocks, Life of the Duke of Wellington, 2 vols., Willison's Works, 1 large volume, and Brown's Bible, 1 large vol.[10]

Certainly not a bad selection. Little Murdoch may learn a great deal out of this library. It is an advantage too, I suppose, that he has free access to it, and take up what book he chooses and at whatever times - except Sunday.

There is a little loch about 4 miles from Kinlochewe on the road to Torridon, Loch Clare & on passing I thought, well, at the other end of that loch, there must be a first rate view of Liagach & Ben Ae & part of the Loch Carron group because they all stand either before it or around it &, if Liagach & the rest looked so beautiful on Wednesday morning, when the summits only were reflected in Loch Rosque, how well they must look when reflected here and seen from peak to base. I must go up the Torridon road again and get to the other end of Loch Clare tomorrow.

Well, that's all as to yesterday. I am now writing after dinner on Saturday 4th July as aforesaid. Instead of going to Loch Clare I took a gig to the lower end of Loch Maree. The day was grey and cloudy but quiet and I reckoned upon a fine evening but the hills manage the matters here and Lowlanders don't understand their manoeuvres; and neither do Highlanders for that as my landlord again assured me that it would be a good day - so it been, rain and all.

The view from the lower end of Loch Maree in coming from Gairloch is very fine. The loch is fortunate in having a most impressive approach at either end and there is no other way for ordinary travellers and tourists of getting to it than either from Glen Dochart or from Gairloch. The numerous long low fir clad islands in the more expansive part of the lake are seen to great advantage from the Gairloch road with the precipitous rocks of Ben Arichaar at their sides and the lowering pinnacles of Sleuch in the distance. These islands have a very peculiar and solemn look quite unlike the islands of Loch Lomond though similar in situation. They put one in mind of a funeral procession and preserve the unity of Loch Maree as perhaps the most sternly and yet beautifully solemn of all our Highland lochs.

The mountains which form the northern side of Loch Maree are first

10  It is interesting that while the collection includes some staples, such as: Arthur Wellesley, *The Life and Exploits of the Duke of Wellington* (London, 1840); *The Practical Works of the Rev John Willison*, (Glasgow, 1846); Rev John Brown, *The Illustrated Family Bible with Self-Interpreting and Explanatory Notes* (London, 1839), there were some more recent arrivals as, for example, James F.W. Johnson, *The Chemistry of Common Life* (S.I., 1855) and Hugh Miller, *The Testimony of the Rocks*, (Edinburgh, 1857), the last only just published.

Burnzieboonie [Beinn a Mhuinidh] (remarkable for its buttress like crags and not unlike Salisbury Crags though much larger); second Sleuach or Sleuch which occupies most of the upper end of the loch on that side; third Ben Lair farther back from the edge of the loch though its skirts come down into the beauty of the scene that they are of such finely varied forms and run so little into each other. On the opposite side at the upper end Ben Ae disappear & MealEwe or Huish occupies the border of the loch almost entirely. The peaked summit of the mountain is not visible from the road but its enormous & wide spreading sheets of naked rock below form a very remarkable part of the place, while the remains of the pine forest already mentioned clinging apparently to the very rock and running up into great fissures as I have ever seen. The glen under Benzieboonie is called Glen Bingastle [Gleann Bianasdail]. The dark little loch which we saw from the top of Sleuach is called Carravack [Garbhaig] & a pretty little hollow green with a small cascade beneath Sleuach is called as nearly as I can spell it Croyanassie [Abhainn an Fhasaigh].

Down came the rain with very little warning; first Sleuach vanished in grey mist, then Ben Arichaar escaped through the side seams, then even the funereal fir clad islands, one by one, faded into nothingness, and the curtain surely fell down, down, down, over everything but the gig and the road and the droukit horse and the drenched riders until, through thick mist and pouring rain, we came almost bump against the gable of the inn at Kinlochewe and were thankful to get 'shifted', and washed, and be at the 'ham and egg' again.

There is really no small comfort in being at a remote Highland inn such as this, even <u>by yourself</u> and on a rainy day, if you have sense enough to be thankful for your mercies, your very loneliness has peculiar advantages. You are lord and master of 'the whole hypothec' as our Scottish lawyers say and for the time being you feel that Mr and Mrs McRae and Maggie the lassie and Hamish the ostler and even Hector the son are all regarding you as something to be thinking about. They are all sitting together in the kitchen this wet evening, as it were under the shadow of your presence in the house, waiting the ringing of your bell to do your pleasure, no otherbody's, in short,

> "You are master of all you survey,
> Your will there is none to dispute,
> You reign with absolute sway,
> And are most assuredly -
> Lord of the <u>fowl</u> and the <u>brute</u> -"

As the aforesaid ham & egg and egg & ham are at your command whenever you choose to call for them.

The parlour I am sitting in is by no means to be sneezed at. A buff papered room about 13 feet square with a glowing peat fire at that state when there's neither smell nor smoke but all a bright glow within a border of white ashes. Six chairs, & an armed one and a sopha [*sic*] covered with plain stripe patterned cotton, a good mahogany sideboard very fairly polished, with two jugs on it containing thyme and sage and wild roses and sweet briar, five pieces of crockery ware on the wooden mantelpiece representing a shepherd and a maid, two dogs and two swans and a lady on horseback (but seemingly very much dissatisfied with her saddle) along with two tumblers full of pink shells from Loch Carron and a large table with a neatly patterned oilcloth on it and a very decent carpet, comprise the furniture and comforts and dimensions of the parlour here. In addition there are four beautiful skins on the carpet, most comfortable things for the feet, one a very large deerskin, and other three goatskins and one in especial remarkably long haired and of a nice grey colour. Many a lady might be justly proud of it in her drawing room.

Rain, rain decidedly at last! I have always found the weather break into rain in Scotland about the first week in July. Well - but something worth seeing may be seen in rainy weather too. A finer play (and on a gigantic scale) of mist and vapour I have seldom beheld than on this evening just before the heavy downright rain came on. I cannot attempt to describe it however. Most assuredly to see such effects, mountain land is necessary, level ground never beholds them and pictures cannot give them (no, not even those of Turner) in one respect. Because <u>motion</u> not merely <u>indication</u> of motion, but actual motion itself, the rapid and surprising changes - wide, instantaneous & startling, are the chief charms of cloud play on a great scale. Often the whole expanse of sky & land, from east to west and from zenith to nadir, changes at once & universal air is a cloud which 'moveth altogether if it move at all' sometimes altering - actually without exaggeration 'swift as a thought'.

For about ten minutes while standing at a little distance on the road from the inn and looking towards Loch Maree, while light and shadows are violently contending for the mastery and the four huge forms of Sleuach, Ben Ae, MealEwe and Benzieboonie were appearing and disappearing every moment, sometimes scarcely indistinguishable from the big clouds & always far larger and loftier than in sunshine & dark forms were whirling up in the boiling firmament & one long white serpent like coil of vapour was twisting and struggling round the base of Ben Ae with exactly a serpent's motion - it really seemed like what the first approach of the Universal deluge might have been with the mountains moved from their places and the windows of heaven opened and the fountains of the deep about to be broken up. It was only for about ten minutes, however, after that all was - <u>rain</u>.

## SUNDAY 5 JULY

Still heavy rain, all day. What we could see of the hills was white with torrents, the rivers more than double what their size was last night and the whole glen resounding with something that might not inaptly be termed the Sabbath psalmody of waters. A deep prolonged roar and yet soft though full; and on listening for a little to it the ear either detected or formed for itself varying tones like the changes of a melody floating through the sustained sound. I sat in the house all the forenoon reading Genesis and Job with Matthew Henry's annotations in a handsome volume belonging to Mr McRae and in the afternoon went with my host to hear a service in English by the schoolmaster at the school house here. The congregation nearly filled the place, rainy as the day was, and appeared attentive and devout. The speaker seemed labouring under great weakness and indeed is going away for some time on account of his health. His knowledge of English was evidently very imperfect and no doubt the defects of the discourse were principally owing to this; but this did not altogether excuse the idiotic like repetitions and savage like groans with which he thought it proper to address his hearers. Three or four <u>grunts</u>, sometimes five or six, like those of a broken winded horse were introduced after every fragment of a sentence, and this was evidently not from the feebleness of his lungs but because he seemed to think there was something impressive in it. He read from that beautiful chapter the 55th of Isaiah and then proposed to "sprake" from it. He repeated "Come ye to the waters" I am sure thirty times at the least - often four times in immediate succession. There was absolutely nothing in the 'speech' except such repetitions and a very few most commonplace remarks. I have no wish to satirize the poor creature's performance. I am only stating the bare truth and as to his intonations it is also the bare truth that they were exactly as follows: Come ye to the waters, waters of salvation / Everyone that thirsteth, Come ye to the waters / Come ye to the waters, to the waters, to the waters.[11]

It was actually intoning the service, and in as wretched a style as anything of the kind could possibly be performed. I pass however from a very unpleasant subject, which in more important respects than those of grunting like hogs and howling like savages in the pulpit - is doing little good, I fear, to the Highlands.

In the evening, though still rainy, I went down once more to the fir and birch wood on the skirts of Mill Ewes and got through it nearly to the foot of the rocks over which the cataracts were then actually thundering, but I saw the sight and heard the sound at the expense of a thorough soaking and was glad at length to be at the side of my peat fire again.

11  The line is set out in musical form.

## MONDAY 6 JULY

I was really sorry to leave my clean snug little bedroom and my obliging host and his household. His bill was very moderate. I got his lad to drive me to Achnasheen and there got the coach to Loch Alsh. I left it before reaching Balmacarra and, shouldering my travelling bag, walked on by Dornie Ferry across Loch Duich to Sheil House Inn.

The drive from Achnasheen to Loch Alsh is not particularly interesting. We saw more cottars houses than is usual along other routes - some of them belonging to <u>Club farms</u> (in which a number of people join their means and work a farm in common) and the driver said that most of them were comfortable and had money in the bank. The Duke of Leeds, however, who is principal proprietor about Loch Carron, wishes to clear them away to make room for deer forest and is beginning, it seems, to clear them out. The houses as usual were wretched. Here, and by the side of Loch Duich, I saw filthy hovels which forcibly recalled to mind the pictures representing the huts of the lowest savages in Cook's voyages.

After leaving Achnasheen we passed Loch Goun [Loch Gowan], Loch Scavan [Loch Sgamhain], - two fresh water tarns; Scuir na Kananshin [Sgurr nan Ceannaichean] a lofty mountain at the end of Morishih [Moruisg] and Corrie Phinerach [Bidean a'Choire Sheasgaich] another very craggy hill at the upper end of Loch Dugal [Loch Dughaill]; then came Loch Carron and Jeantown, a straggling village of miserable huts, then the ferry at Strom and then the drive over a very steep hill to Loch Alsh. A very beautiful view of Loch Duich was the only sight worth seeing on this part of the way.

The walk by Loch Duich-side to Sheil House Inn is well worth the toil of travelling it on foot, even with a heavy knapsack. Eilan Donan castle at the ferry of Dornie is a tolerably picturesque ruin and from some points of view gives additional interest to the lower part of this very noble loch. Just about 16 years ago I gazed upon Skoorpoor [Sgurr Fhuaran] at Glen Sheil for the first time. Often since then have I dreamt of the scene and wished for wings like a bird to fly away thither as if to do so were to be at rest. It is as lovely as ever. Indeed I think more so today than when I saw it formerly.

Not so Sheil House Inn! Dirt, deprivation and discomfort in everything - broken windows - beds with wet plaster fallen from the ceiling and in patches on the coarse blankets - lazy, stupid landlord, slattern landlady, and bewildered serving maid with no washing stand or towels in the bedroom - with no <u>bell</u> to call when you want anything and, among other variety of vexation, a nail sticking up in your chair and tearing your trousers to get at your leg upon which to inflict a 'remember me' likely to continue readable for a fortnight at least. A party of gentlemen, too had 'taken', it seemed, the only sitting room in the house contrary to the rule that such a room, and in an inn situation like Sheil House, must always be open to the traveller who is able and willing to pay for it. Osbaldistone's expostulation "Rob Roy" with the Highlanders who had done the same thing and in similar instance contains the rule and states it fairly. In this case the monopolisers were Englishmen, however. One of them came out while I was trying to make some arrangement with the landlady and invited me into "their" room, nay insisted I should go - but he seemed so very jovial, and the odour and sound from the room so redolent of whisky that, in addition to my unwillingness to acknowledge it as "their" room and of course to appear indebted to them for what was my privilege independently of them, I thought I should be more comfortable alone. So I got a fire in a bedroom and soon had the only good thing about the house - salmon steaks and tea.

## TUESDAY 7 JULY

A most decidedly unlucky day. The mist was heavy on the tops of the hills, but there was no threatening of rain so I determined to take a guide (who was strongly recommended to me by the landlady and old Macrae, the grocer near the bridge) and go over the hills to Loch Hourn. This said guide, Sandy McLennan, I met by chance about 7 in the morning and immediately engaged him to carry my bag and shew me the way, and after breakfast I set out for the expedition. Sandy said he knew the way perfectly, no fear of mistake, had gone over it often, and would land me at Loch Hournehead [*sic*] in three hours. We left the highway near Sheilbridge, and went up the wide high corrie to the South West. Hard work it was. Not certainly so steep in any part, as the first stage of the ascent out of Sleuach, but more continuously toilsome and on the whole more exhausting than that undertaking. As we were labouring up among the rocks, height after height presenting a new difficulty, a less steep corrie appeared to the right and more directly in the line of our journey's end. I asked the guide whether we could not go that way? "Ow yes!" but it was very soft ground and far round about "this way was the shortest". Well, confiding innocently in his knowledge & experience, on I followed and at last got to the top of the ridge and found myself in the middle of the mist. Sandy proposed sitting till the mist should rise, but it was evidently deepening fast. I said we might sit there a month perhaps if we waited for that, so, as he still said he knew the way perfectly, we proceeded. Some high crags above us appeared looming through the fog, but nothing else at a distance was visible. Sandy was evidently dumbfounded. However, he mustered courage, turned a rocky shoulder of the hill, and began our descent into what seemed the largest and widest corrie I had yet seen. But it seemed to me to run so parallel to the one we had just ascended, that surely we could have got into it far lower down, and it gradually became so like the one we had left, that, with a suspicion of something wrong, I remarked the same to Sandy. "Ow yes!" was the reply, "all the hills and corries are very like." Down we went, enormous the gulph was, and its remarkable size gave me confidence it was a new region (for in going down a corrie one sees it more than in climbing it), when at last as we were near the bottom, Sandy came to a dead halt. "We're wrang!" said he. "Never mind", said I, "We'll get somewhere." "No!" said Sandy. "I've brought you back again. That's the Sheil Glen, and we've come back down the same corrie that we gaed up." The absurdity of the thing, and the ludicrously woeful expression of the man's face, made me take a hearty fit of laughter, which Sandy interpreting as great good nature, responded to by a grin, yet more ludicrous than his countenance of woe. Feeling still vigorous and on his assurance that <u>now</u> he could not possibly go wrong, I consented to return, on condition that we went by the lower corrie to the right, about which I enquired when we were going up before. So by that corrie we climbed once more and after two, or nearly three hours' additional labour, we at length turned the ridge of the mountain & got on the other side, looking towards Loch Hourn.

It was very provoking to think that Sandy in leading me back to Sheil, should for three quarters of an hour have been glowering at Skoodoora [*sic*], the hill on which he had been shepherd for 16 years without being able to recognise it, though to be sure the mist lay on the top of it. And it was equally so, to find on the other side of the hill that the whole view was so perfectly different, that a child (who was not a very idiot) might have remarked the difference at once. Through some rents in the cloud we saw the upper part of Loch Hourn gleaming in the distance, and a little nearer, among the moors, a small fresh water loch. Below & between us and the loch was a wide valley stretching from east to west, for about ten miles. The mountain bounding it on the north side was that on which we stood, and appeared, as we saw it by occasional glimpses, to be formed of five or six tall splintered summits, with very steep & stony corresponding corries furrowing the surface from top to bottom. On seeing Loch Hourn to the South West, gleaming beyond the intermediate valley, I said to Sandy, "Should we not go straight down now and make for the loch side at once?" "Oh yes!" (his constant exclamation in answer to every question or remark). "Oh yaes, but that's no the head o' the loch, and it wad be a long way round. The head's here", pointing due East, to the head of the valley. Again confiding innocently, I followed my guiding light, or rather my 'ignis fatuous', who to make a long story short, led me over every one of the stony corries aforementioned, each of them as bad as the side of upper Ben Nevis. Went on till he was at the very top of the long valley, would have gone down a corrie to the north again, if I had not checked him, then stood still, and looked round him gaping, and at length confessed himself "wrang again". It appeared that we should have gone straight down towards the loch side, whenever we caught sight of it and that the part that we did see <u>was</u> the head of Loch Hourn. We had thus more than 10 miles of superfluous work to perform, down a precipitous and craggy watercourse, & along very wet boggy ground by the side of a sinuous stream & after another steep ascent & descent, through a finely wooded gorge between us and our destination, we stood at last upon the shore at the head of Loch Hourn, Sandy having most ingeniously contrived to double the first part of the journey and to more than double the second. We left Sheil at 8 in the morning and reached Loch Hournehead at 4 in the afternoon toiling hard and constantly the whole time.

Our troubles however were not yet ended. "Where's the inn?" "Ow yes". There was <u>no inn</u> although my landlady said so, and Sandy, and Macrae the grocer, and the bewildered servant maid all said there was an <u>inn</u> at Loch Hournehead. Two boys whom we met on the shore said there was a <u>dram</u> house three miles down the lochside but they gave such a description of it and its inmates that to seek lodging there was out of the question. There was one <u>cot</u> in sight belonging to the father of the boys to whom we were speaking, but there was no room there as they all slept in the one and only apartment. There was a tall dismal looking house which had been a farmer's, but it was uninhabited, and the only resource seemed to be Mr Ellis'[12] comfortable shooting lodge which I at first supposed was the inn.

The boys told us that the forester was away but his wife was at home so I thought we might try whether Mr Ellis's accommodations might not help the houseless & helpless to a night's lodging. On going to the door, I saw four or five people in a parlour of which the window was open. After knocking, a servant girl came to the door, picking her nose with her little finger and by no means hospitable looking. On explaining our condition & saying that I knew Mr Ellis and felt sure he would find no fault if we got accommodation for the night, she said, with the finger still in the nose and rather peremptorily, "Oh! I'm sure Mr Ellis could find no fault but there's a house down the loch (the dram shop above mentioned) and the master and mistress are not at home. There's the house down the loch or there's the inn at Tomadoun" (16 miles off). Sandy, seeing how matters stood, and being very hungry (for we had no provisions with us either in meat or drink) asked in Gaelic for at least a drink of milk. I immediately

---

12   Edward Ellice (1783–1863) was an English politician, MP for Coventry, who had purchased part of Glenquoich from Lord Ward.

enquired what he had said, and on being told and without waiting to hear whether the nose picker was disposed to grant his request ordered him to come on and turned our backs as quickly as possible upon the shooting lodge at Loch Hournehead. I have no doubt Mr Ellis would be really most willing to afford accommodation in such circumstances to any respectable traveller - but I think that something like a rule to that effect ought to be laid down for the observance of his servants. (They who are instrumental in making a desert of any country, excepting for themselves, should at least make provision for the proverbial hospitality of the Desert, & not leave travellers to the necessity of sleeping on the hillside, or overtasking their strength to get to the shelter, which common humanity would be ashamed to deny them. And it was no excuse that we were strangers. We had the appearance of decency at least, if not of fashion, and one or two questions on the part of any intelligent individual connected with such establishments, could most easily elicit answers quite sufficient for all safety & security in granting the accommodation required. No man indeed or woman either, is likely to travel thirty or forty miles through a houseless country, or over precipitous mountains, to steal spoons at a Shooting Lodge. I know of nothing else they can be afraid of).

So we had to walk sixteen miles additional, after our heavy day's work to the inn at Tomadoun. It was a fine cool night. The road, though steep for about six miles, was mere child's play compared to the ascent of Corrie Dhu Vainlighan and the labours of the four corries afterwards, and, after passing the loch of Quoich and another lodge of Mr Ellis's we arrived at Tomadoun Inn about 10 o'clock. I gave Sandy 10/-, his supper and bed at night, and breakfast at morning and, saying nothing about his blunders, shook hands with him and parted - never to meet again as guide and follower, I hope. I am glad to see a clear sunshiny day however (today -Wednesday). He cannot perish by the way at least in such weather. A more stupid body in every respect, I have not often encountered. His everlasting "Ow yaes" was almost all I could get out of him.

After a comfortable tea supper, I ordered a fire in my bedroom. It took about two hours to get it on. When I went up, the room was full of peat smoke, more dense by far than the mist on the mountains (when at the worst), to say nothing of the smarting to the eyes, the fragrance to the nose and the deposit upon one's clothes and linens. The peats could smoke with a vengeance but could not flame. The smoke could come out into the room but could not go up the chimney. Through the gloom too I saw that chilliness of the room was owing partly to the lower frame of the window having two shattered panes of glass in it, besides being up to the top and on examining the bed I found the mattress nearly as cold as ice and nearly as hard. Another hour was spent in putting <u>out</u> the fire or rather the smoke and after getting as many flannels and drawers and stockings and shirts on me as I well could I wrapt myself in the blankets, tossing out the damp cold sheets and about 1 o'clock in the morning, I think, lost in forgetfulness for a time all thought of the 'unlucky day'.

One of the most, or rather *the* most provoking disappointment was being obliged to go on without having an opportunity of rightly and leisurely seeing what I had been at so much trouble and expense to see. Loch Hournehead is evidently worth a day or two's examination. What I did see was most beautiful and with character of its own. Finely wooded steeps and intricate ledges of boulder like rocks on a large scale run into the interior while the loch itself and towards the open seas appears closer and deeper in its mountain bounds than usual. So much for another infliction upon the unfortunate tourist who ventures into the Scottish deer forests of English millionaires.

The scenery around Loch Quoich is tame for the Highlands. Mr Ellis's grounds and Lodge are very tastefully managed. On one small sheet of water we saw two swans, one standing by the edge and the other evidentially in great glory and joy swimming hither and thither, now with the shoulders or his wings erect and neck thrown back between them stretching out his head and taking a fierce flight along the surface of the water, then diving repeatedly and the holding up his head and cluck clucking like a pair of castanets. The joy of the creature and the pure white plumage of it delayed me in my tiresome march for ten minutes.

We walked the 16 miles in five hours. Judging at this rate of the distance we had walked previously (beginning at 8 and continuing till 5) deducting about half an hour for rests (and we had no more resting time than that) and making moderate calculation for the very great additional toil of mountain travelling to that of walking on a level road, our day's journey was, I believe, nothing short of 46 miles.

## WEDNESDAY 8 JULY

Rose at 9, Rather stiff about the knees but wonderfully fresh - yet poor Sandy had been away homewards at 5 in the morning. I stayed in the house all day resting, writing up journal and sketching. Nothing particularly interesting about Tomadoun Inn. There are few travellers in this "Land uninhabited" so I have enjoyed a day of quiet after one of toil It has been a lovely day and in the evening I strolled through the neighbourhood; in places like Loch Maree and Loch Hournehead, one feels that the absence of human habitation is natural enough but here, where they ought to be, there is melancholy marking the almost entire absence of them. McDonald of Glengarry's property formerly extended from near Loch Ness to Loch Hournehead. It is now divided between Lord Ward and Mr Ellis.

On Thursday 9th July after breakfast and paying a moderate bill, I got Rory - a kilted laddie to carry my bag, and set out leisurely for Invergarry Inn. The walk was delightful through some of the most lovely birch woods that I have yet seen with some good views of mountain, loch and river scenery. Rory was an obliging well informed boy with a very plain stolid countenance but with an odd habit of always shutting his right eye very close whenever he looked in your face or spoke to you. He diverged from the road to lead me to a very considerable waterfall and through some fine birch woods of Lord Ward's and was altogether worth his hire.

At Invergarry Inn finely situated among these same birch woods and on the side of the river, I found that there was no accommodation for me and thought at the same time that the smart application of a good birch rod from the trees in the neighbourhood might be of essential service to the mistress of the inn and her maids. It was now after 2 o'clock but neither she nor they were either washed or dressed so as to be presentable in decent society. The room into which I was <u>told to go</u> was filthy with dirt and stench, without a carpet and had a rickety beslobbered and unwiped table, with two or three wooden chairs in it. I asked for a bottle of ale. The tawdry servant girl brought a jug full of wretched small beer. I said "Have you no ale in bottles?" "That's a botal", was the answer. "What do I have to pay?" "<u>A shillin'</u>!" I then asked to see Mrs McDonald for a moment. After a while and evidently unwilling to appear (& no wonder) she sidled sulkily into the passage, a fat untidy ill tempered looking concern; "I cannot get a bed here then, I suppose," "Na! There's <u>gentry</u> - with an emphasis on the word - "there's gentry in all the rooms." "Will they stay long? Will any of them be away tomorrow?" "Na, they wunt!" "It's a fine day". The acknowledgement of this remark was a grunt. "Good day, Ma'am". To this there was no answer.

They say courtesy is cheap. Mrs McDonald is evidently of a different opinion. She considers it so dear that she cannot bestow it except upon 'gentry' who must also pay interest at the rate of per cent for it, and that not in courtesy but in hard cash. Her house was full, and she and her slattern maids could indulge their natural incivility to wayfarers who must go on to the next inn.

Rory seemed disgusted at them. "The Master's not at home, sir", said he in a whisper. Certainly the <u>school</u> master was not, as far as manners and cleanliness were concerned. I parted with Rory here, shouldered my bag and trudged on to Fort Augustus.

A very different landlady at the Canal sold me for 4d a bowl of cream and a glass of whisky with bread and cheese on the table into the bargain - clean, tidy and obliging <u>she</u> was, and seemed really unwilling to take the 6d which I thought only a fair remuneration. Good and bad are to be found everywhere else however as well as in the Highlands, and I believe it is equally observable that they are usually very distinct from each other. Where you find incivility and poor accommodation and indifferent fare you will commonly get an overcharged bill to the bargain; where you get attention and comfort you will usually find moderate charges also. The virtues keep together and so do the vices.

At Fort Augustus I found a plain but very comfortable inn and the lowest charges I have found in any bill. I spent the evening in trying a sketch of Fort Augustus and next morning on Thursday 9th July went by steamer to Corpach. Invergarry Castle in ruins is one of the picturesque objects on this part of the journey. It is all too symbolical of the present condition of Highland lairds and chieftains; but the curtain fell here in the shape of rain and little else was visible beside the steamer, and her cargo, and the banks of the canal until we arrived at Corpach Inn. Ben Nevis was, as usual, half shrouded in mist and the evening continued rainy. Were it not for the Ben, this place would be almost as waste and dreary as the middle of the Moor of Rannoch. The inn was tolerably full, having English, French and German tourists in the company. They were very quiet and, at ten, I left them all reading or sleeping or drinking toddy, and retired to a crib and a bed apparently intended for pights [picts] of small stature and not for modern Britons of ordinary size. However I slept until five in the morning when a series of solid thumps, on all the bedroom doors in the long passage, intimated that they who were going by the morning boats had better be moving. An hour's bustle followed and after another hour's repose in peace, I dressed and came down to breakfast alone. The whole covey was off and, as at Loch Maree, I had the inn to myself for a while. I spent Friday, Saturday and Sunday here, sketching and walking, seeing Ben Nevis about three times in all, & for about ten minutes at each opportunity, and having very rainy weather, I attended church on Sunday at Kilmaily [Kilmallie] where we had a very sensible discourse from Mr Clark to a very small audience, and on Monday I left for Greenock in a most comfortable steamer at 5 in the morning. We saw little of the land but the cloud views were superb. The weather improved as the day advanced, and though the Kyles of Bute and the hills of Clyde looked rather tame after Loch Maree and the mountains of Loch Duich, we had a delightful sail, and very agreeable company - and at length landed on the quay at Greenock, with which important event I close my journal of the visit to Loch Maree.

# HENRY UNDERHILL:
## *Tour in Scotland, Autumn 1868*

## *Introduction*

By the third quarter of the nineteenth century, a holiday break of some weeks had become an accepted part of the yearly routine of middle-class and professional society; the question – for many – was not whether a holiday was taken, but 'only' where and for how long. It had become a requirement of life to take a break away from work and business, to have, as the author of this account puts in it in his preamble, a 'complete relaxation for some time'. For Henry Underhill, a middle-aged solicitor in Wolverhampton, the choice of destination in 1868 was Scotland. It was not unknown territory to him; when at Inverary he refers to 'his last visit here', and it was a place which his brother Jem – or James – also a solicitor in the family legal firm, had been on holiday. It was to be a tour of three weeks, in which he had pre-determined 'to do as much as possible'. That meant leaving his wife behind with the younger children, Ethel who was a few years old, and Ernest who was but an infant, and perhaps a trial to his 46-year-old father. They were packed off to Scarborough for their holidays, and Henry took himself to Scotland. With him went his older son, Arthur and his articled clerk, Horatio Brevitt. To complete a cheerful family party, there are his two favourite nephews, Frank (Underhill) who travels with them from Wolverhampton, and the twenty-three-year-old Charles, or Charlie, a medical student at Edinburgh University[1] who joins them in Glasgow.

Their tour takes them up the west coast, from Loch Lomond to Oban, Fort William and the Caledonian Canal, across to Inverness, then Aberdeen, and back by Dunkeld, the Trossachs, Stirling and Edinburgh. The journal is full of colour as to incidents, places and people: locals and visitors; individuals, couples and families; inn-keepers and excursionists; snobs and guides. We share his interest in – indeed astonishment at – the singular old lady on the Loch Lomond steamer, whose passion was geology, and who had that morning been up Ben Lomond – on a pony admittedly – armed with a stone hammer as a walking stick. Foreign visitors are much in evidence, including Canadians, one at Inverness 'doing the British Isles', another – a politician and his family – at Oban and again at Blair Atholl. Scotland

---

1    According to Edinburgh University, there are two entries for Charles E. Underhill from Tupton, Staffordshire, who matriculated in the Faculty of Medicine in 1867–68, and again in 1868–69. But he did not graduate, nor was he present at his uncle's funeral in 1882, which suggests an early death.

may have seemed a large country, but tourists when 'doing Scotland' tended to follow a fairly tightly defined and restricted schedule. On the main tourist routes or circuits, even in the height of the season as this account shows, there was a fair likelihood of finding friends who were also in the north, like Stratford Lovett and his wife. Or running across time and again the same new acquaintances, particularly if they were on the same clockwise tour from west to east, such as the Jewish family from London, the Beddingtons. By an extraordinary coincidence, which again reflects the herd instinct of tourists, Henry Underhill was to meet up again with the Beddingtons in the following year's holiday at Lucerne, when he (this time accompanied by his wife) was spending the 'lawyers' vacation month of August on the Continent.[2] And travelling broke down, or at least relaxed, the normal stuffy conventions. As Henry remarks, 'there is great fraternisation on a tour like this'. Manners were changing, and old gender barriers dissolving: 'The English are losing their accustomed reserve and all, even to the most starchy or timid young lady, are willing to enter into conversation if a neighbour will break the ice.'[3] You mixed with whom you met, and as well as being pleasant it was useful: you could exchange up-to-date information about what to see and where next to stay. There are indications in this account, and also from his journal of the next year's holiday, 'A Month On the Continent, 1869' which follows the Scottish tour, that he was a seasoned traveller. He refers to the Scottish sky being as clear as that of Italy, and his Continental Journal talks of the time that he had spent time in Paris in 1867. Henry's observations on tourists and tourism are of weight, even if opinionated and not always complimentary. In his journal entry for Zurich, Henry observes how he had often met women tourists, either travelling alone or in pairs without the slightest inconvenience, but adds 'but then they had lost all bloom and beauty and were noted simply for their massive understandings'.

The final phase of the Scottish tour of 1868 was cut short abruptly by a telegram recalling him back to Wolverhampton for an important political meeting. As well as his legal practice, Henry was heavily involved in local politics and civic affairs, as alderman, clerk to the school board, and from April 1869 town clerk to the Borough of Wolverhampton. His health, undermined by excessive work (or so informed opinion held), was never good, and was further affected by the death of his first wife in October 1873. He remarried in 1879 a woman twenty years his junior. Neither that, nor a three months' sabbatical in the south of England at Bournemouth in the spring of 1881, reversed his decline, and after a stroke he passed away on 26 February 1882 at the age

---

2   Henry Underhill, 'A month on the Continent, 1869' (the manuscript account of which follows the Scottish tour ): '[at Lucerne] where we met 'much to our astonishment the gentle jews, as Charlie christened them, that is the Beddingtons whom we met in Scotland last year'.
3   See entry for '*Tour in Scotland*', Monday 10th August.

of 59.[4] There was a large civic funeral, and amongst the mourners were some of his fellow travellers from the 1868 tour in Scotland: his oldest son Arthur, now a barrister, his nephew Frank, and Brevitt. The younger son, Ernest, who as an infant had been taken to Scarborough in 1868, was an articled clerk in the family firm.

## Note

This diary is held in the Special Collections department of Glasgow University Library. There are 121 pages, illustrated with many photographs or 'scraps' pasted throughout, which were, one assumes, purchased en route. Punctuation has, on occasion, been introduced to assist in reading.

# *Journal*

For months I have been anticipating this journey with a desire no one but a hard worked man can appreciate. A few years ago I resolved that I must either slacken speed or have complete relaxation for some time, at least once in the year, and as the first was impossible, I have religiously adhered to the latter.

When we first determined on Scotland for this year's tour, my wife was to accompany my eldest son Arthur and me, but fearing her health would scarcely permit the fatigue consequent on a journey in which we determined to do as much as possible in three weeks, she arranged to take the children to Scarborough during their holidays and leave Arthur and me to our Autumn wandering.

We first had to make up our party and this was soon settled by my old articled Clerk Brevitt (a most jolly companion) and my two favourite nephews Frank and Charlie Underhill volunteering to join us, the two former starting with us from Wolverhampton, the latter who is at Edinbro' University, meeting us at Glasgow.

We left the North-Western Station at Wolverhampton on the night of the last day of July by the 11 o'clock train hoping to get seats in the Limited Mail at Stafford which would have landed us in Glasgow at 7.25 on Saturday morning. We had as companions a talkative young Irish man who appeared to concentrate all his powers of concentration into a very small picture of Manchester Races and his return therefrom, and a fellow who seemed a cross between a Commercial Traveller in the Linen Trade and an Attorney's out of door Clerk, and who, being a little screwed, judged (because I started with my pipe) we intended a course of dissipation to Glasgow and kept reiterating his desire that we should get an apartment to ourselves in the mail. We mentally resolved to avoid the companionship.

4 'The Late Town Clerk of Wolverhampton' in *The Wolverhampton Chronicle*, 8 March 1882, I am grateful to Mr A. Russell of Wolverhampton Archives for this reference.

On arriving at Stafford the Station Master (who had previously promised me the first seat if any were vacant) met me on the platform with a telegram stating the mail was quite full and we must wait an hour and three quarters and go on by the Auxiliary Mail. There was no help for it so as the night was warm we promenaded the Station and examined the Mail and its passengers as they arrived. Amongst them was Mr W. Hunt the Chancellor of the Exchequer[5] whose size alone would have made him remarkable had he not been an instance of those numerous cases of men rising to distinction by their force of merit and work. He was the son of a Northamptonshire Clergyman of some note, educated at Eton and Christchurch, taking his degree as a first class classic, and then coming on to the Oxford Circuit; doing nothing there he obtained a seat in parliament and now after some 15 or 16 years has forced himself into one of the foremost places in the nation.

Away went the Mail and we kicked our heels until our train was prepared and, fortunately being able to shirk our former companion, we got a comfortable carriage to ourselves and fairly started for the north. I confess to being almost oblivious till we arrived at Carlisle at 6.30 a.m. when a cup of tea and a hot cake wonderfully refreshed me, and being a fine morning we woke up, admired what scenery we caught glimpses of and chatted on until we came into the Scotch coalfield in the immediate neighbourhood of Glasgow. The very appearance of the furnaces and plant as you obtain a hasty glance show what the capital of such men as the Bairds and others can do and made me regret the marked difference between this and some parts of the South Staffordshire District. However we passed them rapidly and soon reached Glasgow arriving at McLean's Hotel, St Vincent Street, about 10.30. We were well prepared for a good breakfast and after making a refreshing toilet we set to work. My nephew Charley had just arrived from Edinbro' looking as manly and chatting as agreeably as usual. He joined us and after making an early meal he became our guide to the city of St Mungo.

We first visited the Cathedral, the exterior of which is plain but the interior is the finest piece of early English architecture I have seen, very perfect and excellently preserved. The immense quantity of stained glass is remarkable but all modern, placed there with few exceptions by the trade Magnates of the place. I am no judge of such works of Art but with the exception of some two or three windows they did not please me. The coloring was not rich and did not blend well together. There is a good organ screen but no organ, owing to the vexed question still existing in the Scotch Church 'Music or no Music'. From the Cathedral we passed the Barony Church (where Dr McLeod preaches), the Infirmary, a large substantial building, to the Necropolis, most romantically

5   George Ward Hunt had been appointed Chancellor on 29 February 1868.

situated on the side of a high rocky hill, but wanting that verdure and woodlike scenery that makes our own country so pretty.

We had no time for a minute inspection but the monuments including one to John Knox, which towers above all the rest, looked massive rather than beautiful. After leaving the Necropolis we went to the University, a dull ugly set of buildings (which it is said are to be replaced by a new College of some beauty in another part of the city) then walked through the chief streets, admired the Exchange a very beautiful structure with pure fluted Corinthian columns and on to George's Square, an oblong place surrounded by buildings principally hotels with no architectural beauty, but having a few good statues.

Glasgow is on the whole a dirty city, and the very lowest class as dirty as the Irish and we were glad to get away, starting by a train leaving at 4 pm to Balloch the lower end of Loch Lomond. We intended to economise and therefore rode third class and as the day was fine and warm the carriage was very comfortable. The lads were chatty and agreeable and Arthur occasionally indulged us with a pun so our ride of an hour and a half was very enjoyable. Arrived at Loch Lomond we had to wait some half hour whilst the boat came down the Loch and took in passengers for the return journey.

The foot of the Loch is comparatively tame, at least it would be so but for the many lovely islands dotted here and there. It is not unlike the lower end of Windermere but on a much larger scale. Our voyage to Tarbet was most pleasant, quite fine but not too hot, though Ben Lomond was just capped with cloud. Some dozen sea gulls followed the boat quite tame and when a piece of biscuit was thrown overboard it was astonishing from what a height they would see it and at once swoop down and take it, scarcely touching the water. There was a singular old lady on board who looked from 60 to 70 at the least. She had been up Ben Lomond in the morning (on a pony of course) and was armed with a stone hammer which she used as a walking stick. She dealt in the scientific, but geology was her especial study. She was nevertheless a genial old woman and a grandmother and was evidently fond of narrating anecdotes of her three living generations. They were all travelling together on the lakes and very sensibly each chose his own excursion for the day, the old lady taking Ben Lomond *solus*.

We reached Tarbet about 7 o'clock too late for Table d'hôte but found our rooms ready. They were small but clean and comfortable. Mine looked over the lake on Ben Lomond and I anticipated the beauties of a glorious sunrise on the morrow. The Landlord is a young well educated and bustling man taking great care of his guests.[6] He soon had dinner ready, commencing with the inevitable

---

6 According to Black's *Picturesque Tourist*, 17th edn (Edinburgh, 1865), A. McPherson was the proprietor.

Hotch pot, a remarkably good and comforting soup. Afterwards the lads had a row on the Loch and I wrote my wife a short description of our journey thus far. On their return we had a night cap of 'toddy' and were in bed by 10 o'clock.

## SUNDAY 2 AUGUST

As I jumped out of bed I was delighted to see Ben Lomond without a cloud and as the sun was then low every object in the landscape was distinctly defined. The outline of the hills was clear yet saved from harshness by that soft blending with the atmosphere you so rarely get to perfection save in nature. This was just the day to climb the mountain if but soft clouds would pass over the sun shielding us from the intense heat and gleamy glare that would otherwise be inevitable towards noon. There was no appearance that we should be so favoured for the sky was as clear as Italy and the sun was mounting hotter and hotter. Nothing daunting we determined on the ascent and after breakfast a party was made up consisting of an American a very intelligent fellow, a young Irishman, a most agreeable companion, a London talkative snob (who nevertheless was amusing) and two officers from Edinbro who were also gentlemen.

Being Sunday there were no steamers on the Lake so we abandoned the idea of making the ascent from Rowardennan, 4 miles below Tarbet, which is by far the easiest route and where we might have had ponies, and determined to cross the Lake commencing the ascent directly opposite the Inn. The Landlord had no Sunday scruples but found us a boat and a guide and we started about 11 o'clock. I had given notice that I should go only a part of the way and it was well that I did, for the others on landing started at such a pace that it was impossible a 14 stone man like me could keep up with them. I therefore wished them good speed and followed at my leisure. With great difficulty I reached the first range but was dead beat, not from fatigue but from loss of breath and intermittent palpitation of the heart. Here I found the benefit of a good large umbrella for there was not a span of shade for a mile on either side but throwing myself on the grass and unfolding my friend I indulged in a practical pun by reposing 'sub umbra ella'. I lay for an hour admiring the glorious landscape beneath and the mountains across and at the head of the Loch, smoked a pipe, read a short paper in the Holiday number of 'London Society' and quite refreshed, mounted another range coming into view of Ben Lomond and just catching sight of our party as they were at the last and steepest ascent. Here I had another half hour's solitary but luxurious rest and started for the third point but entirely lost the path and found myself wandering in what would have been a bog but for the extreme dryness of the summer which had left it a perfect springy carpet. Rapidly going over it I came to an almost perpendicular ascent but finding good footing in the rock and plenty of fern and heath to cling to I fairly climbed to the top but with an amount of exertion that took me back to my school days when I was as athletic as anyone. I was so elated at my success that after another rest I determined I would reach the top when looking at my watch I found it nearly 3 o'clock and although I could see nothing of the others I knew by the hour they must be descending and inwardly confessing my defeat by 'old father time' I clung to the idea that I was as good a man as ever tho' a little slower. But conscience told me I was attempting to humbug myself, before I got to the bottom of the hill.

Turning to descend I found I had lost all landmarks and was compelled to trust to my imagination and to the knowledge that the route lay to the right. I found it however even more trying to get down than ascend and what with the climbing and jumping I was dreadfully shaken and forced to admit that 46 and 14 stone could not compete with 18 and half that weight. However, struggling on I reached the white cottage at the foot of the mountain and found poor Brevitt who owing to his boots pinching had been compelled to give in earlier than I. He was dreadfully disgusted with himself but like a true philosopher was consoling himself with unlimited quantities of whiskey and milk. I soon joined him and nothing could have then been more grateful. In less than a quarter of an hour the whole party came straggling in very much distressed but delighted they had succeeded in gaining the summit from which they had a glorious view though limited owing to the glare of the sun on the distant mountains. Whiskey and milk was in great request and after a little rest we got to the boat crossing the Loch and sending for cloths from the hotel had a most delicious and refreshing bathe before dinner.

Table d'hote at 5 our party sitting together and enlivening the Company by our chat and jokes, our Cockney friend talking as if he would never cease and making himself the hero of every tale. Nor could he be silenced by our chaff nor even by the remark of an old cock who sat near that horse racing and whist was a strange kind of talk for a Sabbath evening. I only recollect one good thing said and that by Frank who retorted on Brevitt that 'Brevitt is the soul of wit'.

Having enjoyed the morning with mundane pleasure we determined we would be good and go to Kirk in the evening but on enquiry we found the village kirk was being rebuilt and that the Minister had performed service in the morning in a barn attached to the hotel, but had been so exhausted by his exertions that he was unable to repeat the dose of an hour and a half sermon. We however consoled ourselves with a 'loaf' in the shade and a pipe till about 8 when the sun going down we took a boat with our Irish friend (an excellent and most amusing companion and a great rower) and pulled up to Inversnaid about 3 miles from the hotel and on the other side of the loch. We merely stayed to look at the Waterfall (a most diminutive affair) owing to the long drought, some going up to the bridge beyond it and returning to Tarbet. And a glorious ride back it was, deliciously cool after the intense heat of the day whilst the rich brightness of a full unclouded harvest moon lit up the Loch and mountains with picturesque beauty. Arriving at the hotel about 10 o'clock we turned in and if the others felt as I they wanted no rocking.

## MONDAY 3 AUGUST

Breakfasting at 9 we strolled about the grounds till half past 10 when the coach was announced for Inverary and we wished good bye to our Landlord a very superior young fellow, well educated, not above his business, but actively engaged in making his guests comfortable. The hotel arrangements were all excellent and altho' the bed rooms were small they were remarkably clean and the beds good.

We soon reached the village of Arroquhar [Arrochar] situated very prettily at the head of Loch Long and about 2 miles from Tarbet and then winding round the head and skirting the western side of the Loch we turned to the right and approached Glen Croe. The road is excellent, one of those many in the Highlands formed by the military under General Wade. The ascent is very steep up to a stone at the summit known as "Rest and be Thankful" and here you get the best view of the entire glen. On the left you look back in the direction of Arroquhar and on the right towards Inverary and it is difficult to say which half is the grander. It is magnificently wild and lonely and altho' the width is great and mountains not very precipitous their majestic height from the intervening valley forms a splendid picture.

You then descend the glen passing the ruined castle of Ardkinglas, the village of Cairndow and Downdown [Dunderaw] Castle, another ruin as you wind round the head of Loch Fyne and reach Inverary the residence of the Duke of Argyll. Inverary is a small and dirtyish town having only one hotel 'The Argyll Arms' and that not the best, for though the charges were moderate, the fare was of the simplest, the bedrooms indifferent and the waiters wretched. We reached Inverary a little after 2 o'clock and whiled away the time till dinner at 5 by a walk in the Ducal grounds which are open to everyone without charge and without attendance, and where you may wander as you like and as if they were your own. They are beautiful and undulating with vast woods and a salmon river, high hills almost attaining to mountains and the castle lying at the foot and facing Loch Fyne having beautiful views up Hell Glen and in the direction of Glen Croe. The Castle is a square stone building flanked at each corner with a round tower. It is not open to the public.

Our Jew friends (a family we met at Tarbet) had preceded us to Inverary and we joined them at dinner. The wife is a well educated and extremely agreeable and motherly woman and I quite enjoyed her conversation. They are evidently City people and very well off and appear a united and happy family. After dinner, Arthur and Charley manned a boat and rowed the Jew and me on Loch Fyne till both of us grew rather funky at the swell when they put us ashore and started again alone. I then found I had a budget of letters to answer and set to work in earnest writing also to my wife and my brother Jem. The lads were all away and I finished the evening by a pleasant conversation with the Jews whose names I could not yet learn.

The youngsters prowling about for amusement were attracted to a small inn 'The George' by hearing music and on entering found some University men and quickly chumming with them formed a musical party and kept it up most hilariously till midnight.

TUESDAY 4 AUGUST

Up and at the dock at 7.30, took out a boat and had a delicious saltwater bathe with only one drawback, the getting in the boat afterwards. This to me, a fat man, was an arduous matter, but the boatman made me a rope stirrup and with much exertion I contrived to get on board but with a mental reservation that I would shy all boat bathes in future. At breakfast we made our calculations that we could post to Oban as cheaply as going by coach and accordingly ordered our carriage to be ready for a start at 11 o'clock. Before going Frank suggested a walk to the top of Duniquoich (a large and steep hill close to and overlooking the castle) and the others at once concurring away they went like a lot of young mountaineers. I stayed behind and looked for them on the summit for they could not be seen while ascending owing to the trees. They must have kept up a tremendous pace for in half an hour they were at the top resting by the old watch tower. The hill is 700 feet high rising abruptly from the lake and most tourists ascend it by a less fatiguing road through the Castle grounds. Whilst they were away I got the luggage in the carriage and the bill paid, which was reasonable, as it should have been considering the accommodation was bad. The Landlord Mr McPherson was not a bad sort of fellow, for on the return of the climbers with a cry for beer in any quantity, he insisted on giving the stirrup cup himself and at his own expense.

The drive from Inverary commences in the woods of his Grace and runs for about 6 miles up Glen Aray. The Woods are exceedingly beautiful and were relieved by the river running on the right of the road most of the way. There are the finest fir trees, scattered about, almost as large as a good sized oak in girth and running to a great height. The shade in the wood was most grateful the day

being as hot as those preceding it. From the head of Glen Aray the view of Loch
Awe and its surrounding mountains is magnificent, Ben Cruichan [Ben
Cruachan] towering above the others.

The view but slightly varying extends to a place called Gladdich [?Cladich],
10 miles from Inverary where there is a small Inn standing out of an exceedingly
picturesque mountain tarn almost choked with huge boulders, and descending
with rapidity to the Lake. I well remember that at my last visit here we climbed
on to the boulders in the midst of the stream and there luxuriated and smoked
like heathens. We stayed a few minutes at the Inn for a pull at the everlasting bar[7]
(here enriched by ginger cordial) which the youngsters pronounced excellent but
I reserved myself for the next stage.

Proceeding from Gladdich we descended a glen richly wooded to Dalmally
one of the most beautiful spots we have yet seen. There is a comfortable Inn kept
by a Nottinghamshire man who also farms a large tract of land and has the
command of a salmon river. If I were a fisherman there is no place I have seen I
would rather stay at. The scenery was so rich so beautiful and grand we were
charmed we had selected this the longest route instead of cutting off 10 miles by
crossing the ferry near to Gladdich. At first we feared we should not get horses
but when the landlord found we were determined to go on with those that had
brought us from Inverary he sent to the hayfield for a pair rather than lose his
posting charges. While they were being harnessed we lunched off a first rate pie
made, as the Frenchman describes it, of "savage" rabbit and a reasonable modicum
of beer; we felt quite fortified for the further journey of 20 miles. On leaving
Dalmally we skirted round the right side of Loch Awe passing a ruined castle
called 'Kilchurn Castle' and at the foot of Ben Cruachan.

In the course of a few miles our driver found us a glorious spring with water
ice cold and very refreshing and in return I gave him a pull at my brandy which
was evidently a novelty to his whiskey throat. In about an hour and a half we
reached the head of the Low Country at a place called Bonaw where live the
family of the Kellys, our Wolverhampton acquaintance. The house is prettily
situated in a thick plantation close to and overlooking Loch Etive. We saw old
Mr Kelly and a young man, probably one of his sons, busily superintending
haymaking in a very large meadow forming almost a farm of itself. At this spot
are the celebrated Lorn Furnaces at which is made the Lorn malleable pig iron,
the ironstone being sent by ship from Ulverston [Lancashire] for the sake of the
charcoal produced from the innumerable forests of small scrub which are here
cultivated for the purpose and periodically cut down.

7   A phrase meaning 'to take a smoke'.

Leaving the bold and magnificent scenery of the Awe the country becomes much tamer through Bonaw to Taynuilt and so on to Oban, only enriched by the beauties of Loch Etive lying on the right of the road. We changed vehicles and horses at Taynuilt and with the thirsty souls of travellers made no slight inroad onto the whiskey and milk which the Landlord's pretty daughter soon got ready. We had a most intelligent driver from Taynuilt who told me all about the Kellys and enlightened me on the duties of the Minister, gave me a description of his house, his glebe and his stipend which for a bachelor was not bad, viz £100 a year in addition to his manse and glebe and the former he let off for two months each year at £60 going into cottage lodgings himself in the meantime. His duties our driver summed up concisely with "one day's work and six days play and payment for the seven."

The road from Taynuilt soon descends to Loch Etive, very pretty with fringes of wood and one or two good flowers and in the Loch when the tide is low and about half way to Oban the channel is very narrow and a rapid is found on other side by a reef of rocks. This has a beautiful appearance and greatly heightens the scenery of the lake. We arrived at Oban about 8 o'clock somewhat tired with our long hot drive and glad to find our beds were ready and a refreshing ablution did full justice to a meat tea.

## WEDNESDAY 5 AUGUST

The Great Western Hotel at which we are staying is newly built, commodious and admirably conducted.[8] The bedrooms are clean and roomy, the Coffee and drawing rooms large and handsomely decorated and furnished, the feeding good and plentiful and the attendance first rate.

We were out and bathing at half past 7 this morning and just as we were prepared for a dive some ladies sent a request we would remove a little further up to enable them to have a dip. We requested their patience for a few minutes, plunged in, soon dressed and left the women who quickly followed our example. The water was cool and delicious but owing to the rocky ground the shingly beach and the shallow water it is not very good bathing ground. After breakfast we determined on a boating excursion to explore the beauties of the neighbourhood and soon hired a good boat of which I took the tiller leaving the younger and more energetic youths to do the pulling. Oban at first does not strike you as being more than an ordinary sea side little town but as you explore the isles and country round you perceive its full beauty for whilst there is nothing of grandeur (except the ruins of Dunnolly Castle which stand on a most

8   Black: 'new and very good', 443.

commanding and precipitous rock) it is surrounded by charming bits of undulating and rocky scenery varied by the rich green intervening valleys, and little bays and headlands form a lovely picture. We had a long pull of six hours varied by an occasional landing to spy out the beauties of the place. Luncheon found us at a small cabin the hut of a ferryman where we hoped to get some refreshment but were told by a shockheaded young Highlander in everything but disposition a savage that he dared not give us anything "as the woman was away to Oban." Charlie whose resources never fail him at once invaded the cabin and found plenty of milk and butter and part of a loaf of delicious bread and seized it. The young savage then managed to find a gill of whiskey and so we lunched sumptuously. Returning to the hotel for dinner we renewed our acquaintance with our Jew friends whose name we had been unable to find out but a young fellow with whom we had made a tourist acquaintance informed us he was the head of the veritable firm of Moses & son, a Minories[9] notoriety who having adopted Christian habits had assumed the name of Alfred Henry Beddington,[10] but whether "Moses or Beddington", Jew or Gentile, we found him a very good natured agreeable fellow and his wife and daughters well educated and lady like.

## THURSDAY 6 AUGUST

Not caring to encounter the hazard of seasickness and finding the youth and spirits of my party a little too trying I resisted all their persuasions and started them at 8 this morning for Staffa and Iona determined to have a day's quiet and answer my correspondence. The Beddingtons left at the same time by another boat for Ballahulish [Ballachullish] with much regret on all sides that we were parting company and Papa gave me his card with a pressing invitation to all of us to call at Lancaster Gate Hyde Park when next in London this I shall most certainly do.

I received a most amusing letter from my wife giving me a description of a grand fete of Foresters in which poor Robin Hood was overtaken by drink and had to be propped in his saddle and my dear little daughter also gave me a most interesting account of the wedding of Dick Rutter[11] and Miss Deakin not

---

9    The Minories is an area of London near the Tower of London which was a Jewish quarter. See C. Dickens, *Dickens's Dictionary of London* (London, 1879).

10   The 1881 census gives Alfred Henry Beddington, aged 45, born London, living at 8 Cornwall Terrace, Marylebone, with his wife Isabel (40) and daughters Estelle (19), Lilian (15) and Mabel (9). In 1868 Alfred would have been 32, his wife 27, Estelle 6 and Lilian 2. The Beddingtons were to meet up again with the Underhills quite by accident in Switzerland the next year.

11   Richard (Dick) Rutter (then aged 24) and his new bride make a further appearance later in the journal when they are sighted in Edinburgh. Rutter was a fellow solicitor in Wolverhampton.

forgetting a full description of the dresses worn by the bride and her maids. I spent the day very quietly but most pleasantly in sauntering about the hills, writing home and to some few business correspondents and getting up the arrears of my diary and am now waiting the return of my lads to dinner from whom I am to have a full description of the wonders of the Island.

I had almost forgotten to narrate a little adventure of last night. After dinner we determined to stroll to Dunnolly Castle and taking no heed of a notice board warning trespassers of the due rigor of the law we crossed a stone dyke into the park leading to the ruin.

Charlie with Arthur led the way some 100 yards in advance but suddenly a gentleman jumped from a boat and ran up to them remonstrating urgently (but as a gentleman) on their disregarding the warnings not to trespass and asking civilly if they thought dykes were made for climbing over. Before we could come up, Charles with a suavity which seems part of his nature had so mollified his interrogator that we found him actually apologising for closing his grounds as "Glasgow Fair had been lately held, and so many excursionists invaded the place committing all manner of damage." I afterwards discovered that the gentleman was Captain McDougall the proprietor of the place and the direct descendent of the chief of the great clan of McDougall, lords of Lorn. After a little conversation with him, he actually invited us to see the Castle and ran up to his house lying very snugly near, brought us the key and left us to ramble about the old place alone. This is another of the many thousand illustrations "that a soft answer turneth away wrath." The view from the keep was magnificent commanding the lower part of Loch Etive and all the craigs of Oban with the mountains of Mull in the distance.

The youngsters returned a little before 7 o'clock having enjoyed the trip amazingly.

Of course I had a full description of the voyage and all pertaining thereto but as Black is far more diffuse and accurate than I should be and the photographs below more graphic I shall not attempt a recapitulation of the extraordinary rocks and caves of Staffa nor the ancient wonders of Iona. Suffice it to say that the fare by Steamboat was dear as they and the coaches always are in this neighbourhood but the lads were amply repaid by a pleasant day's excursion.

Last night it rained heavily for the first time during the tour but altho' it threatened a continuance this morning the sun broke out and we had a fine warm but not hot day. After dinner we strolled up into the town and were amused by some wretched tricks and songs in a booth put up by a party of itinerant actors. In chatting over the events of the day and canvassing our friends the Jews we agreed that no doubt Moses on getting rich had determined to adopt the name of Beddington and had as clearly dropped the Jew to which Arthur (who will never leave off punning) added they evidently became "genteel and Gentile" at the same time.

## FRIDAY 7 AUGUST

Breakfast at 6 o'clock paid our bill which was large but not more so than was fair for the accommodation which was first rate and started for Ballahulish at ¼ before 7 by steamboat. The sun broke out but the mountains as we neared Glen Coe portended rain. The voyage was lovely as we commenced and became grand as we neared Ballahulish entering loch Levin [Leven]. This is not the Loch Levin of Scott's romance and is far more beautiful. It is indeed wildly picturesque as it runs up towards Glen Coe. We arrived at the landing place at half past nine and shouldering our knapsacks walked on to the hotel about a mile distant to secure our beds for the night. Here the old landlady who did not appear the most amiable of her sex insisted she had not heard from me altho' I wrote some two posts before, but finding her obdurate I suggested it was useless discussing the shortcomings of the post but could we have beds? To which with some reluctance she assented as we were bachelors and some could manage with double bedded rooms. Leaving our luggage we jumped on the coach to convey us to Kings House at the extremity of Glen Coe from which we intended to walk back and admire the magnificence of the scenery which is by far the better way to see it as I had been strongly recommended by my brother Jem. We soon found the comfort of being armed with good Scotch plaids for it rained more or less from the time we started until we reached our destination, a good 16 miles from the Inn. On our arrival we wrung our plaids and put them to dry, warming ourselves by a capital kitchen fire made of half coal and half bog whilst our dinner of herrings and chops were preparing to which we shortly did ample justice.

After smoking our pipes in great comfort and imbibing huge quantities of milk slightly tinged with whiskey we paid our bill which was most reasonable and prepared for our long pull of 16 miles down the Glen. For the first three miles or so the path is an uninteresting moorland at which point the upper portion of the scenery commences by an immense precipitous mountain on the left, not standing alone but grouped with others slightly lower and banked on the right by high declivities. From each of these mountain rylls swollen by the rain of the morning (and which in winter would be torrents) leapt in cascades to the vale, forming a fine salmon river which in winding reaches finds its way into Loch Leven. The first half of the pass is wide but gradually narrows as you reach the centre which is divided from the lower pass by a ridge of some little width. On descending from this ridge the three sisters of Glencoe hang towering above,

Plate 1
*Glasgow cathedral.
With the Royal
infirmary to the right,
this was first on the
schedule for most visitors
to Glasgow.*

Plate 2
*Glasgow Necropolis.
The statuary of such
cemeteries was a draw
for many, with this vista
dominated by John
Knox's column.*

ABOVE
Plate 3
The University.
The Old College, just
prior to its demolition
and the University's
move to grander
premises at
Gilmorehill.

RIGHT
Plate 4
George Square.
The neatly laid out
centre of Glasgow,
before the present day
City Chambers,
complete with flower
beds and statues.

*Plate 5 Glen Aray. A picturesque view, looking over a semi-ruinous dyke and a very basic wooden gate. No fences or barbed wire here.*

*Plate 6   Waterfall at Cladich. A hermitage, or viewing point, is visible to the left.*

Plate 7 Oban. Oban was described in contemporary language as the great rendezvous for tourists arriving and departing by sea (this is before the railway) for tours in the Highlands.

Plate 8 Great Western Hotel. One of the many new big hotels being opened in the Highlands, principally to cater for the tourist trade and busy only for four months in the year.

*Plate 9  Staffa; Fingal's cave. One of the renowned attractions of the area, Fingal's cave was a 'must-see' for not just for geologists but for all visitors.*

*Plate 10   Staffa; boatmen at rest. In calm weather small boats took passengers from the Oban steamer into the cave itself.*

*RIGHT*
Plate 11   Iona. Celtic Cross, with the
Cathedral Church in the background.
Either a Guide or the photographer's
assistant in front with the inevitable small
boy hanging about.

*BELOW*
Plate 12   Glencoe. Looking up towards the
site of the massacre; gamekeeper on hand
offering some information.

*Plate 13  Steamer at Ballachulish. Hutcheson's evening boat waiting to take back to Oban those who had taken a coach ride inland to Glencoe.*

*Plate 14  Falls of Foyer. Underhill shared the Victorian enthusiasm for waterfalls, and this was, some held, one of the finest in Scotland until in the 1890s an aluminium scheme reduced its flow.*

*ABOVE*
Plate 21 Dunkeld. Not an
attractive village, though a
striking location, but a good
array of shops, Black's guide
reported.

*RIGHT*
Plate 22 Dunkeld. An
extraordinary trolley, on
which the attendant is
lounging, in front of what was
the 'fine old ruin' of the
Cathedral.

LEFT
*Plate 19  Killiecrankie. The
Soldier's leap with the new
Highland Railway viaduct of
1865 a spectacular addition to the
landscape.*

BELOW
*Plate 20  Birnam Hotel; card
kept, perhaps, by Underhill
because of the excellent service
that the party received there, it
would have carried the tariff and
facilities on the reverse.*

*Birnam Hotel.*

*RIGHT*
*Plate 17   Linn O' Dee Bridge.*
*As the plaque at the centre of the*
*arch records, this new bridge was*
*opened by Queen Victoria in*
*September 1857 – another*
*contribution to 'Royal Deeside'.*

*BELOW*
*Plate 18   Guide and family.*
*The local guide at Killiecrankie,*
*and his family, all of whom are in*
*their Sabbath best.*

*LEFT*
*Plate 15 Aberdeen. Looking across the graveyard and façade of St Nicholas Church to Union Street, this confirms why Aberdeen was already known as the 'Granite City'.*

*BELOW*
*Plate 16 Aberdeen Castlegate. A place of markets and meetings, the area around the Market Cross is remarkably empty apart from one cart and a few cabs. The Town House (ahead to the right beyond Simpson's Fine Athenaeum building) was shortly to acquire an additional and much grander tower.*

*Plate 23   Loch Katrine. A view from above the steamboat pier —the wake of the Rob Roy is visible — of this loch made famous by Scott.*

*Plate 24   Stirling Castle. Looking up to the castle from the cemetery; a view perhaps sold to him by the chattering guide whom Underhill so much disliked.*

*Plate 25   From Stirling Castle esplanade. Looking over the cemetery and the King's Knot and in the middle distance the new suburb of King's Park.*

*ABOVE*
Plate 26 *Edinburgh Waverley Station. A panorama from the Castle to the Calton Hill; Waverley station before its several enlargements in the later nineteenth century.*

*RIGHT*
Plate 27 *John Knox's House. Yet to be worked up to its full tourist potential, this recently repaired property was nevertheless a key attraction.*

a cluster of mountains with glorious summits and steeply precipitous sides the glens dividing each being inaccessible to any but the stoutest climber.

A lovely waterfall which when swollen would be magnificent bounds from height to height till it falls turbulently into the river. In the last of the three mountains you see high up in the precipitous rock a large coffin shaped cave which is pointed out as the cave of that mythical poet Ossian whom the genius of McPherson has embodied into a reality.

Descending still lower as you approach the vale you find yourself in the scene of treacherous massacre of Glencoe so admirably described by Macaulay. There you see some faint traces of the dwellings which have been swept away and the cabins of the murdered dead. You think not of the excesses of the robber band but the barbarous policy by which they were half annihilated. Leaving the plateaux where this wretched slaughter was perpetrated, you fall rapidly to the Leven and enter the village of Ballahulish divided into two separate hamlets by an enormous slate quarry finding occupation for a large number of workmen. The cottages are very low miserable huts most of them thatched but some few covered with slates. They are dirty looking places, and the accumulated filth adjoining makes you wonder how the numerous progeny you see everywhere can be as healthy as they evidently are. No doubt the sea breezes and the mountain air with the simple but plentiful diet counteract the effect of the crowd and dirt of the huts.

We had just the weather one would desire to see this magnificent glen. The mist on the distant mountains which did not obscure the view, the most brilliant sunshine varied by showers and storm heightened the effect of scenery which is grandly wild and beautiful whilst the historic poetry of the silent wilderness added to the sublimity of the landscape. But notwithstanding these aids to grave meditation the way was enlivened as usual by the chaff and puns of my young companions each vying with the other in the gaiety of his sayings. Frank who was particularly lively remarked of his brother Charley who was clothed from head to heel in macintosh that he looked uncommonly like "a varnished chimney sweep", a pleasantry received as such pleasantries should be by a due acknowledgement of the witticism. Frank and Brevitt pushed on before us from the vale of Glencoe evidently determined to show their pedestrian powers, but when Charley, Arthur and I reached Ballahulish I was so dead beat I was delighted to be a [sic] able to make a bargain with two boatmen to row us to the hotel, for 13 miles of mountain walk find out the man of sedentary habits with 14 stone to carry.

On arriving at the hotel we found our rooms small but comfortable and after a hearty meat tea I was glad to jump into bed at 10 o'clock. The walk down the glen from King's House occupied a little over 5 hours.

## SATURDAY 8 AUGUST

Finding we could not get on to Inverness and the day being ushered in with rain we determined to 'loaf' about Ballahulish till the evening boat at 7 could take us on to Fort William. This is a sweetly pretty spot and just the place for the newly married to spend their "sub-lunar"', as Charlie calls the honeymoon. It lies embosomed in mountains and ranges of hills falling down to the very edge of the loch which when the wind is high portrays the rage of a miniature sea. I was dreadfully tired with my Glencoe walk, Charlie full of life ascended one of the near mountains obtaining a magnificent view whilst Arthur and Frank took a boat and had a long tough pull on Loch Leven. Brevitt was '*non est*' and it is believed slept most of the day in his bed chamber. We all assembled for dinner at 4 o'clock and the usual racy conversation enlivened our end of the table. Brevitt ventured to suggest that Charlie (who was admiring as usual all the good looking girls) was "*captus amore*" to which he replied that he was only "*captus a* Mary", not very bad for a semi classical pun.

Altho' the bedrooms we occupied were miserably small they were very clean and the feeding plentiful and good and the charges exceedingly moderate as Lake charges go. In the evening we shouldered our knapsacks and walked to the pier taking the boat and steaming up Loch Eil to Fort William. Here we made our first mistake by staying instead of going on to Banavie. We walked up to the Caledonian Hotel as it is called but which appeared very much like a third rate Commercial Inn. Its outward aspect did not belie its inward accommodation for a more dirty unsavoury place I never was in. As to eating in such a hole (after seeing the filth of the kitchen as I passed) was impossible, but as we had written for beds and it was doubtful if we should get in at the Lochiel Arms Banavie[12] even if we could get our Landlord to send us there, we determined to make the best of it and after a glass of toddy get to bed, rising early in the morning and getting to Banavie for breakfast. On entering the wretched den called the coffee room which put in mind of the line: "In the worst Inn's worst room",[13] we found a party of low Glasgow snobs at tea and very convivial. The leader at the head of the table had evidently been imbibing something stronger than the mild refreshing beverage "which cheers but not inebriates" and was bent on showing off what he thought his wit and making us his butts. Commencing with a complaint that there was no billiard room or other place of amusement he impudently turned round and suggested we should stand on the sofa and give the company a quintet. I thought I should have satisfied him with my answer that we

---

12   Black, 491: 'the hotel was built by Sir Donald Cameron of Lochiel and occupies a fine position ...'
13   Alexander Pope, *Epistles to Several Persons*, Lord Bathurst, 1733.

were not in the habit of making fools of ourselves if he was; but returning to the charge in a few minutes he hoped ironically we would excuse his keeping his back on us, to which I replied with studied politeness, "By all means, we prefer it." This quite shut him up and so astonished his companions who had been vociferously grinning at his small jokes that they dropped off one by one leaving us in possession of the room. We drank our toddy, strolled about the town smoking our pipes and doing a little shopping till 10 when we turned in, each determining to keep his candle alight to scare off the bugs.

## SUNDAY 9 AUGUST

We kept our resolution to leave early and met at half past 7 but it rained so heavily we ordered a carriage which after much delay came round and took us to the Lochiel Arms at Banavie in time for breakfast and where we found they could bed us for the night.

We had the previous evening walked thro' the dismantled fort from which Fort William takes its name. It must in the days when ordinance was in its infancy have been a strong place and Black says it stood two sieges in 1715 and 1745 from the rebellious Highlanders. It is still in good order but has lately been sold by Government to a local proprietor. After breakfast the rain gave symptoms of ceasing and the glass went up but, as Ben Nevis was wrapped in mist, Frank and Charlie joined a large party from the hotel and went to the Episcopal church at Fort William and reported they had heard an excellent sermon. As the rain ceased Brevitt and Arthur had a walk along the canal whilst I wrote to Ethel and Ernest and afterwards strolled to see a glimpse of Ben Nevis and see the ruins of Inverlochy Castle and a very fine mansion[14] of Lord Abinger, who is the owner of considerable estates in this neighbourhood. The glass told truly, the rain ceased and the sun bursting out betokened a fine day. The clouds speedily arose and gave a splendid view of Scotland's highest mountain.

It is certainly very wild and imposing but did not strike me as possessing the majestic beauty of Ben Lomond or the barren grandeur of Ben Cruachan. Probably the high chain of mountains adjoining detract from its magnificence.

As I was writing Charlie, Arthur and Brevitt came to the sudden resolution of walking up the mountain and when I went to look for them I found them gone without a guide. I felt somewhat uneasy but as the afternoon was beautiful and I had every reliance on Charlie's athletic qualities and discretion, I hoped it would be all right. Frank and I dined at table d'hote at half past 4 and as we finished dinner the weather again changed, rain came down and the mist

14 New Inverlochy Castle.

gathered on the mountain. My fears again arose for the safety of the lads lest they should be unable to move or if they did get into danger and much to my surprise I found they had not even taken a plaid with them. The weather grew worse and a terrific storm with thunder and lightning came on and the mountains were absolutely lost to view. I was now downright alarmed and as it was getting late was debating with myself whether I should wait a little longer or take some guides and seek the wanderers when I was delighted to see them emerge from the mist and coming to the hotel at a rattling pace. Of course they were drenched but after a good rubbing down and a change of clothes we got them to a first rate hot dinner and heard their adventures. As they ascended Charley outstripped and missed the others who struggled on to the nearest summit and had a magnificent view, fortunately retiring to the Lower Plateau before the storm came on. Charley on the other hand got quite out anything like a path and had to make his own way literally climbing towards the top which he had nearly reached when a stone to which he clung gave way, his stick broke and he was all but precipitated down a frightful declivity. He could not further ascend but with great difficulty managed to retrace his steps and on reaching the plateau fell in with his companions. They describe the thunderstorm as magnificent in the extreme and amply repaying them for their exertions.

Pipes and a solitary glass of toddy closed the evening and rising early we breakfasted about 7 o'clock and found ourselves on the boat for Inverness starting at 9 from the top of the Locks about 200 yards from the hotel. The Lochiel Arms is a most comfortable house and altho' we had small bed rooms in the garret they were clean and the beds all right. There is unfortunately no ladies drawing room, merely the coffee room where eating is always going on and a smoking room in which the men do congregate.

## MONDAY 10 AUGUST

What is called the Caledonian Canal consists of a series of canals connecting Loch Eil at Fort William with Beauly Firth at Inverness and using in its passage the three lochs, Lochy, Oich and Ness. The ride is extremely beautiful the entire distance of nearly 60 miles. There are various stoppages as you proceed caused by the locks connecting the various water levels. As you leave Bonavie up the canal and along Loch Lochy which is ten miles in extent, you leave behind you the dark ridge of which Ben Nevis is the centre and on which even in this unusually hot summer you could see with the naked eye huge masses of snow. The country then becomes less wild, the mountains more cultivated at their base and with verdure nearly to their summits and here and there a shooting box or other residence peeps from the trees. A canal of about 2 miles connects Loch Lochy with Loch Oich which is much the smallest of the three lochs but excessively pretty. You pass the ruined castle of Invergarry and a very handsome new house nearly completed, now with the large property adjoining belonging to a Mr. Gilbert Ellice. This is called the Glengarry property and was some little time back the shooting estate of Lord Dudley. The old castle was burnt by order of the Duke of Cumberland after the rebellion of 1745. You soon run through Loch Oich and enter another part of the canal which descends into Loch Ness at Fort Augustus. Here we were transferred into a larger boat waiting at the foot of the locks for an excursion party returning to Inverness.[15]

Having to wait here some half hour we passed the time by visiting the Fort which like Fort William was erected to keep the Highlanders in check, but which is now also dismantled. In the fort on the parade ground we found the excursionists dancing polkas and gallops, for they appeared to prefer as much the English dances as the English dress and out of some 400 or 500 persons not one was clad in highland costume. Indeed I may say that through all the country we have passed everyone but the children of the poorest peasants have forsaken the tartan and they only appear to use it as a convenient child's dress. Now and then it was adopted by a tourist as adding to his picturesque appearance and the tourist so clad almost invariably turned out an Englishman. A lady joined the boat a little below Loch Oich who had been to the celebration of the 21st birthday of some young laird in that locality. She was returning alone to Aberdeen and of course we took pity on her loneliness, Brevitt opening the trenches by assisting to wind a skein of wool. She was an extremely well educated and well informed girl and I was surprised when she said she was Scotch for her accent was as pure as an Englishwoman and it was only now and again when she transposed the "shall" for "will" that I could have detected even a lengthened residence in Scotland.

After leaving Fort Augustus and taking on board the excursionists we had a great deal of noise from a large and very bad brass band accompanying them but at my request the Captain kept them well in the bow of the boat so we had very little annoyance. Not a few had imbibed pretty freely and this brought out at last a reel or two but no highland fling and the favourite dances were evidently the polka and gallop. In the course of an hour or so we arrived at the place where tourists land to see the Falls of Foyers and were allowed three quarters of an hour for that purpose. Of course we all went up Arthur and Frank beating us hollow to show their extraordinary agility. The lady accompanied Charlie who

15  *The Inverness Courier*, 13 August 1868, noted the arrival on the Monday of a large party of excursionists from Elgin by special train, who had had a trip up Loch Ness by steamer, accompanied by a brass band, which played on their way. I owe this reference to Eileen MacAskill.

had made an impression and I followed; a pretty good burst it was before getting to the top but we were amply repaid by the fall which is decidedly the finest we have seen in Scotland and was well filled from the rain of last night. There are two falls the higher about 30 feet with breaks in the fall and an arch surmounting it whilst the lower which is far the more beautiful descends in an uninterrupted stream of from 80 to 700 feet. It is prettily situated in the well clad hills and is a splendid cataract. The lady proved an admirable climber and in the descent she went down the steep incline like a gazelle.

After a long pull up Loch Ness of about 30 miles which is extremely beautiful and well wooded, we approached Inverness in the neighbourhood of which there are some excellent modern villas and amongst them on either side of the lake are two, one an Italian and the other Moorish, not very appropriate as it appears for the North of Scotland but looking very lovely in the woods by which they are surrounded.

We arrived at the landing place at Inverness about 5 o'clock and after some chaff with the owner of the omnibuses who robbed us by his charge of 1/- fares and would not let us start till we had paid, we safely landed at the Station Hotel, Charlie having seen his lady friend safe to the railway. We found very good beds and bed rooms allotted to us and had a fair but only a fair dinner. Here I found an accumulation of letters requiring answers and occupied part of the evening in correspondence, afterwards joining the lads in the billiard room for the toddy and smoke enlivened by the usual jokes and repartees. I had almost forgotten an excellent pun of Charlie's at Inverary which I now recall. A fisherman was throwing some salt over a cart load of herrings and I enquired the reason of salting fresh fish intended for immediate sale. He replied that he had merely thrown over them a few grains to keep them sweet from the heat of the weather, when Charlie at once suggested he sold his fish *"cum grano salis."*

We have had some very pleasant companions in our tour and some snobs, one of the latter Charlie styled "the retired sirloin" to which I added "or the butcher on half pay." A Canadian gentleman of about 40 was exceedingly agreeable. He had never been in England before this visit and was now doing the British Isles. He was the very type of Canadian loyalty and heartily loved the old country. He was prepared to admire everything and was particularly struck with the enterprise of the people and the height to which agriculture had risen. He gave me some interesting accounts of Canada. He was singularly like pope in appearance and manner but without those peculiarities which detract from the parson. The system of common room and table d'hote seem telling on the English for they are losing their accustomed reserve and all, even to the most starchy or timid young lady, are willing to enter into conversation if a neighbour will break the ice. This is certainly more pleasant than to continue the dummies of former days and besides the agreeableness of the change you obtain information as to routes and beauty of scenery, hotel accommodation etc which "Black" does not impart, and not infrequently you meet with much travelled intelligence from your companions.

## TUESDAY 11 AUGUST

As we rose this morning it rained steadily as if it would continue the whole day as indeed it did, and we should at once have been off to Aberdeen but tourists, like armies, have their impediments and a general wash was absolutely necessary and as the laundress could not return the linen till late in the evening we were compelled to spend a day here.

The town is moderately large, having several apparently fair hotels, some of the new streets are handsomely built of stone and it is a clean place. There is however little for the tourist to see beyond what is left of the field of Culloden. A large lunatic asylum stands on a hill to the north west of the town affording accommodation to the three counties of Argyll, Ross and Inverness. A few churches, like most Scotch churches not worth looking at, and a turreted building erected on the site of the old castle and overhanging the river Ness, used as County jail and public offices.

One of our tourist friends, a clergyman and master of a school at Norwich, was most anxious to see Culloden and we made up a party of six to go notwithstanding the inclement weather. The waiter had told us the cab fare was 2/- per hour and that we could do it all in a couple of hours. After driving between 4 and 5 miles we came to about two acres of moor (the residue having been enclosed and planted) with the public road running through the centre. On the left of the road was an accumulation of large stones evidently intended to erect a memento of some kind for an attempt had been made on a large square basement the stones of which were simply piled one on another without cement or mortar. On this heap was placed a mere stick about as thick as one's finger about three yards' high and having a shred of plaid looking very like an old garter dangling from it. The guide book says, on other parts of the field now enclosed and cultivated are large stones marking particular phases of the battle etc, on one of which the Duke of Cumberland breakfasted but we did not trouble ourselves to find them and that which I have described is literally all that is left to mark the spot on which Highland loyalty and gallantry fought its last battle for a well loved but worthless race. And perhaps it is well it should be so for where nations like England and Scotland are blended together as one people the fewer tokens of former variance the better.

On our return to Inverness we found we had to pay the usual cab fare of 1/- per mile and half price back very much to our disgust for had it not been for the apparently moderate charge according to the waiter's information we certainly should not have wasted the money on so sorry a sight. We however consoled ourselves by a stroll in Mr McDougall's Tartan Warehouse, a place visited by every tourist and well worthy of inspection. The shopmen are most civil and you see every variety of wool manufacture from the most brilliant royal Tartan plaid to a mere necktie. The lads bought a few souvenirs, and I purchased a lovely shawl for my wife, a plaid dress and sash for Ethel and a plaid for Ernest, ordering for myself a winter travelling coat made after my own design. The remainder of the day was spent in billiards, reading and writing, and we were not sorry to get to bed, with the prospect of a long railway journey on the morrow. This hotel is by no means first rate, the bed room accommodation being by far the best part of it, but the charges as charges go in the Highlands are moderate.

### WEDNESDAY 12 AUGUST

Determined to do the economical we resolved to travel to Ballater third class and booked for Aberdeen (where we had to stay an hour) starting a little after 10 and arriving at 3.45. The journey was most tedious and as at the earlier stations there was a general holiday our carriage was at times overloaded and not with the most pleasant companions. The country thro' which we passed is uninteresting (except for its state of cultivation which for its climate and soil is very good) until near Aberdeen and there we had some pretty views of grouse moors and hill well wooded. We dined at Aberdeen and the lads ran off to see the college and whatever else the time would allow and on their return reported it to be a beautiful city and almost entirely built of granite.

We started at 5 for Ballater having prince Arthur in our train. The country is undulating and very pretty all the way with immense tracts of moor and deer forests. On our arrival at Ballater we had a very good view of the prince who was in an open carriage waiting for his governor who was giving directions. He is a slim good looking gentlemanly fellow, bearing a family resemblance to the prince of Wales but looking far more the gentleman. We stayed at the Invercauld Arms where we had good beds but indifferent feed, by no means a first class hotel. The place itself is a small village not remarkable or pretty but the country round appears more picturesque, though not at all equal to what I had imagined it. Byron spent his early days in this neighbourhood and gathered inspiration from its scenes. Finding there was no prospect of getting into Balmoral Castle owing to the prince of Wales and other members of the Royal family being at Abergeldy we determined to drive from here by coach to Braemar on the following morning.

## THURSDAY 13 AUGUST

The morning was dull and misty and appeared like rain but fortunately none fell till the evening. We got 5 good seats together and started from the Inn but soon pulled up at the Railway Station to wait the arrival of the train which was late. We got down and had some beer and banter to keep ourselves warm and in good temper, and after more than half an hour's delay we started fairly and with four good horses. The road lay along the banks of the Dee almost the entire way and sufficiently elevated to give us an excellent view of the surrounding scenery. It differed materially from any we have seen, no high rocky mountains, picturing desolation, but masses of mountainous hills covered with forest and heather without even the speck of a sheep, showing plainly the game preserve where deer and grouse were plentiful. Although this is the general character of the scenery, its many undulations, lovely vistas, abrupt precipitous crags and ever present river vary the landscape and render it very beautiful. We passed Abergeldie Castle the property of the late Duchess of Kent, now occupied by the prince and princess of Wales and their family, a plain stuccoed, turreted building with straggling outhouses, having no pretensions to architectural embellishment or antiquity. Had it not been castellated one might have taken the place for a small highland village and the house for the residence of some unknown laird. It is situated about 3 miles from Balmoral.

As you approach the royal residence the creation of prince Albert, the beauty of landscape increases and impresses one with the taste which dictated its selection and added to its adornment. It is everyway suited for the summer retirement of a Queen. Lying in a charming valley on the borders of a lovely winding river, sheltered on all sides by the most verdant hills, with distant views or lofty mountain ranges, it is simply superb. The road winding with the river but at a high elevation gives the tourist an ample opportunity of inspecting the exterior of the Castle and grounds and no painting or drawing I have seen does justice to the original.

Passing the Queen's estates we enter the noble property of Mr Farquharson, the representative of one of the oldest of the Highland families, whose picturesque residence is seen from the road. We then pass the old house of Inver Castle which tho' uninhabited is well preserved. It appears comparatively modern and is rather in the style of Abergeldie Castle. Just before entering the village of Castleton in Braemar you pass a small Roman Catholic Cemetery (the Farquharsons and a large number of the population are Catholics); we mooned away half an hour at the inscriptions and epitaphs on the tombs. One records the death of a Peter Grant at the age of 110 years. None of us believed the fact. One old lady died at the age of 90 surviving her husband 50 years. I wonder if affection or even the remembrance of it lingered so long.

On reaching the hotel the Invercauld Arms we found our letter bespeaking rooms had not arrived but fortunately we got the last 5 unoccupied beds and I should think mine was the last, for a harder, more uncomfortable straw mattress could not have been made. The rooms however were clean and the feeding very good. We soon started for a walk and after a little time found ourselves in what is called the Queen's drive, from an especial liking Her Majesty has taken to it, and no wonder for it is exquisite. Forests of firs with silver birch intermingled, the mountains not lofty but rudely precipitous and overhanging, just such a landscape as my wife would revel in, neat, verdant, beautiful and bold.

We called at the post office and found lots of papers and all the illustrated witticisms of the week sent by Emma with some few letters which I spent the afternoon in answering and also in giving my wife a further detail of our progress. When we returned from our walk the ladies were complaining of the bitter cold in whispers to each other. I at once enquired if they would like a fire to which they instantly assented but doubted if they would get one. I at once rang the bell and ordered the waiter to have one lighted. He looked surprised but on my saying, "Now look quick about it, for these ladies are half starved", he promised obedience and in a short time one was burning brightly. Mem; the ladies were snobs for not one had the civility to thank me for making them comfortable though they crowded round the fireplace at once excluding all the gentlemen. The rain commenced about 6 o'clock and descended in torrents thro' the night.

### FRIDAY 14 AUGUST

As I rose at 6 o'clock the rain was still pouring down and I began thinking it was simply absurd to walk thro' Glen Tilt and was devising another mode of getting to Blair Athole but in about an hour the sky broke and the blue and sunshine appeared and the entire day was warm bright and delightful. Starting at 10 o'clock punctually we drove in a break with capital horses to the falls of Corriemulzie about 3 miles from Braemar. They lie close to the road and we had simply to walk to the bottom of a narrow glen to obtain a full view of them. They are exceedingly pretty and like all the other falls we saw today were in full force owing to the heavy rain of last night. The feeder passes under the bridge carrying the road and greatly heightens the picturesque beauty of the place. An artist, an exceedingly good looking young fellow was making a finished painting of the landscape, occupying a rustic arbour half way down the fall.

About 4 miles further on we came to the Linn of the Dee. This is a foaming cataract caused by a sudden narrowing of the broad river between two precipitous and rocky embankments and as sudden a fall in the level of the bed.

The rush of water as it passes under the bridge is beyond measure grand and gives one a notion of the power of the winter stream to carry down the huge boulders which the summer tourist sees dotting the rivers while wondering how they got there.

Proceeding on our way we met a man in a light cart his horse appearing frightened and exhausted who pulled up and told us our carriage could not pass thro' the river as he had had the greatest difficulty and been nearly lost, so on reaching it we left the carriage for our walk across Glen Tilt, passing the river by a frail wooden bridge and thence proceeding to the keeper's lodge at the north entrance of the glen. This gave us some mile and a half further walk than we had agreed on. The keeper at first seemed inclined to be uncivil but as we treated him civilly and told him a carriage would be waiting at the end of the glen for us, he altered his tone and pointed out the route, which is no more than a sheep track but with a little care cannot be lost. The drive from Braemar had been very lovely thro' well wooded hills which however did not destroy the view, but now it was at every step becoming more beautiful. Bounded on each side by mountains with colours varying from the richest greens to deepest purple and in one instance to the darkest blue, and as we advanced the gorges swollen by last night's rain formed natural falls and cascades at each declivity. In the background Ben Mich Dui [Ben MacDui] and the Cairngorm mountains closed the glen as if fairly shutting us in. Thus for five miles we penetrated, crossing several streams now swollen into small rivers, not without difficulty until we came to that which we had been told would probably stop our advance.

This was a point where another river falls into the Tilt barring all progress. Usually in summer weather it is readily fordable, not deeper than the knee, but Fisher the landlord at Braemar at starting had told us he did not think we should be able to get across and illustrated the difficulty by a tourist's tale. In the summer before last (these tales are always recent to give the greater appearance of truth) two gentlemen left his hotel intending as we did to do Glen Tilt and after similar rain the night before. Towards the close of the day one alone returned much exhausted, and on being asked where he had left his companion he answered "that the last he saw of him was going down the Tilt." He had lost his footing and the current had carried him down. Happily he succeeded in getting on one of the boulders in the middle of the river and there he was found the next morning by the searchers sent to look after him. We deemed the tale apocryphal till we neared the river and then we saw at once that such a thing might be. The river was roaring over the large stones and treacherous holes might be seen on every side.

But our party of young ones were not to be daunted and it was not for me to check their spirit of adventure. We took off all our lower garments but our boots (for no less tender feet than a Scotchman's could have withstood the stones) and tried to wade across. It was soon evident we could not get over in the direct course and so determined on a double crossing. With care we managed the first but to get into the path on the other side was a different matter. The holes were so numerous, the current so strong, and the boulders so large we had to work our way foot by foot and with our heavy knapsacks on our shoulders it was no easy task to keep our balance. Once Brevitt fell but fortunately on a large stone which enables him to recover himself with no injury but a slight wetting. I was nearly upset fairly tottering and within an inch of falling and had I done so with a 30 lb knapsack on my shoulders, I should have gone down the Tilt like the hero of the landlord's tale, but I fear I should not have been equally fortunate in getting to a rock of safety. The water was up to our middle but after an exhausting struggle we gained the bank, Frank leading, followed by Charlie, Arthur, Brevitt and me, and heartily glad I was for all of us on reaching *terra firma*.

We walked on for about half a mile till we came to the Queen's luncheon place, a rude rock on the mountain side where we discussed our adventure over our sandwiches, whiskey and some delicious water from an adjoining spring. It had taken us an hour from the time we reached the river till we were safely over. We were soon ready for another start having 5 miles before reaching the keeper's lodge at the south end of the glen. As we advanced the scenery became much more magnificent, the mountains closing in till the end of the glen looked a mere defile. We plodded quietly on admiring everything as it came in view, not forgetting the lodge which seemed a haven of rest. As we neared the end of our walk we passed a man in Tartan flirting with a showily dressed woman and afterwards learned they were the valet and maid of the Duke and Duchess of Athole. About a quarter of a mile before reaching the lodge we saw a remarkably handsome woman dressed in the perfection of taste for a ramble standing on a mass of rock overlooking the river. It was a lovely picture and had we not passed so near was one to dwell upon. It was Helen McGrigor without her ferocity and an artist could have chosen no better study. When we reached the lodge we were told it was the Duchess of Athole who was staying there whilst her husband was shooting that part of the forest. She shortly returned to the lodge passing us and acknowledging our salute with graceful courtesy.

We were delighted to find the carriage we had ordered waiting for us, with an intelligent and well mannered driver, who pointed out the various objects of interest as we drove to Blair Athole. It is the most charming drive in Scotland. You pass thro' the woods at a high elevation, the river bounding at the foot of lofty precipitous banks, here and there a waterfall, here and there a lovely river break. We left the carriage several times to admire various points of interest, such as the salmon leap and the falls of Fender, and reached the Athole Arms[16] about 7 o'clock after passing 30 miles through the finest scenery and spending the most enjoyable of all the pleasant days we have had.

## SATURDAY 15 AUGUST

Very comfortable feed at the Athole Arms, my room fair, but the bed terribly hard, and the others (from that gentle desire to please the ladies which appears inherent in them) had to be content with one room and three beds, hard comfort after a day so toilsome. But young blood does with little when the spirit of adventure is strong and no complaints were made. We met here a Canadian family who had been staying at Oban when we were there. The father a remarkably fine man 6 feet 4 inches high, a member of the Assembly (who was not a little proud to write himself in the visitors' books an 'honorable'), an insignificant wife and two pretty daughters and a very good looking son, who was an equally good fellow and with whom we had previously struck up an intimacy. There is great fraternisation on a tour like this, and we naturally renewed our acquaintance.

Feeling so proud of our yesterday's exploit, we determined to march, luggage and all, thro' the pass of Killiecrankie to Pitlochry and there take train for Dunkeld and away we started at 11 o'clock having first sauntered to get a view of Blair Castle the Duke's residence with which we were greatly disappointed. It appeared little better than a collection of large staring [*sic*] whitewashed houses, very much inferior to any workhouse in England of any pretension. As we approached Killiecrankie the train with our Canadian friends rushed by but not without a recognition on both sides. <u>The walk began to tell on my feet which were very sore from the previous day's</u> exertions and I was almost determined to take train at once but found none stopped at that station till 6 p.m. *Nolens, volens*, therefore I was compelled to go on and after the exertion was over I was glad that I did so or I should have missed the glory of the pass. On reaching the cottage near the head of the pass, we found the guide who rejoiced in the highland name of Macintosh, but wore the tartan of Athole, who humbugged us and all Englishmen to our hearts' content, that it would have disgusted us had it not been that poor human nature loves flattery and we (at least I) felt the full force of such affection. We however found him extremely useful for whilst abusing all other scenery, he had an eye to the beauty of his own lovely glen. To describe it with any accuracy requires almost an addition to one's vocabulary for

16 Which Black describes as 'very good'.

it is a concentration of beauty and grandeur. It is but about a mile in length but every step is exquisite, from the bold rocky river bed at the "Soldier's Leap" to the sylvan landscape of the Queen's [**** ?Birnam] view. It is literally a pass and not a glen, for the river and path occupy nearly the entire space between the precipitous hills clothed with forest trees feathering to the water's edge, whilst at the northern end stands out in giant proportions one of those mountains nameless but to a Scotchman from which the gallant Dundee defended the pass and received his death wound at the moment of victory.

We could have lingered here all day, but the train like 'time' waits for no one, and we pushed on to Pitlochry, under the enlivening strains of Charlie's merry singing and the tales and jokes of the whole party who keep up my spirits wonderfully when they flag. Arthur amused us by a sketch of the obtuseness of two of his dinner companions of the previous day. A lady had taken lamb, the gentleman called of mutton, which was brought him, but after a careful inspection he pronounced the mutton lamb, when Arthur suggested the animal might have attained its second childhood (not a very good joke) it fell dead on the apprehension of the stump. Brevitt chaffed Charlie on the extent of his vision which he said was only bounded by the horizon, but Charlie replied it was often bounded by his inclination. These and such like jokes carried us on to the Station and we found we had no time to give to the falls of the [**** ?Tummel]. But as we had seen many as fine, and had all the beauties of Dunkeld to explore we did not much regret the loss. The train soon reached this beautiful place, beautiful by nature and ornamented by art under the care of Sir William Stewart and the late Duke of Athole. We were fortunately able to get accommodation at the Birnam Hotel[17] (situate just opposite the Birnam Wood of *Macbeth*) and a better hotel we have not met with. It is as good as the Great Western at Oban and better situated. I was far too tired to explore the town, lying half a mile away, and whilst the youngsters went off loafing there I enjoyed the repose of a nap. We had an excellent dinner at the table d'hote and enjoyed our pipes as usual afterwards.

## SUNDAY 16 AUGUST

We all rose early with the exception of Brevitt who justified his sluggishness on the ground of its being Sunday, but I have a strong idea he was like me footsore and terribly done up with his two days' exertion. The three lads went with their usual energy to the top of Birnam Hill and enjoyed the view whilst I

17   The card, with frontview, of the Birnam Hotel, Mr Pople, is here inserted. According to Black (1865 edition, 253), 'This elegantly built hotel is both beautifully situated and well adapted in every respect for the comfort of tourists.' The Highland Railway had recently (1863) reached Birnam as part of the route from Perth to Inverness.

walked to the town to inspect the buildings and a very handsome fountain erected by the townspeople and others to the memory of the late Duke who appears to have been much more popular than his successor.

The river runs through the estate improving materially the landscape. The old house the former residence of the family is turned into offices and the Duchess resides in a very homely and very ugly yellow cottage wherein our Queen is an occasional visitor. A small fir is shown as having been planted by Her Majesty and every care is taken of it. The Cathedral the greater portion of which is in ruins adjoins the cottage and is a very good specimen of the transition in Architecture from the early English to the Norman. Charlie and Frank were learned on the subject but I confess my extreme ignorance.

After breakfast our landlady (who with her husband are very good sort of people and conduct their hotel admirably) sketched us a drive which turned out most beautiful. We first drove to Murthly Castle and grounds the property of Sir William Stewart but in the occupation of a tenant with a proviso that the public have an opportunity of the fullest inspection without fee or the annoyance of an authorised guide. The old Castle alone is occupied. The new one built by the predecessor of the present owner is magnificent both in size and splendour but is a mere shell roofed in, Sir William declining to spend so vast a sum as would be necessary to complete it on the same scale as was originally designed. The two great features of the place are the avenues of choicest firs and cedars running down sloping terraces to the edge of the broad and rapid Tay, and a Roman Catholic Chapel built by the present owner in a style of unique magnificence rarely if ever seen. It is a mass of gorgeous colour and gold but so admirably blended that nothing offends the eye. Over the altar is a splendid painting of the conversion of Constantine and although the cicerone[18] could not give us the name of the Artist, it was evidently painted by a master hand. The design is powerfully telling. Constantine is leading his host of warriors when he sees the cross in the sky barring his way, speaking as it were the story of his conversion. Over the altar piece is a St Catherine's wheel in stained glass of crimson, green and dark blue the colours most brilliant and as if their beauty required heightening, some large diamonds have been introduced into the stems of the green flowers for what reason except an additional outlay none of us could imagine. Miniature paintings of saints exquisitely finished adorned the walls whilst the chairs within the Altar were a mass of velvet, painting and gold.

Leaving the Chapel and admiring the varied views from the grounds we drove through a rich undulating country dotted with small lochs and having very much

18  A guide who shows antiquities and sights.

the characteristics of English scenery till we came to the grounds close to Dunkeld occupied by the Dowager Duchess of Athole. They are open to the public each party being attended by a guide and 1/- fee charged per head. This looks shabby but the explanation is that the guides are family retainers too old to work and the money goes to pay their wages. This (if guides are necessary) seems fair as it would be scarcely just to impose on the Duchess a tax for the enjoyment of the visitors. The grounds are very beautiful and art has aided nature without injury.

We walked on under the care of the guide admiring the old trees and rough grottoes in the grounds which extended some two miles till we came to a ferry boat kept by the Duchess to transport the visitors across the Tay to another part of the property. The boat was pulled in first rate style by a young girl and it required some experience to get well thro' the current which runs extremely strong. She was the most taciturn of females, even declining to answer our "good morning." After leaving the boat we had a walk of about a mile passing under a very ornamental railway bridge to the Hermitage. This is a building of some pretension erected on the edge of a deep declivity and overlooking a magnificent waterfall on the river Braan, divided into three equal cascades all falling together into a deep turgid pool and issuing therefrom into the river by a narrow channel enclosed by rocks.

It is very fine and well worth a visit. The grotto or hermitage is richly decorated with paintings and mirrors but appeared to me quite inconsistent with the character of the surrounding scenery which is wild and rugged. We then drove to the falls of the Rumbling Bridge about three miles from Dunkeld a very fine bold fall and much of the same character as those at the hermitage aided in effect by a bridge thrown over the stream from which the best view can be obtained.

Having thus occupied the entire morning we returned to our hotel much pleased with our excursion and in time to dress for table d'hote at 5. We had seats at table near some very agreeable people. An old Colonel of Engineers was near me. He stays here for some time every year and is well acquainted with the neighbourhood for miles. He was most communicative and gave us no end of information about the Duke and Duchess, Sir William Stuart, and their lovely properties, not to be found in any guide book. Charlie who always finds himself near a petticoat was fortunate in getting up quite an interesting conversation with a Mrs Farrer, the wife of a brother of one of the masters at Harrow. She was a most charming woman and evidently enjoyed Charlie's conversational powers and was amused by our party for she joined us in the evening whilst taking our grogs and having a talk over the events of the day. We indulged in a little luxury at dinner, taking a bottle of Claret, the first wine we have had since our start! After dinner we tried the Athole Brose, a mixture half honey and half whiskey, very potent but not to be despised if taken simply as a liquor. We then adjourned to the garden with young Macpherson and lying in the grass on the margin of this beautiful river, spent the early evening in conversation and the joys of the weed.

## MONDAY 17 AUGUST

Charlie was up betimes this morning and left us to join a college friend in some grousing[19] a few miles from Pitlochry. I hope he will enjoy himself, he is such a good fellow and so fond of sport. He joins us again at Edinburgh. We started at 10 o'clock for the Trossachs by train to Aberfeldy 18 miles intending then to coach or post the remaining 52 miles.

When we arrived at Aberfeldy we found the coach was being crammed and at once engaged a break and pair to take us to Killin and as there was ample room, we allowed four other tourists to accompany us, a gentleman with his two sons from London and another gentleman from Lancashire whom we could not make out. They were all very agreeable travelling companions and entered fully into the wild spirits of our own party. This ride from Dunkeld is remarkable for thro' the entire 70 miles there is not a mile of tame scenery. We pass to Aberfeldy through the beautiful valley of the Tay and then enter the magnificent territory of the Earl of Breadalbane whose noble residence of Taymouth Castle, lying at the foot of a splendid range of mountain scenery and having the river in foreground is an object of great interest as you look down on it from the road leading to Kenmore.

Kenmore is an exceedingly pretty village at the end of the park and at the foot of Loch Tay having a good Inn covered with creepers and ivy. From thence you wind round the north side of Loch Tay to its head at Killin at such an elevation as enables you to see in its full beauty this noble Loch, the scenery of which much resembles Loch Lomond, but without those islands which so much adorn the latter. From Killin you drive through the vale of the Dochart and see the river Dochart (which empties itself into the Tay) rushing with frantic volume over the singularly abrupt rocks which form its bed and then passing thro' the gloomy and narrow Glen Ogle where you fully realise you are again in the heart of the wildest Highland scenery. You come down upon the beautiful Loch Earn. Here the posting house was crowded but we managed to get an omnibus and a pair of black hearse horses on to Callander. We were followed by another vehicle (which from the arrangement of its seats should be called a quartet break) filled by a lot of young girls with papa, mamma, and uncle, and of course our youngsters at once commenced a telegraphic communication with the young ladies which was as quickly responded to. This resulted in an

19  The grouse shooting season would just have started on 12th August, 'the glorious twelfth'.

exchange of songs from the two vehicles which was heartily encouraged by *mon pere*, but *ma mere* looked grim and dissatisfied.

The road to Callander skirts Loch Lubnaig and runs thro' the pass of Lenny, enriched by mountain scenery and gloomy rapids. At Callander we improved the acquaintance of our fair friends and having obtained a relay of horses got on through the Lady of the Lake scenery to the Trossachs, where we arrived at 9 o'clock and if such magnificent landscape could weary we certainly ought to have had enough of it. The first persons we saw on reaching the coffee room were Stratford Lovatt and his wife, late pretty Mary Davenhill of Compton.

## TUESDAY 18 AUGUST

We employed the day in exploring the varied beauties of Loch Katrine and the Trossachs. After walking to the strand we took a boat and Lovatt and his wife joined us in a row to Ellen's Isle whilst I read them the first canto of the *Lady of the Lake*. We landed and explored the island.

It is a very pretty spot covered with birch and firs and almost matted with ferns, broom and heather, but Scott's illusion is soon destroyed, when we picture this small isle as the citadel in which all the non-combatants of the Clan Alpine took refuge on the eve of the battle. But it is not fair to the gifted author nor pleasing to our own imagination to reduce poetry to prose by such criticism. On reaching the landing place we boarded the steamer and sailed to the head of the loch and back again the description whereof has been given even to satiety. We were glad to find the works of the Glasgow Water Works had not destroyed but rather aided the beauty of the place, by the erection of an ornamental cottage overlooking the small dam through which this delicious water runs to supply the thirsty citizens. Nor does the consumption in any apparent degree lower the immense mass of water descending from the vast watershed surrounding the loch. On returning the lads went off to the hotel for luncheon preparatory to the ascent of Ben [****] whilst I mounted a craggy rock on the Ben Ann side and endeavoured to recall the poetic visions of early youth by reading the *Lady of the Lake*. The young ones soon returned and scaled their mountain, Frank gaining the summit in 50 minutes and the others within the hour. After exhausting the beauties of the wizard I strolled home thro' the wooded Trossachs, and we met again at dinner. The dining room of the hotel (apart from the house) is a large wooden shed covered outside with moss and the interior ornamented with rough rustic work but a very beautiful effect is produced from the roof by hanging therefrom short branches of the weeping birch which have the appearance of having penetrated from the outside, and in the gloom of the building (for it is very dark) give the notion you are dining *al fresco*. We had a very good dinner and the waiting at this hotel is first rate. I got up a talk with a vulgar flannel manufacturer from Rochdale, and his bride not a bad looking girl and well dressed, and as long as she contented herself with simple monosyllables she passed muster, but on exciting her to a little more detailed conversation she betrayed the northern dialect and manners so completely as to lead to the simple conclusion that she was a mill girl, whose fascinations (hidden to my eye) had been too seductive for resistance by the blanket man. In the evening a most glorious sunset invited to another walk, and so closed our day at the Trossachs, for as the lovely young ladies of yesterday had returned to Callander, our equally larky young men could find no one for a night's flirtation.

## WEDNESDAY 19 AUGUST

Arthur and Frank with Lovatt out at 7 for a long walk the former staying at Loch Katrine for a bathe. They accomplished 7 or 8 miles before breakfast. Paid our bill and got the best seats on the coach for Callander. This hotel had the reputation through the highlands as being most extravagant in its charges. We found it as high as Tarbet but not more so. It is admirably managed by a Mr and Mrs Blair, who are young and handsome, particularly the landlady. The waiting is very good, the bedroom accommodation excellent and the feeding all that could be desired.

The old coachman who when I was last here chanted snatches from *The Lady of the Lake* all the way to Stirling has gone where all coachmen go, but our driver was a civil communicative fellow. We soon left behind us the pretty Loch Achray, and the more beautiful Venacher, improved as to size and depth by the handsome embankment of the Glasgow Waterworks and saying adieu to the Highlands caught the train at Callander which landed us about one o'clock at Stirling. We were much disappointed with the place and the more so to find the armoury of the Castle which contains many relics of olden warfare was closed, the only portion of the interior now shown is the Star Chamber where Douglas was killed, and the small adjoining room through which his body was dragged and thrown from the window. The man in charge is a chattering liar, who does a large trade in wood ornaments and photographs and who amused us by a tale of the destruction of some highland clan telling us they were absolutely 'annihilated'. We wandered round the Castle walls admiring Wallace's[20] unfinished monument at the distance and regretting the want of public spirit that would have it so. The view from the walls is magnificent, the eyes wander over a rich champagne

20  The National Wallace Monument had been a project long in the making. Dogged by difficulties in raising enough subscriptions, it was to open fully in the following year. A photograph is inserted here.

country bounded by the nearer mountains of Perth and Argyleshire with the field of Bannockburn before you, very lovely it is. We walked thro' the adjoining cemetery where there is a well executed monument by Ritchie of Margaret Wilson the martyr of the Solway and her sister with an angel in the background, very well designed.

We left Stirling by the 3.13 train arriving in Edinbro' little before 5 pm. On leaving the country for the town our spirits flagged as in regret at parting from the land of the mountain and the flood and in dreary silence and half asleep we continued our journey. On reaching Edinbro' we went to the Edinburgh Hotel[21] but as I had forgotten to write for rooms we found the hotel full. However on hearing we intended to stay a day or two they promised to make us up beds in some way for the night and give us more comfortable quarters on the morrow. After dining at the table d'hote where we met Mr Mellor and the Spencers (the gentlemen who joined us at Aberfeldy). The lads with Mellor went to the theatre, whilst I answered a lot of correspondence which I found lying for me at the post office. The elder Spencer turned out to be the manager of Brooks' Bank in Lombard Street and he gave me a pressing invitation to call on him when in London. I found a most comfortable bed made up for me in a large sitting room and enjoyed a good night's sleep.

THURSDAY 20 AUGUST

After breakfast and calling at the Post Office (a very noble building in Prince's Street) for letters we went to the National Gallery to see the paintings. The building is a fine Ionic erection standing back from Prince's Street behind the Royal Institution. It is just the building for an exhibition of paintings the rooms being low enough to enable one to obtain a good view of all the paintings and is lighted from the roof. For the size of the collection it is the best I have seen. It contains good specimens of most of the old masters such as Rembrandt, Titians, Guido etc and some good modern painters amongst which those I admired the most were two by Noel Paton, the subject being the quarrel and reconciliation of Oberon and Titania. We could not obtain admission to the Royal Institution but the exterior itself is amply worth even a prolonged visit. It is a pure Doric building of exquisite workmanship and is quite as near my idea of what a public building should be as the Madelaine at Paris.

In fact Edinburgh for its size contains more public buildings of genuine architectural beauty than any city I have seen. Passing up Princes Street and again looking at Scott's monument, the Post Office and the Record Office we

21  36 Princes Street, opposite the Station.

came to the cemetery where David Hume the historian is buried and if he <u>were</u> a deist he took an odd way of showing it, for in an inscription to the memory of his wife, 'he hopes soon to join her through the merits of Christ'. On passing the city prison which is a magnificent pile of castelated building we were reminded of the ironical inscription we saw yesterday over the main entrance to Stirling prison, viz, "No admittance except on business."

It was now nearly 12, the hour at which we expected Charlie to arrive and we therefore went to the station to meet him. The train soon came in and he appeared with a lot of grouse in token of his manhood on the moors. After luncheon we drove to Holyrood and saw the oft described pictures of Scotland's kings with noses in sets of three, the rooms of Mary and Darnley, the spot of Rizzio's murder, the bloodstains and all that is so glibly described in the guide books. Barring the associations they recall, the sight is worthless but not so the remains of the chapel, which altho' crumbling away rapidly are well worthy a visit. It is a specimen of more than one order of architecture but the early English predominates and one arch is particularly beautiful.

On leaving Holyrood we inspected an admirably carved fountain erected by Prince Albert before the principal entrance to the palace and then walked to the summit of Arthur's Seat where all the glories of this beauteous city and the riches of the Lothians lie below and ruminating under the influence of the thought inspiring weed we conjured up the battles of the plain, the histories of the city and the romances of the dearly beloved novelist and lived for a time another life with the same surroundings. But neither tobacco nor its reflections help on the tourist and on descending from the pinnacle of the plain we made our way round the Queen's drive to the Canon gate, renewed our intimacy with the old tolbooth, the Regent Murray's house, the few residences of the old nobility still left, but turned to the uses of very ignoble trade, and lastly John Knox's house, which altho' restored is made to serve the turning of an honest penny in the shape of a Tobacconist's shop.

From thence we passed over the principal bridge connecting the new and old towns and so on to the Calton Hill to admire the wonders which the oddities and taste of the citizens have from time to time erected, of which the chief the ruined Parthenon (an intended memorial to Waterloo) is not and never will be completed. We had previously inspected the beauteous monument to Scott in the gardens in Princes Street and the statues to Burns and to Wilson. After a hard day's work we returned to our Inn and I was heartily tired and in the evening left the young spirits to the delights of Christy's Minstrels and other gaieties of which I made no enquiry.

## FRIDAY 21 AUGUST

I received a telegram announcing an important meeting of the Conservatives supporting Messrs Smith Child and Meynell Ingram to be held at Stafford on the morrow and requiring my presence.[22] We at once arranged to return home by the night mail and occupy the day in seeing as much as possible of Edinbro'. Charlie was our guide and first walked us thro' some of the principal streets of the new town all built in stone uniformly and in good taste. This is owing mainly to the power of the governing body of the city who exercise a very large control over the building. We then saw Donaldson's Hospital, a noble building, one of those scholastic institutions for which Edinbro' is so celebrated. It is admirably situated at the outskirts of the city on an eminence commanding an extensive view of the surrounding country. Her Majesty was at one time anxious to purchase it but the Trustees declined to treat. There is also another college near completion in this quarter of the city not so magnificent in scale but still very beautiful.[23] We then passed over to the old town and reached the Castle, saw a parade of the garrison, inspected the small chapel (one of the stars of the place), the rooms of Mary in which our James the 1st was born, the regalia and the monster cannon Mons Meg. The regalia as such is scarce worth seeing except from its association, the crown having been worn by many Scottish monarchs and last by the unfortunate or wicked Mary. On looking at the gun it struck me as somewhat curious that we should have returned to the same style in the manufacture of the ordnance, as it is made first by the welding of lot of bars longitudinally and then surrounding this with a wrapper of bar iron also welded together. Of course the workmanship is rough but the principle of manufacture appears identical with Armstrongs.

Leaving the castle, Arthur whose love for astronomy is remarkable was attracted by Short's Observatory and induced the others to climb up a huge tower from which they descended vowing vengeance at the disgraceful "sell". Whilst they were away Dick Rutter and his bride drove by me on their way to the castle. They did not observe me and as they were so recently married I would not disturb the privacy of the honeymoon by offering my congratulations. After seeing the Free Church Hall, the building wherein the general assembly of the Church of Scotland meet, St Giles and other churches, we paid a visit to the old cemetery of Edinbro', the Grass Market and High Street noting the remains of

22 According to his obituary in the *Wolverhampton Chronicle*, 1 March 1882, Underhill was the county agent for the Conservatives, and it was chiefly due to his 'zealous services' that the Conservatives won that election in 1868, unseating the two Liberal candidates.
23 Fettes College, for which David Bryce was the architect, opened in the autumn of 1870.

the city of the old Scotch Nobles and then went to see Charlie's school, the University. It is a handsome but not remarkable building, but the library, the chief feature, is an excellent one, adorned with busts of eminent professors. We then paid a visit to the Museum of Science and Art adjoining the University containing many interesting things and afterwards to Heriot's Hospital, a school the funds of which provide gratuitous education, clothing and maintenance to 320 children and in school houses in other parts of the city where as many as 3000 and upwards are annually and gratuitously educated. It was late in the afternoon when we returned to princes street to purchase some small gifts for the children and servants, and having paid our bill at the Edinburgh adjourned to Charlie's lodgings at 6. Having dined during our morning's excursion, grog and tobacco amused us whilst I read the diary which appeared to interest the heroes of the story. At eight we fortified ourselves for the night journey with a meat tea, tongue, sardines, and the best of marmalade, and at 9 my two nephews accompanied us to the Caledonian Railway Station and wished us a hearty good bye.

We soon arrived at Carstairs junction after which we had the carriage to ourselves and with little interruption slept to Crewe. We were half an hour late which we made up between there and Wolverhampton, but arriving at the Station at 7.30 we found my wife with her usual thoughtfulness had sent us a car into which we quickly jumped and whilst delighted with our tour were even more delighted to regain our home and find all well and receive the warmest welcome from my dear wife and children.

# MARY ALLISON:
# *Uncle and Aunt's trip to Butterbridge, July 1881*

## *Introduction*

How fortunate Maggie Ferguson, in service at Inveraray,[1] must have counted herself to receive such a lengthy twenty-page letter from her Aunt Mary, which along with family news, describes and illustrates a holiday spent by Mary and James in July 1881 with Maggie's parents at Butterbridge, near Rest & be Thankful. And equally how fortunate we are that this remarkable letter, which is held in private hands, has survived, albeit with the doubtful aid of sticky tape. It sheds light on the kind of holiday-making that those who did not have much free time or disposable income could enjoy, a few days taken at minimal cost – their steamer fares only – during the Glasgow Fair, visiting family and relaxing in a change of scene. Mary Allison and her husband James lived in a two-room flat in a Glasgow tenement in an artisan area at 20 Hill Street, Anderston. According to the 1881 census taken just a few months' previously,[2] he had a steady job, as a storekeeper to a railway engineering business, perhaps the St Rollux works.

What is striking is how late in the proceedings they decide what to do with his customary annual break from work. They had family – grandmother, aunt and uncle – not too far from Glasgow at Greenock, whom they visit on the Thursday, and they receive an invitation to spend the weekend there. But good weather on the Friday morning, and it does seem to have been decided only then, encourages them to make more of the Fair. They opt for a more extended time away, but travel very light: an unannounced visit of a week to her older sister and her family in Cowal, whence Mary originated. Alexander Ferguson was a shepherd who had recently shifted to a new farm[3] – which explains why despite directions, they have some difficulty in locating the house. The lack of forewarning appears to present no problem at all either for catering or accommodation, and the welcome is warm.

---

1   Margaret Ferguson, aged 16 was a housemaid at Rhunacraig house, Inveraray, in the service of John Campbell Maclullich, the local procurator fiscal, and his sister Colina.
2   On the weekend of 3 April 1881.
3   Perhaps from Blairmore where the children had been born.

There were six children in the Ferguson family but only the youngest three, Katie aged 14, Fergus aged 12 and the nine-year-old Alexander – or 'Alec' – were still at home. The older girls had had to find paid work as soon as they could, and that meant domestic service. Bella had a place at Lochgoilhead and Maggie at Inveraray, and the 15-year-old Jessie was working at the Post Office,[4] in Lochgoilhead; as it happens she was back with the family for the weekend of the visit. There was a spare cot bed or two (as the drawing on page 224 shows).

The time away is precious and enjoyed, despite the rain with which the Glasgow Fair has always been associated. Mary counts each day as a holiday, day by day, until they have to return, as shown by her final line to the proceedings for the Saturday: 'and so ended our third holiday'. They walk, they talk, they climb, they visit Cairndow, they meet a travelling fiddler. They would have visited Maggie at Inveraray, but James has to be back at his work on the Thursday, and so the niece gets this lengthy, loving and well-composed letter instead. There is a very strong sense of family throughout, and of happiness at this stage of her life with James. She teases him, but gently, about his lack of musical ability; or his waving his stick 'like an old fool'. What adds poignancy is that Mary Allison had had, and was to have, a number of tragedies in her life. When she and James had married in October 1865, she was already a widow after a short first marriage[5] with a three-year-old daughter,[6] Mary Hunter, who was living with the Allisons at 10 Nicholson Street when the census was taken in April 1871. She features in the letter to Maggie, both at the beginning and at the end, with a day trip to Arran. James and Mary had a son whom they called Stewart Miller Allison,[7] who had been born in December 1870, but he died in their house, as so many working-class children did, before his first birthday. She therefore knows in 1881 when this account is written what she has lost; she knows not what she is yet to lose. They make modest progress in life to a larger flat in Shaftesbury Street.[8] But in December 1894, James's body was found early one morning in the water at the Glasgow wharf of the Forth & Clyde Canal, an accidental drowning, which left Mary widowed for a second time and her life on a downwards path. The last glimpse that we have of Mary a few years

4    Campbell's the Grocer, where Mrs Mary Campbell was the postmistress and her son the telephone clerk.
5    She had been married on Rothesay at the age of 20 on 19 March 1861 to Hugh Hunter, a 27-year-old farm servant in North Bute. Her occupation is given as domestic servant, living at Colubhill Place, Rothesay.
6    There may perhaps have been more than one: 'I used to let my own girls lie long enough when not working'.
7    Stewart Miller was the name of her late father, a farmer.
8    According to the 1891 census, their flat at 4 Shaftesbury Street was three-windowed, and they had three lodgers: two carters and a steam engine fitter.

later in March 1901 is very sad – perhaps inevitable – as an inmate,[9] working as a seamstress in the 'house of industry for indigent women', part of the Blythswood Night Asylum for the destitute and homeless in North Frederick Street, Glasgow. She at least was not alone; next to her name is that of a Catherine Ferguson, who is the same age as Mary and from the same parish in Argyleshire; surely part of her extended family.

There is another aspect to the background. What is remarkable about this extended letter, composed over a week, is that she was able to write it at all, given that at her marriage to James in 1865, she was able only to sign the register with a 'mark'. Mary, a Gaelic and English speaker, must have learnt to read and write as an adult – so often assumed to be something that only men achieved – and as her letter to Mary shows, to much more than an elementary level. Poetry was a taste that she shared with James: we find Scott, Campbell and even an allusion to Keats. She uses Scotticisms carefully, draws on a good vocabulary, and her grammar is mostly solid, with the odd miscue; 'we seen them' for 'we saw them', and 'both her and her friend were sick' for 'both she and her friend'. But when, why and from did she learn? Perhaps, and this is largely speculation, the marriage in 1865 was the springboard for both of them to better themselves. For her part, there is an educational transformation. For his, from being a spirit dealer, not a respectable occupation, James becomes a timekeeper and storeman at a locomotive works, both positions with responsibility. It may that the church played a part: James, for instance, while interested in the music from good choirs and organs, according to Mary liked 'real well' to enjoy good old fashioned services in quiet out of the way places. We know for certain only that they were married in Greenock by the Rev. Peter Carmichael,[10] who had just splintered away from the Reformed Presbyterian church. A vigorous pastor, he may have provided the stimulus. Or not, as the case may be. They did not follow him in his total commitment to the Temperance cause: they drank a dram or two of whisky while they were away. Of course, people on holiday often suspend their normal practice without any penalty to their principles!

But what we have here is a treasure. The line drawings are a pleasure, whether the view of the chimneys from her tenement windows, or the 'wee refreshment' on the road from Lochgilphead, or the bicyclists, one of whom is riding the old 'penny farthing'. That heavy machine for the muscular was soon to be pushed aside by the safety bicycle for the many. So also were sketching skills, which withered as the

---

9   This is drawn from the census account taken on the night of 30 March 1901 of the Blythswood Night Asylum.

10   W. J. Couper, *The Reformed Presbyterian Church in Scotland* (Edinburgh, 1925), 113. They were married in their own home.

picture postcard and the box brownie arrived. Overall, this account of a few days away shows what by the early 1880s trade and works holidays could mean to the less well-off, to artisans and domestic servants. It shows how time away, using family, could be both cheap and enjoyable to visitor and visited alike; a hospitality that was reciprocated at holiday time and throughout the year.

## Note

This delightful account runs to twenty pages of text with a number of drawings and likenesses inserted at intervals. The text is well-written in a clear hand, but time and adhesive tape have taken their toll which means that a few words, particularly towards the end, are missing. The manuscript is retained in private hands, in the possession of the Crawford family of Upper Blarghour near Dalmally, and I am grateful to them for allowing its reproduction.

*List of line drawings:*
Prospect from our window
Bella welcomed us kindly
A little refreshment
On the road to Butterbridge
Washing in the mountain stream
Bicycling
Katie
Going to Church
From four till half-past eight on Monday morning 18th July 1881
Climbing Ben Ime
On top of Ben Ime
The wandering minstrel
Butterbridge
Bella
Jessie

# *Letter*

20 Hill Street,
Anderston,
Glasgow
5-12 August 1881

My Dear Niece -

I must commence my letter with an apology, for I feel that I owe such to you, inasmuch as the holidays have come and gone and I am at home again without having gone the length of Inverary. I will speak more of this further on. In the meantime, my dear niece, do not doubt the strength of my affection. As a substitute for my presence I will give you a few details of how uncle James and I spent the holidays, and how we were kindly entertained by the dear friends at Butterbridge.

You may depend upon it, dear Maggie, we were right glad in the prospect of a few days absence from the dreary prospect of house - roofs and chimneys as seen from our window. Only those city pent mortals like ourselves can appreciate fully the beautifully refreshing sight of country scenes, such as you enjoy, day after day. I have tried to give you an idea of how we are surrounded by chimneys, but I cannot get half the number in. But I must begin with my letter proper. On Thursday the 14th July uncle James got released from his duties, and we proposed taking a leisurely stroll through the town, but we changed our minds and proceeded to get ready for the four o'clock train for Greenock, which we managed to do. We went to Uncle 'Sandy's shop' as we were not acquainted with the address of their new house. After waiting a short time we went to the house, in Inverkip Street, and Aunt Agnes gave us a real nice tea. There were just the four of us present - your grandmother, aunt Agnes, and ourselves. Grandmother was looking pretty well, considering her great age, and she made us laugh by telling over again the comical journey of herself and Mary Hunter[11] from Wishaw to Greenock. They wished us to remain for a few days at Greenock but we had not our door at home properly secured, so we had to get home the same night. We bid them goodbye with the promise if weather on the morrow was not very promising we would return them and stay over Sunday. We reached our chimney-surrounded dwelling about 10 o'clock. Finis our first holiday.

Friday morning opened up beautifully, and we did not take long to make-up our minds that we would go to Butterbridge. I confess, Maggie, that the thought of the long walk among the hills did give me some uneasiness, but I thought

---

11  Mary Hunter was, it is suggested, her daughter by her first marriage.

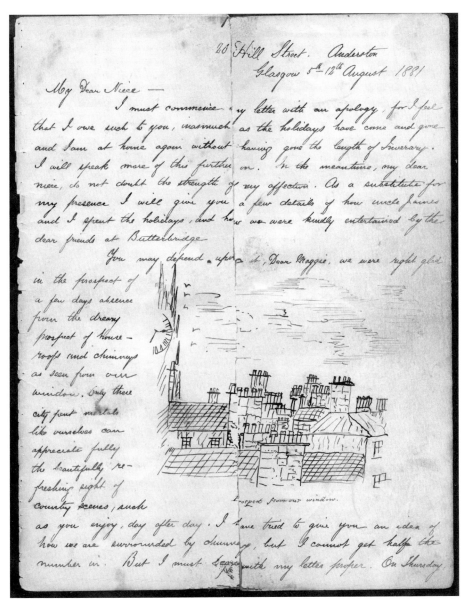

20 Hill Street. Anderston
Glasgow 5th–12th August 1881

My Dear Niece —

I must commence my letter with an apology, for I feel that I owe such to you, inasmuch as the holidays have come and gone and I am at home again without having gone the length of Inverary. I will speak more of this further on. In the meantime, my dear niece, do not doubt the strength of my affection. As a substitute for my presence I will give you a few details of how uncle James and I spent the holidays, and how we were kindly entertained by the dear friends at Butterbridge

You may depend upon it, Dear Maggie, we were right glad in the prospect of a few days absence from the dreary prospect of house-roofs and chimneys as seen from our window. Only these city pent mortals like ourselves can appreciate fully the beautifully re-freshing sight of country scenes, such

*Prospect from our window.*

as you enjoy, day after day. I have tried to give you an idea of how we are surrounded by chimneys, but I cannot get half the number in. But I must proceed with my letter proper. On Thursday,

Figure 1. Prospect from our window

again the day was long and we could take our time, so half past ten found us on board the "Edinburgh Castle" bound for Lochgoilhead.[12] It was very pleasant our sail down the Clyde, all the piers were thronged with pleasure seekers, relieved like ourselves for a brief time from daily toil. We had, happily, no adventure on our passage worth noting. A few mistaken souls were not long on board till they showed their appreciation of a holiday by getting tipsy, but there was no quarrelling. After leaving Greenock and Gourock the boat struck across for Dunoon and Innellan then by Blairmore. We tried to get a glimpse of your old home. Uncle said he saw it, but I could not say I did, and I will match my eyes against his any day. We then proceeded up Loch Long and into Loch Goil. James has so often deaved me with Campbell's poem of Lord Ullin's Daughter that I asked him to show me the place where the ill-fated lovers were drowned, but he could not do so but he assured one if he could not tell me the place in the water where they went down, this hills were the same that the hapless pair must have seen as they were overwhelmed by the angry waters.

> "'Oh! haste thee, haste'! the lady cries,
> 'Though tempests round us gather,
> I'll meet the ragings of the skies,
> But not an angry father!'" [13]

After touching at Ardentinny and Carrick Castle we reached Lochgoilhead about three o'clock. It is certainly a beautiful place. Uncle James was quite taken up with it. A little enquiry soon brought us to Bella's and she welcomed us real kindly. We chatted with her for a least an hour. She told us Jessie was at home for a few days holiday. After we had rested well she put on her wrapper and came a bit of the road with us and after giving us full instruction she returned, and we were fairly on our way to Butterbridge. But for all the instructions we got, Maggie, we took the wrong road, that is we took the left side of the stream where the trees and bushes line the way, instead of the other road through the meadowland. But we did not go very far wrong, for we crossed the bridge at Drumeyricheg (the name is something like that) on to the right road again. After crossing the bridge our way was all among the hills, and we were not too tired at

---

12 According to Alan J.S. Paterson, *The Victorian Summer of the Clyde Steamers, 1864–1888* (Newton Abbot, 1972), 76–7, *The Edinburgh Castle* belonged to the Lochgoil & Loch Long Steamboat Company and had entered service on this route two years previously. She was to spend her entire working life from 1879 to 1912 on the Glasgow to Lochgoilhead route. There were two daily sailings from the Broomielaw during the summer.
13 Thomas Campbell's popular poem *Lord Ullin's Daughter* was written after a visit to Mull in 1795, reworked in 1804 and published in 1809.

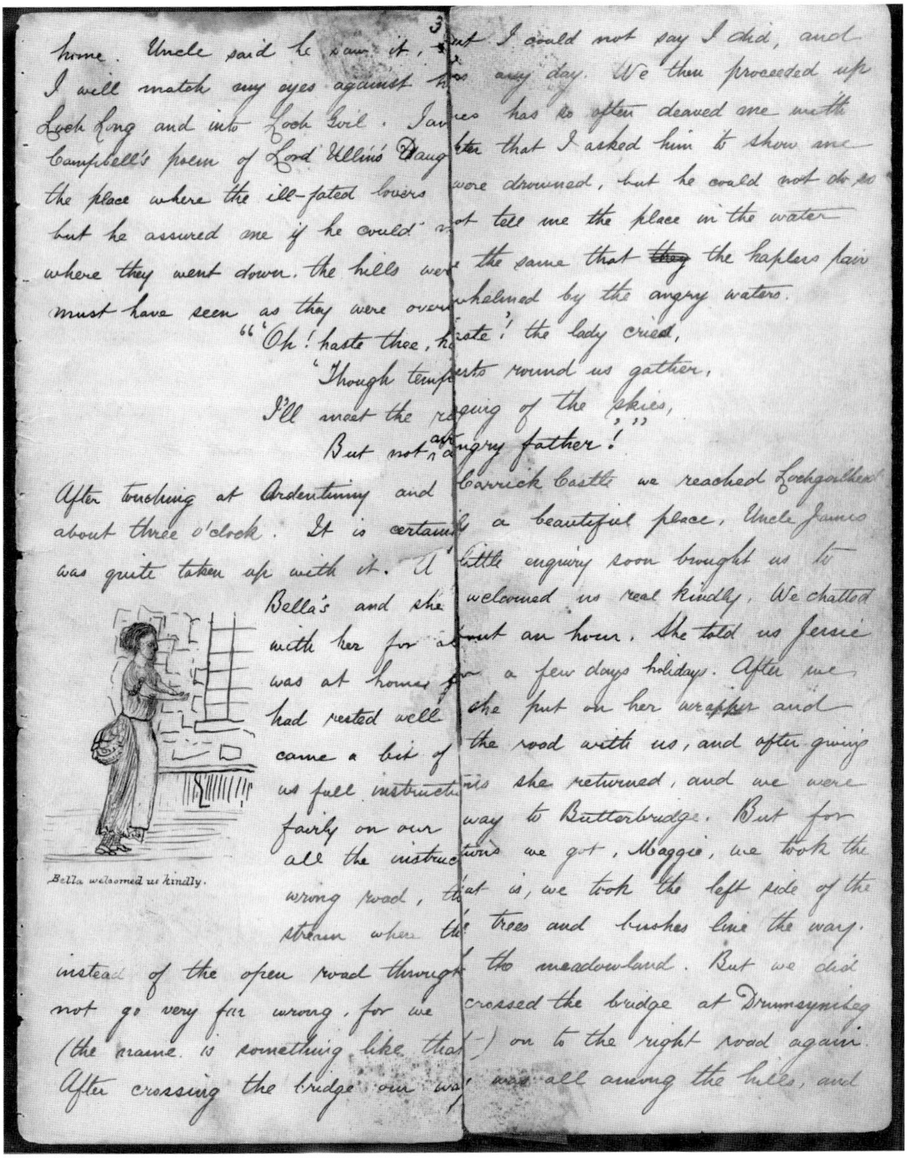

home. Uncle said he saw it, but I could not say I did, and I will match my eyes against his any day. We then proceeded up Loch Long and into Loch Goil. James has so often deaved me with Campbell's poem of Lord Ullin's Daughter that I asked him to show me the place where the ill-fated lovers were drowned, but he could not do so but he assured me if he could not tell me the place in the water where they went down. the hills were the same that ~~they~~ the hapless pair must have seen as they were overwhelmed by the angry waters.

"Oh! haste thee, haste!" the lady cried,
'Though tempests round us gather,
I'll meet the raging of the skies,
But not an angry father!'"

After touching at Ardentinny and Carrick Castle we reached Lochgoilhead about three o'clock. It is certainly a beautiful place. Uncle James was quite taken up with it. A little enquiry soon brought us to Bella's and she welcomed us real kindly. We chatted with her for about an hour. She told us Jessie was at home for a few days holidays. After we had rested well she put on her wrapper and came a bit of the road with us, and after giving us full instructions she returned, and we were fairly on our way to Butterbridge. But for all the instructions we got, Maggie, we took the wrong road, that is, we took the left side of the stream when the trees and bushes line the way. instead of the open road through the meadowland. But we did not go very far wrong. for we crossed the bridge at Drumsynieg (the name is something like that) on to the right road again. After crossing the bridge our way was all among the hills, and

*Bella welcomed us kindly.*

*Figure 2. Bella welcomed us kindly*

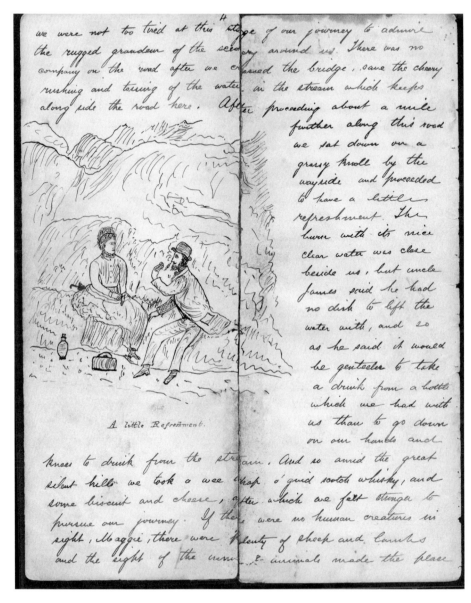

we were not too tired at this stage of our journey to admire
the rugged grandeur of the scenery around us. There was no
company on the road after we crossed the bridge, save the cheery
rushing and tossing of the water in the stream which keeps
along side the road here. After proceeding about a mile
further along this road
we sat down on a
grassy knoll by the
wayside and proceeded
to have a little
refreshment. The
burn with its nice
clear water was close
beside us, but uncle
James said he had
no dish to lift the
water with, and so
as he said it would
be genteeler to take
a drink from a bottle
which we had with
us than to go down
on our hands and

A little Refreshment.

knees to drink from the stream. And so amid the great
silent hills we took a wee drap o' guid scotch whisky, and
some biscuit and cheese, after which we felt stronger to
pursue our journey. If there were no human creatures in
sight, Maggie, there were plenty of sheep and lambs
and the sight of the unnn & animals made the place

Figure 3. A little refreshment

this stage of our journey to admire the rugged grandeur of the scenery around us. There was no company on the road after we crossed the bridge save the cheery rushing and tossing of the water in the stream which keeps alongside the road here. After proceeding about a mile further along this road we sat down on a grassy knoll by the wayside and proceeded to have a little refreshment. This burn with its nice clear water was close beside us, but uncle James said he had no dish to lift the water with, and so as he said it would be genteeler to take a drink from a bottle which we had with us than to go down on our hands and knees to drink from the stream. And so amid the great silent hills we took a wee drap o'guid scotch whisky, and some biscuit and cheese, after which we felt stronger to pursue our journey. If there were no human creatures in sight, Maggie, there were plenty of sheep and lambs and the sight of the innocent animals made the place seem not so very lonely. After walking some time longer we began to be on the outlook for Butterbridge, but not a house appeared to gladden our eyes. We had been told to keep by the side of the Lochan, but no Lochan could we see, unless as uncle James said that was the name given to the stream by the wayside, if so we certainly were keeping by the side of the Lochan very faithfully. I remarked to James, when we came in view of a very high hill that some one was lighting fires up there, for it was covered with smoke. He laughed a deal at this, and when the laughing was done he told me it was not smoke but clouds that capped the mountain top. The road is very zigzag twisting and turning in a provoking manner, and then hiding from one's view behind some hillock or other. Uncle James was not as displeased with the road as I was. He said he could walk all day on such a road with such a fine stream beside it as this one on the road to Butterbridge. It was such a merry stream, with such an abundance of pools and waterfall and such fine rocks and boulders. He declared it beautiful, but I was wearying for Butterbridge. We had been told to be careful that we did not take the road to Arrochar, but we both got so uncertain of being on the right that we would not have been surprised had Arrochar appeared to our view at any moment. We had still some spirit of fun left in us however, for we were just jesting about which hill we would lie down on for the night when the real Lochan came upon our view. We felt sure this was the water spoken of by our guides, and knew your father's house could not be far off. We were both somewhat awed by the dark and treacherous look of the water. The great black rocks that rise up behind it cast their sombre shadows on the water, and gave me a desire to get away from the place as soon as possible. After we passed the Lochan we came in sight of two cows grazing near the road-side, and I said "These are Janet's cows." In a short time we came in sight of a house, but there was no roof on it; only four bare walls, however,

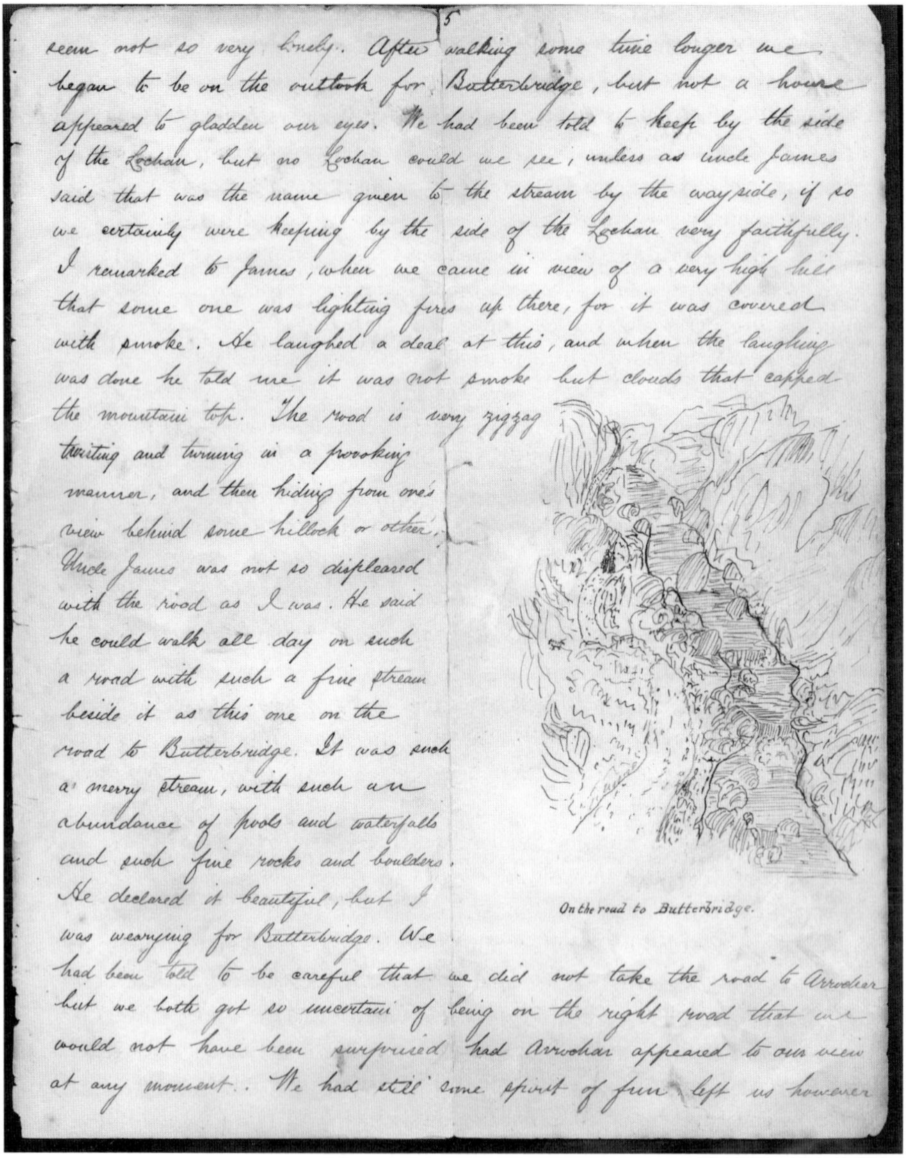

seem not so very lonely. After walking some time longer we
began to be on the outlook for Butterbridge, but not a house
appeared to gladden our eyes. We had been told to keep by the side
of the Lochan, but no Lochan could we see, unless as uncle James
said that was the name given to the stream by the wayside, if so
we certainly were keeping by the side of the Lochan very faithfully.
I remarked to James, when we came in view of a very high hill
that some one was lighting fires up there, for it was covered
with smoke. He laughed a deal at this, and when the laughing
was done he told me it was not smoke but clouds that capped
the mountain top. The road is very zigzag
twisting and turning in a provoking
manner, and then hiding from one's
view behind some hillock or other,
Uncle James was not so displeased
with the road as I was. He said
he could walk all day on such
a road with such a fine stream
beside it as this one on the
road to Butterbridge. It was such
a merry stream, with such an
abundance of pools and waterfalls
and such fine rocks and boulders.
He declared it beautiful, but I
was wearying for Butterbridge. We

On the road to Butterbridge.

had been told to be careful that we did not take the road to Arrochar
but we both got so uncertain of being on the right road that we
would not have been surprised had Arrochar appeared to our view
at any moment. We had still some spirit of fun left us however

Figure 4. On the road to Butterbridge

the roofless house was something to be thankful for, and spoke of some sign of life amid the dreary hills. Possibly the next house we saw would have a roof on it, and as it proved for in a few minutes we saw one with some sign of life about it (McLean's)[14] and shortly afterwards another; and this last proved to be your father's. But we could see no way to get at it, so I waved my umbrella, that whoever were the dwellers in the house, they might come and give us some information about Butterbridge. In a short time we saw your mother whom I recognised, at her door, and then hurrying down to meet us Fergus and Aleck were with her, but they soon left her behind and running down, guided us up to your mother who greeted us with no common kindness. In a few minutes more our travel was ended and we were comfortably seated and in a few more your mother had a nice tea before us, and we felt ourselves at home. We now learned that Jessie and Mary were at Inverary on a visit to yourself and were staying with you till the following day (Saturday). It was about seven o'clock when we reached the house, and your father came in about eight, and if he did not welcome us kindly call me a Dutchman - I mean a Dutchwoman. During the evening we all had some very comfortable chat about friends far and near; about times past and times present, and with a wee drap o' whisky and sugar we closed the evening and retired. And so, dear Maggie, closed the evening on our second holiday.

You may depend on it I had curious sensations on rising on Saturday morning and finding myself surrounded by hills. Instead however of rising early as we should have done we lay in bed till about eight o'clock, and then one at a time we went out to the mountain stream to have a wash, and what a novelty that was. James was particularly taken up with it, and said it beat washing in a basin all to sticks. Your father had gone out early so he was not in at breakfast. After that meal was over, the two boys, uncle James and myself went out for a climb up the hills behind the house. After climbing for about an hour I gave it up, and rested on a hillock overlooking the stream. In less than an hour the others returned, and they had not been halfway up either. Uncle was woefully cheated in his estimation of hill climbing. He had fancied half an hour would suffice to climb Ben Ime, but when he returned beaten he excused himself by saying it threatened to rain.

After coming down from the hill we had an hour or two's rambling about the stream that comes down from the Abysinian [sic] direction, and down by the bridge, looking for blaeberries, but there were none to be found. Being the Glasgow Fair Holidays, we observed a great many people riding on bicycles. They were

14 Donald McLean (a shepherd) and May, aged 28 and 31, with three young children, are listed in the 1881 census.

had some very comfortable chat about friends far and near; about times past and times present, and with a wee drap o' whisky and sugar we closed the evening and retired. And so, dear Maggie, closed the evening on our second holiday.

You may depend on it I had curious sensations on rising on Saturday morning and finding myself surrounded by hills. Instead however of rising early as we should have done we lay in bed till about eight o'clock, and then one at a time we went out to the mountain stream to have a wash, and what a novelty that was. James was particularly taken up with it, and said it beat washing in a basin all to sticks. Your father had gone out early so he was not in at breakfast. After that meal was over the two boys, uncle James and myself went out for a climb up the hills behind the

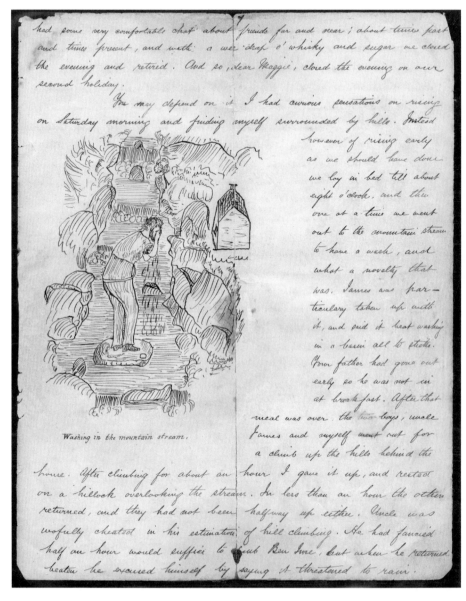

Washing in the mountain stream.

house. After climbing for about an hour I gave it up, and rested on a hillock overlooking the stream. In less than an hour the others returned, and they had not been halfway up either. Uncle was woefully cheated in his estimation of hill climbing. He had fancied half an hour would suffice to climb Ben Ime, but when he returned beaten he excused himself by saying it threatened to rain.

*Figure 5. Washing in the mountain stream*

After coming down from the hill we had an hour or two's rambling about the stream that comes down from the Abyssinian direction, and down by the bridge, looking for blaeberries, but there were none to be found.

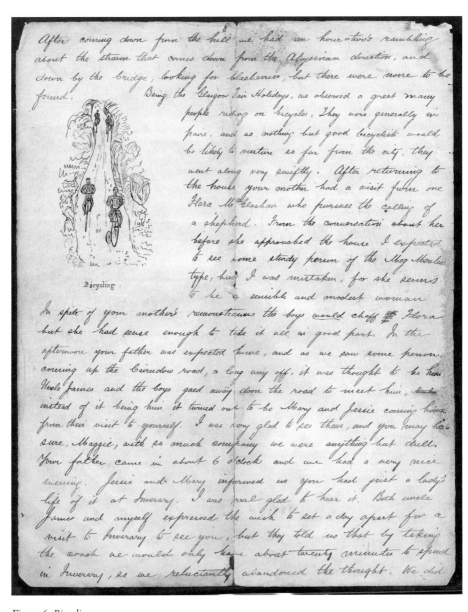

Being the Glasgow Fair Holidays, we observed a great many people riding on bicycles. They were generally in pairs, and as nothing but good bicyclists would be likely to venture so far from the city, they went along very swiftly. After returning to the house your mother had a visit from one Flora McGloshan who pursues the calling of a shepherd. From the conversation about her before she approached the house I expected to see some sturdy person of the Meg Merrilies type, but I was mistaken, for she seems to be a sensible and modest woman.

Bicycling.

In spite of your mother's remonstrances the boys would chaff Flora but she had sense enough to take it all in good part. In the afternoon your father was expected home, and as we saw some person coming up the Cairndow road, a long way off, it was thought to be him. Uncle James and the boys gaed away doon the road to meet him, but instead of it being him it turned out to be Mary and Jessie coming home from their visit to yourself. I was very glad to see them, and you may be sure, Maggie, with so much company we were anything but dull. Your father came in about 6 o'clock and we had a very nice evening. Jessie and Mary informed us you had just a lady's life of it at Inverary. I was real glad to hear it. Both uncle James and myself expressed the wish to set a day apart for a visit to Inverary to see you, but they told us that by taking the coach we would only have about twenty minutes to spend in Inverary, so we reluctantly abandoned the thought. We did

*Figure 6. Bicycling*

generally in pairs, and as nothing but good bicyclists would be likely to venture so far from the city, they went along very swiftly. After returning to the house your mother had a visit from one Flora McGlashan who pursues the calling of a shepherd.[15] From the conversation about her before she approached the house I expected to see some sturdy person of the Meg Merilees[16] type, but I was mistaken, for she seems to be a sensible and modest woman. In spite of your mother's remonstrations, the boys <u>would</u> chaff Flora but she had sense enough to take it all in good part. In the afternoon your father was expected home, and as we saw some person coming up the Cairndow road, a long way off, it was thought to be him. Uncle James and the boys gaed away doon the road to meet him instead of it being him it turned out to be Mary and Jessie coming home from their visit to yourself. I was very glad to see them, and you may be sure, Maggie, with so much company we were anything but dull. Your father came in about 6 o'clock and we had a very nice evening. Jessie and Mary informed us you had just a lady's life of it at Inverary. I was real glad to hear it. Both uncle James and myself expressed the wish to set a day apart for a visit to Inverary to see you, but they told us that by taking the coach we would only have about twenty minutes to spend in Inverary, so we reluctantly abandoned the thought. We did really think it vexing that we were so near you and still were to be denied the pleasure of seeing you. But we were granted the pleasure next to seeing yourself - that is a look at your card,[17] for though we had seen it before it was a pleasure to look at it again. And every one in the house had, of course to see it again and again, and every expression was of pleasure and admiration. Your father particularly, dear Maggie, took a long look at it, and more than once. But this must be in confidence, Maggie, for if your parents were to know that I was telling these little actions of the domestic circle, surely they would shut their door on uncle James and I. Katie is a very pretty girl. In a playful mood she put on one of the boy's caps and she looked so nice and jaunty withal that I have attempted to give you an idea of how she looked on the left of this page. When I think on Katie I cannot help seeing the cap too. We had another nice evening of chat, but I must not attempt to enter into it here for my ink would fail me. So with a "good night" all round we retired, and so ended our third holiday.

15 According to the 1881 census, the 53-year-old Flora, who is listed as a 'shepherd's wife' and her daughter of 18, also called Flora, lived at Artgatan Lodge, Lochgoilhead.

16 In Walter Scott's novel, *Guy Mannering* (1814), Meg Merrilees is a gypsy nurse.

17 By the early 1880s, *cartes-de-visites* – a photographic image mounted on a card – were cheap and popular.

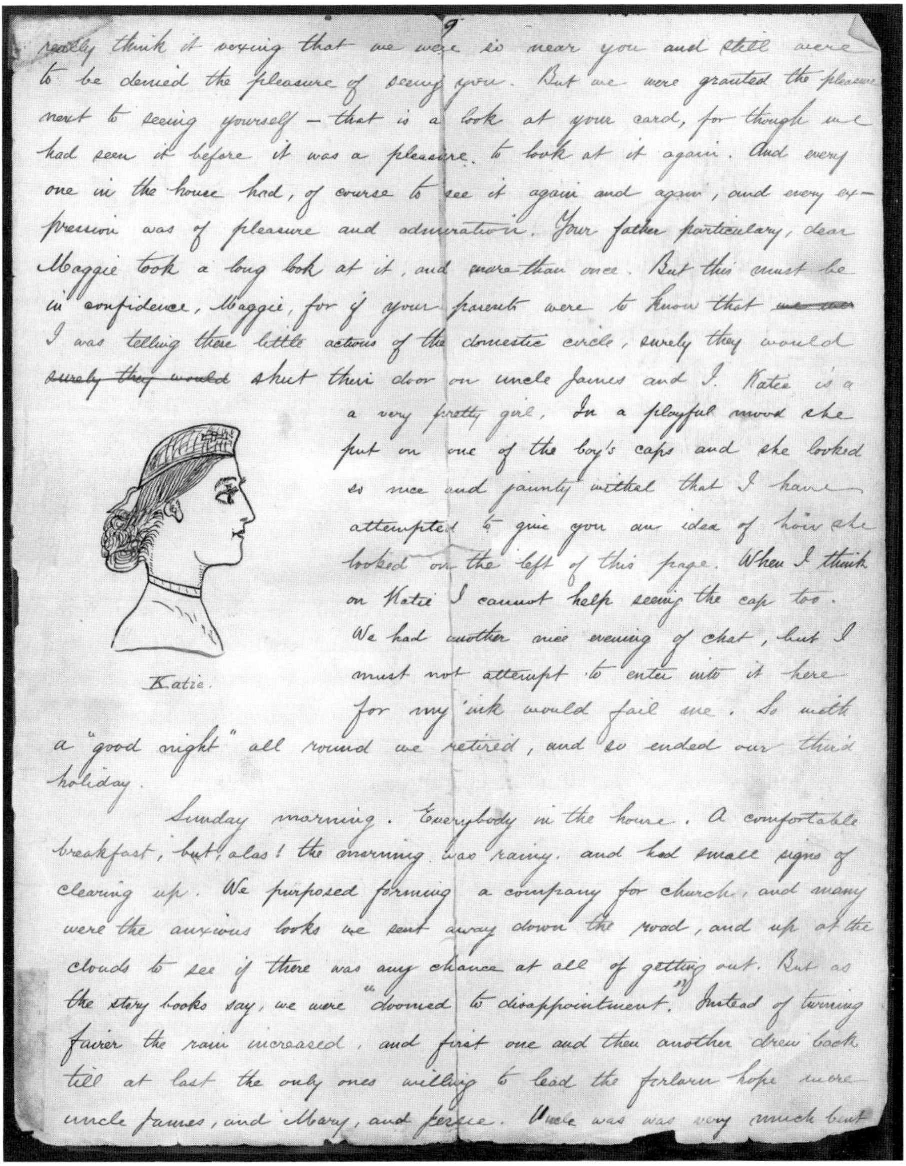

really think it vexing that we were so near you and still were to be denied the pleasure of seeing you. But we were granted the pleasure next to seeing yourself — that is a look at your card, for though we had seen it before it was a pleasure to look at it again. And every one in the house had, of course to see it again and again, and every expression was of pleasure and admiration. Your father particulary, dear Maggie took a long look at it, and more than once. But this must be in confidence, Maggie, for if your parents were to know that ~~we can~~ I was telling these little actions of the domestic circle, surely they would ~~surely they would~~ shut their door on uncle James and I. Katie is a

Katie.

a very pretty girl. In a playful mood she put on one of the boy's caps and she looked so nice and jaunty withal that I have attempted to give you an idea of how she looked on the left of this page. When I think on Katie I cannot help seeing the cap too. We had another nice evening of chat, but I must not attempt to enter into it here for my ink would fail me. So with a "good night" all round we retired, and so ended our third holiday.

Sunday morning. Everybody in the house. A comfortable breakfast, but, alas! the morning was rainy. and had small signs of clearing up. We purposed forming a company for church, and many were the anxious looks we sent away down the road, and up at the clouds to see if there was any chance at all of getting out. But as the story books say, we were "doomed to disappointment." Instead of turning fairer the rain increased. and first one and then another drew back till at last the only ones willing to lead the forlorn hope were uncle James, and Mary, and Jessie. Uncle was was very much bent

*Figure 7. Katie*

Sunday morning.

Everybody in the house. A comfortable breakfast, but, alas! the morning was rainy and had small signs of cleaning up. We purposed forming a company for church, and many were the anxious looks we sent away down the road, and up at the clouds to see if there way any chance at all of getting out. But as the story books say, we were "doomed to disappointment". Instead of turning fairer the rain increased, and first one and then another drew back till at last the only ones willing to lead the forlorn hope were uncle James, and Mary, and Jessie. Uncle was very much bent on seeing service in the little church at Cairndow, for although he is fond of the music from good choirs and organs and he likes real well to see the good old fashioned service in quiet out-of-the-way places. Well although it was raining hard when they started it was only the hope that it would eventually clear up which urged them on. Katie put a shawl on to go down a bit of the road with them. The boys also proceeded to convoy the three of them a wee bit. They were a queer sight, as we seen them from the window. Katie was under the umbrella with her arm round Jessie's neck. Fergus stuck in for [**** ?a] share of uncle James' umbrella. We thought every minute they would turn back, but they stuck out right away over the bridge, but we were glad to see them at last take refuge in McLean's. After waiting there in a vain hope that it would clear up they came out and retraced their steps home again. Well, Maggie, it rained all day, so there was nothing for it but to remain in shelter of the house. I think there was none of us very sorry, for we spent a very happy day. Your mother had a fire put on in the room, and we sat there all day very easily, as we had plenty to talk about. Eventually we retired and so ended our fourth holiday.

Monday morning opened up with promise of a better day. We got up somewhere about eight o'clock. I daresay it would be half past eight. But your mother was up long before that hour. Your father was out very early in the morning, and I heard your mother working away at the kirn when I am sure it could not be past four o'clock, but I as well as the others slept on till the time mentioned.

If your mother's daughters are not early risers they cannot say their mother showed them a sleepy example. (*[sic] Dear Maggie I do not mean here to cast any reflection on the girls for sleeping as long. Jessie had a long walk before her that day. Mary was almost an invalid, and Katie - well, I used to let my own girls lie long enough when not working). After breakfast, as your mother required certain necessary things from Cairndow, Mary and I proceeded to get ready for the journey. We had a real nice day and I admired the place very much. After we were gone uncle James and the two boys resolved to make another attempt to ascend Ben Ime. After being furnished with a pair of your father's boots, and a coat of hardier material than his own, and each one with a stout stick in his

on seeing service in the little church at Cairndow, for although he is fond of the music from good choirs and organs, he likes real well to see the good oldfashioned service in quiet out-of-the-way places. Well although it was raining hard when they started it was only the hope that it would eventually clear up which urged them on. Katie put a shawl on

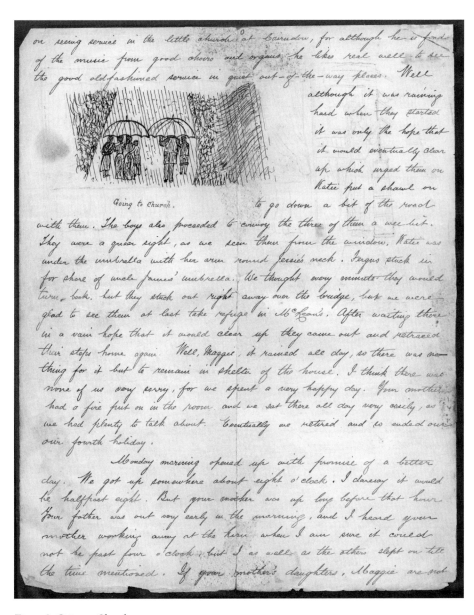

Going to Church.

to go down a bit of the road with them. The boys also proceeded to convoy the three of them a wee bit. They were a queer sight, as we seen them from the window. Katie was under the umbrella with her arm round Jessie's neck. Fergus stuck in for share of uncle James' umbrella. We thought every minute they would turn back, but they stuck out right away over the bridge, but we were glad to see them at last take refuge in McLean's. After waiting there in a vain hope that it would clear up they came out and retraced their steps home again. Well, Maggie, it rained all day, so there was nothing for it but to remain in shelter of the house. I think there was none of us very sorry, for we spent a very happy day. Your mother had a fire put on in the room and we sat there all day very cosily, as we had plenty to talk about. Eventually we retired and so ended our our fourth holiday.

Monday morning opened up with promise of a better day. We got up somewhere about eight o'clock. I daresay it would be halfpast eight. But your mother was up long before that hour. Your father was out very early in the morning, and I heard your mother working away at the hens when I am sure it could not be past four o'clock, but I as well as the others slept on till the time mentioned. If your mother's daughters, Maggie, are not

*Figure 8. Going to Church*

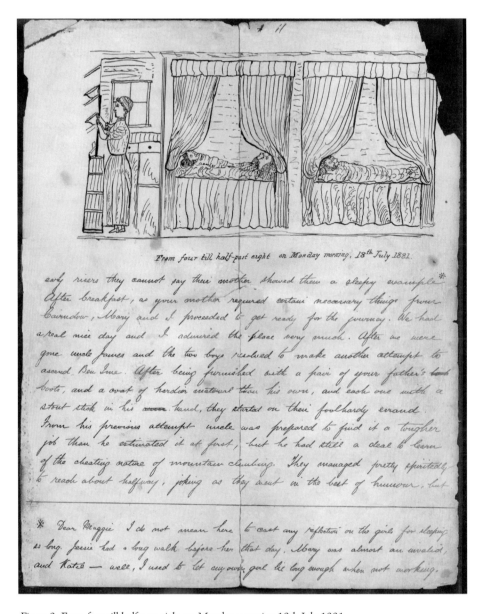

*From four till half-past eight on Monday morning, 18th July 1881.*

early risers they cannot say their mother showed them a sleepy example *

After breakfast, as your mother required certain necessary things from
Cairndow, Mary and I proceeded to get ready for the journey. We had
a real nice day and I admired the place very much. After we were
gone uncle James and the two boys resolved to make another attempt to
ascend Ben Ime. After being furnished with a pair of your father's ~~boots~~
boots, and a coat of hardier material ~~than~~ his own, and each one with a
stout stick in his ~~own~~ hand, they started on their foolhardy errand.
From his previous attempt uncle was prepared to find it a tougher
job than he estimated it at first, but he had still a deal to learn
of the cheating nature of mountain climbing. They managed pretty spiritedly
to reach about halfway, joking as they went in the best of humour, but

* Dear Maggie I do not mean here to cast any reflection on the girls for sleeping
as long. Jessie had a long walk before her that day, Mary was almost an invalid,
and Katie — well, I used to let my own girl lie long enough when not working.

*Figure 9. From four till half past eight on Monday morning 18th July 1881*

hand, they started on their foolhardy errand. From his previous attempt uncle was prepared to find it a tougher job than he estimated it at first, but he had still a deal to learn of the cheating nature of mountain climbing. They managed pretty spiritedly to reach about halfway, joking as they went in the best of humour, but after that their fun got scarce. The first half of the ascent is very easy, being covered with sheep pasture but after that is past, there is nothing but rocks, large and small, through and over which one has to pick his steps rather cautiously. But they were resolved to reach the top, and at it they went. Fergus had one or two slight stumbles, but both he and Aleck surprised uncle with their pluck and powers of endurance. Long before they reached the top they found they had made a great mistake in leaving home without providing themselves with as much as a bite of bread in their pocket. So I think they (I mean the boys, not that blockhead of husband of mine) must be formed of the stuff that heroes are made of, for in spite of the hunger gnawing within them, they had no thought of giving in, and returning till they reached the top. The sight of a small flock of ptarmigans diverted their attentions for a while, and they made some useless endeavours to strike some of the harmless birds with stones. At last success rewarded them and they stood on the top of Ben Ime. They found a circular building of stones on the top, and another smaller one built up from the centre of the larger one. Up this our little band clambered, and then in the exuberance of their triumph they waved their caps from the top of their sticks. Uncle took out his handkerchief and tying it to the top of his stick waved it high over his head, like an old fool. They told us afterwards they saw Mary and I approaching the house through the bog, and that they waved and shouted, but, of course we never heard them, nor had we any idea they were in such a place. They said we appeared just like mice crawling along; and the house itself looked the size of a dog-house from their elevated standpoint. It was awful cold and blowy so high up, and Fergus got as "white as a clout". And they got terribly hungry. They rung an imaginary hotel bell and ordered a dram of whisky and some biscuits and cheese, but it was a real barmicide's feast.[18] The only good thing was the view, and it was splendid. All the surrounding hills lay below them and Loch Fyne was visible from end to end, and Inverary was plainly descried on the far side to the loch. After they thought they had enough of it they descended at a galloping speed, and, without mishap reach house and made your mother's scones and cake and milk disappear as if by magic. Next time they ascend Ben Ime I rather think they will see their pockets are not empty. In our absence Jessie had gone away to her place at Lochgoilhead. I had tried to get her to stay over Monday night and

18 Procession of imaginary dishes. An interesting choice of word, given her background.

after that their fun got scarce.
The first half of the ascent is
very easy, being covered with
sheep pasture but after that
is past, there is nothing but
rocks, large and small, through
and over which one has to pick
his steps rather cautiously.
But they were resolved to reach
the top, and at it they went.
Fergus had one or two slight
stumbles, but both he and Aleck
surprised uncle with their pluck
and

*Climbing Ben Ime.*

*On the top of Ben Ime.*

TOP: *Figure 10. Climbing Ben Ime and* ABOVE: *Figure 11. On the top of Ben Ime*

we would go down the road together, but she could not see her way to do this. Katie went along a bit of the road with her. After your father came in and had supper, we assembled in the kitchen and had some more chat. Your father told some stories. We tried to get uncle James to sing a song, but though he sings away at snatches of songs at home, the stupid fellow has not a complete song in his memory. Mary has a sweet voice, but I think she has not been at the trouble to commit many songs to memory. So passed the evening of our fifth holiday.

Tuesday morning was somewhat wet and unpromising. Uncle and the two boys went out to fish, but all they catched was three small trout not worth pulling out of the water. After they came in and got a little refreshment in the shape of milk and scones, they went off again to the hillsides. Uncle was very fond to be about the hills, and he gambolled and ran and jumped like a young colt - the old fool. As the day advanced it showed signs of clearing up, and as uncle had a strong desire to see Cairndow, Mary and I proceeded to go along with him. He wished your mother and Katie also to go, and let the boys stay at home to watch the house and the kye, but some one remarked they would have the house on fire if left to themselves, and your mother was afraid of the long walk, so she drew back and Katie remained with her. Then seeing these two remain at home, uncle wanted the boys to get, and Fergus was particularly glad to go, but your mother would not let him, and in case he would go in spite of orders to the contrary she ran out after him, and after a struggle, stripped him of his jacket. He was for going as he was in his shirt sleeves and did go about the length of McLean's, and Aleck also, but at that point they returned home. The day proved very fine, and uncle relished the walk exceedingly. The quietness of the road between the great hills had a perfect fascination for him. We had purposed coming home by the coach, but just as we were turning the bend in the road near Cairndow, we met the coach on the return journey; so we had to make up our minds to foot it both ways. Uncle was delighted with Cairndow, while Mary and I were in the wee shop getting some necessaries for your mother he was outside drinking in the beauty of the scenery. When we came out he showed us St Catherine's away down the loch, and he said if he had known it was as near he would have made me walk it someday, and get the ferry across to Inverary, so that we could have had two or three hours with you. If it had not been that we have had to return on the morrow (Wednesday) nothing would have detained him from drawing as many as would have ventured with him to St. Catherines, and thence across the water. He told me "Maggie would not have grudged a walk of that length to see aunt Mary if she was as near her house." We sauntered for half-an hour in the little churchyard at Cairndow, and then leisurely proceeded homewards. When we came to the road which branches off for St. Catherines, uncle looked quite wistfully down the road as if he fain would have us away that way, for Inverary to see you. Shortly after we passed that road we met a wandering minstrel in the shape of an old man with a fiddle. At our request he sat down on the roadside and gave us some music from his instrument. It sounded strange to us, there amid the silence of the great hills with no being but ourselves in hearing, to hear this wandering musician discourse some highland airs. James says it recalled to his mind those nice lines in the opening of Scott's 'Lay of the Last Minstrel.'

> His withered cheek and tresses gray,
> Seemed to have known a better day'.
>
> x x x x
> The last of all the Bards was he.
> Who sung of Borden Chivalry
> For, welladay! their date was fled
> His tuneful brethren  all were dead.
> And he, neglected and oppressed,
> Longed to be with them, and at rest.
>
> No more on prancing palfrey borne,
> He caroll'd, light as lark at morn,
> No longer courted, and caress'd,
> High placed in hall, a welcome guest,
> He poured to lord and lady gay,
> The unpremeditated lay:
> Old times were changed, old manners gone
> A stranger filled the Stuart's throne:
> The bigots of the iron time
> Had called his tuneful[19] art a crime,
> A Wandering harper, scorned, and poor
> He begged his bread from door to door
>
> x x x x
> And much he wished, yet feared to try
> The long forgotten melody,
> Amid the strings his fingers strayed,
> And an uncertain warbling made,
> And oft he shook his heavy head,

---

19 Mary's memory slightly betrays her: it should be 'harmless'.

was for going as he was in his shirt sleeves, and did go about the length of McLeans, and Alick also, but at that point they returned home. The proved very fine, and uncle relished the walk exceedingly. The quietness of the road between the big hills had a perfect fascination for him. We had proposed coming home

The wandering minstrel.

in the opening of Scott's "Lay of the Last Minstrel" —
His withered cheek and tresses gray,
Seem'd to have known a better day;

The last of all the Bards was he,
Who sung of Border chivalry,
For, welladay! their date was fled,
His tuneful brethren all were dead.

*Figure 12. The wandering minstrel*

> But when he caught the measure wild,
> The old man raised his face and smiled,
> And lightened up his faded eye
> With all a poet's ecstasy!
> In varying cadence, soft and strong,
> He swept the sounding chords along
> The present scene, the future lot
> His toils, his wants were all forgot.

After we parted with the old minstrel, whom should we meet but Fergus. He had gone up to the garret at home and donned some old cast-off jacket, and took the road, for Cairndow. We were right glad to see him, and a bit nearer home, we fell in with Aleck.

In due time we came in sight of Butterbridge, and so ended as pleasant a walk as ever James and I remembered to have had. We had another nice evening of chat. Uncle James was quite chagrined that he could not give even such a snatch of a song. He has nothing much of a voice, but as he says himself any reasonable sort of singing would have been better than none. But he says the like shall not happen again for he is going to study a few songs to be ready at any further time. About ten o'clock we retired and so ended our sixth holiday.

Wednesday morning was very showery, and we were in 'twenty swithers' whether we would make up our mind to stay another day or not. Your father was not at work on account of the weather. They were all wishing us to stay and very kindly urged us to but as it showed signs of [**** ?drying] at midday we resolved to take the road. Uncle had to be at his work on the Thursday, so unless it was a very wet day we thought it best that he should be in on the day appointed, than have to make an excuse for delay. Uncle was out with the boys jumping about the burn and the house till it was about time to start. All holidays come to an end, Maggie, and the vexing "good-byes" must be spoken. After we were ready, and your mother had put a big roll of beautiful butter in my bag, we bade goodbye to Mary and Katie in the house. Your father and your mother and Fergus and Aleck came away with us to give us a start on the road. After seeing us a good bit beyond the Rest-and-be-thankful we took goodbye with them also, and we were once more alone on the road, 'homeward bound'. Except some slight showers, we had a nice afternoon and the road did not seem to so long as at first. That was, I suppose, because we knew where we were and of the whereabouts of the end of the journey.

We reached Lochgoilhead about three o'clock and of course went straight to Bella's. I assure you, Maggie, it was a pleasure to think, on our journey that your two sisters were in Lochgoilhead ready to greet us when we got there. It is nice to

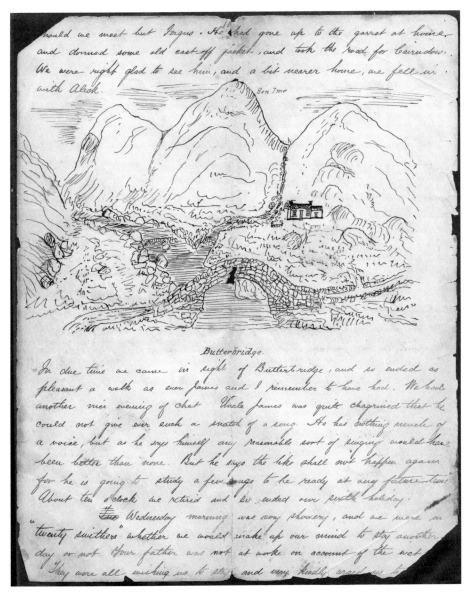

*Butterbridge.*

In due time we came in sight of Butterbridge, and so ended as pleasant a walk as ever James and I remember to have had. We had another nice evening of chat. Uncle James was quite chagrined that he could not give ever such a snatch of a song. He has nothing much of a voice, but as he says himself any reasonable sort of singing would have been better than none. But he says the like shall not happen again for he is going to study a few songs to be ready at any future time. About ten o'clock we retired and so ended our sixth holiday.

Wednesday morning was very showery, and we were in "twenty swithers" whether we would make up our mind to stay another day or not. Your father was not at work on account of the wet. They were all wishing us to stay, and very kindly urged us to

*Figure 13. Butterbridge*

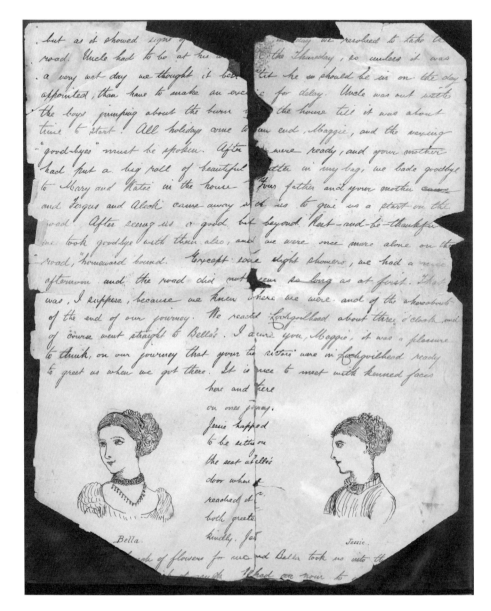

but as it showed signs [...] [...] day we resolved to take the
road. Uncle had to be at his [...] the Thursday, so unless it was
a very wet day we thought it bet [...] it he so should be in on the day
appointed, than have to make an exc[...] for delay. Uncle was out with
the boys jumping about the burn [...] the house till it was about
time to start! All holidays come to [...] an end, Maggie, and the evening
"good-byes" must be spoken. After [...] were ready, and your mother
had put a big roll of beautiful [...] in my bag, we bade goodbye
to Mary and Katie in the house [...] our father and your mother came
and Fergus and Aleck came away [...] us to give us a start on the
road. After seeing us a good bit beyond Rest-and-be-thankful
we took goodbye with them also, and we were once more alone on the
road, "homeward bound." Except some slight showers, we had a nice
afternoon and the road did not seem so long as at first. That
was, I suppose, because we knew where we were and of the whereabouts
of the end of our journey. We reached Lochgoilhead about three o'clock and
of course went straight to Bella's. I assure you, Maggie, it was a pleasure
to think, on our journey that your two sisters were in Lochgoilhead ready
to greet us when we got there. It is nice to meet with kenned faces
here and there
on ones jorney.
Jessie happod
to be sitt on
the seat atellos
door when [...]
reached [...]
both greeted
kindly. Je[...]

Bella.                                      Jessie

[...] of flowers for me and Bella took us into th[...]
[...] 1 had ou now to

LEFT: *Figure 14. Bella and* RIGHT: *Figure 15. Jessie*

meet with kenned faces here and there on one's journey. Jessie happened to be sitting on the seat at Bella's door when we reached it. Both greeted us kindly, Jessie had a nice bunch of flowers for me and Bella took us into the [****]. We had an hour to chat and we had of course to tell of our adventures at Butterbridge. Bella got ready and they both went with us to the boat. We kept in the boat till we reached Glasgow about eight o'clock, and so ended our holidays which have left impressions of nothing but pleasure to both uncle James and myself. These pleasant impressions are due in some degree to the reasonably fine weather, to the novelty and the quietness of the great hills but in by far the greatest degree are they due to the exceeding and uniform kindness with which we were treated by your dear parents and the other members of the family. In after years our memory will recall with pleasure the various little incidents, and the hearty welcome we received on our trip at Butterbridge.

Dear Maggie, I hope you are keeping in good health and pleased with your situation. Do not forget that I will be looking for you, when you get a day or two to yourself. I suppose it will not be till the November term. Now don't forget.

We have just got a letter from Mary Hunter. She was away on a trip to Arran on the 20th July. That was the day we left Butterbridge; but she did not enjoy herself very much as both her [**** ?mistress] and the girl she was with were seasick all the time they were in the boat. But it is likely she will have told you all about it in a letter. Her mistress has asked her to remain through the winter with her, but she has not decided yet. We had a visit from uncle Sandy and his wife on Monday last (August 8th). Grandmother is looking well.

Dear Maggie I must draw to a close this rambling letter. Uncle James wishes to be kindly remembered to you, and always think of me as ever.

Your affectionate aunt

Mary Allison

# Bibliography

## Works cited

AUERBACH, Jeffrey A., *The Great Exhibition of 1851* (New Haven, CT, 1991)

BLACK, A. & C., *Picturesque Tourist of Scotland*, 17th edition (Edinburgh, 1865)

BUCHAN, Dr William, *Domestic Medicine* (Glasgow, 1819)

CHAMBERS, Robert, *The Scottish Songs* (Edinburgh, 1829)

CORMACK, B., *A History of Holidays* (London, 1998)

COUPER, W.J., *The Reformed Presbyterian Church in Scotland* (Edinburgh, 1925)

DAVIES, Kenneth, *The Clyde Passenger Steamers* (Ayr, 1980)

DENBY, Elaine, *Grand Hotels. An Architectural and Social History* (London, 1998)

DURIE, A.J., *Scotland for the Holidays* (East Linton, 2003)

GARD, Robin, *The Observant Traveller. Diaries of travel in England, Wales and Scotland* (London, 1989)

GEIKIE, Sir Archibald, *Scottish Reminiscences* (Glasgow, 1906)

HACHE, Jean-Didier, *The French Macdonald. Journey of a Marshall of Napoleon in the Highlands and Islands of Scotland in 1825* (Isle of Lewis, 2007)

LACH-SZYMTRA, Krystyn, *From Charlotte Square to Fingal's Cave. Reminiscences of a Journey through Scotland 1820–1824.* Edited by Mona Kedslie McLeod (East Linton, 2004)

LUMSDEN, James, *Edinburgh Poems and Songs* (Edinburgh, 1899)

MACBRAYNE, David, *Summer Tours in Scotland* (various editions, Glasgow)

MACCULLOCH, Dr John, *The Highlands and Western Isles of Scotland* (London, 1824)

MCRORIE, Ian, *To the Coast. One Hundred Years of the Caledonian Packet Company* (Fairlie, 1989)

MURRAY, Sarah, *A Companion and Useful Guide to the Beauties of Scotland* (Hawick, 1982)

MUNSELL, Walter A., *Two on a Tour* (Paisley, 1909)

PATERSON, A.J.S., *The Golden Years of the Clyde Steamers* (Newton Abbot, 1969)

PITTOCK, Murray, *The Reception of Sir Walter Scott in Europe* (London, 2006)

POPE, Alexander, *Epistles to Several Persons* (London, 1733)

ROBINSON, Arthur R.B., *Seeking the Scots. An Englishwoman's Journey in 1807* (York, 2006)

SINCLAIR, Sir John, *Statistical Account of Scotland* (Edinburgh, 1798)

SLATER, Isaac, *Commercial Directory of Scotland* (Manchester and London, 1867)

TAYLOR, John, *Medical treatise on St Bernard's Well* (Edinburgh, 1790)

WALKER, David, 'Inns, Hotels and Related Building Types', in Geoffrey Stell, John Shaw and Susan Storrier (eds) *A Compendium of Scottish Ethnography*, vol. 3: *Scotland's Buildings* (East Linton, 2003)

WALTON, John K., *Blackpool* (Edinburgh, 1998)

WORDSWORTH, Dorothy, *Recollections of a Tour Made in Scotland 1803.* Introduction by Carol Kyros Walker (New Haven, CT, 1997)

WORDSWORTH, Dorothy, *Journal of my Second Tour in Scotland*, ed. E. De Selincourt (London, 1943)

## *Further reading*

CLYDE, Robert, *From Rebel to Hero. The Image of the Highlander 1745–1830* (East Linton, 1995)

GRENIER, Katherine Haldane, *Tourism and Identity in Scotland 1770–1914: Creating Caledonia* (Aldershot, 2005)

HAGGLUND, Betty, *Tourists and Travellers Women's Non-Fictional Writing about Scotland 1770–1830* (Bristol, 2010)

KELLY, Stuart, *Scott-land. The Man Who Invented a Nation* (Edinburgh, 2010)

# Index of Significant People and Places